STRUCTURAL DYNAMICS OF INDUSTRIAL POLICY

STRUCTURAL DYNAMICS OF INDUSTRIAL POLICY

Edited by

Bodo B. Gemper

Transaction Books
New Brunswick (U.S.A.) and Oxford (U.K.)

Copyright © 1987 by Transaction, Inc., New Brunswick, New Jersey 08903.
Original edition copyright © 1985 by Verlag Weltarchiv GmbH, Hamburg,
West Germany.

All rights reserved under International and Pan-American Copyright Conventions. No part of this book may be reproduced or transmitted in any form or by any means, electronic or mechanical, including photocopy, recording, or by any information storage and retrieval system, without prior permission in writing from the publisher. All inquiries should be addressed to Transaction Books, Rutgers–The State University, New Brunswick, New Jersey 08903.

ISBN 0-88738-679-2
Printed in the United States of America

Library of Congress Cataloging-in-Publication Data

Industrial policy.
  Structural dynamics of industrial policy.

  Reprint. Originally published: Industrial policy.
Hamburg: Verlag Weltarchiv, 1985.
  Includes index.
  1. Industry and state. 2. Laissez-faire. I. Gemper,
Bodo B. II. Title.
HD3611.1385   1987   338.9   87-5023
ISBN: 0-88738-679-2

Industrial Policy by Waxing and Waning Structural Change

A Foreword

Preparing the way for the future: by chance or by consciously guided industrial progress? This is the question. The conscious shaping of the future presupposes both, vital intuition and farsightedness. Innovation has to become a tradition to bring about the "economics of change". The Walberberg System Symposia, arranged by The Independent Institute for the Jurisprudential, Social and Economic Sciences, Bonn (IRSW Bonn), provide a setting for the debate of crucial issues, which the Federal Republic of Germany and her Atlantic partners face.

This organization, a non-government, non-profit research institution, was established in 1976 to encourage the free exchange of information on legal, social and economic problems. Its purpose is to serve as an international forum which promotes co-operation in the study of common interest. The published papers and remarks of the Walberberg System Symposia provide profound discussions of contemporary socio-economic challenges. Most of the papers in this volume were discussed during the 12th Walberberg System Symposium, held at the Dominican Monastery St. Albert, Bonn/Bornheim-Walberberg, West Germany, March 1985. This international symposium furnished a timely contribution to an important public policy issue which has not yet received the comprehensive treatment which it deserves in West Germany.

The following questions arise:

What are the main reasons to establish an industrial policy in a free market economy, even in the most developed industrial countries? What are the main goals? What currents of thought influence and inspire a new approach? What are the results of international experience in this ongoing debate? What has been achieved so far and what problems remain to be resolved? Especially what kind of an industrial policy should the market economies actively pursue under the pressures of accelerating change in order to strengthen the market mechanism without ignoring social welfare goals? Do we need new tools for tomorrow? If yes, which?

The aim of this symposium on industrial policy was to create a better understanding of the pros and cons of such a policy in a free market economy. As *Karsten's* analysis for the applicability of an industrial policy for the United States points out, an industrial policy needs to be evaluated in terms of its "meaning" and "validity".

What we have to learn is to avoid the danger of being locked into a given structure which makes advanced economies not responsive to change. Industrialized economies have to fashion devices which enable them to shape the development of the changing structures. This ability has to be cultivated all the more in the face of the magnitude of rapidly increasing change. The depth, the pervasiveness and the speed of the changes which we are experiencing by far exceed any previous one. For example: The move to the urban civilization began a little more than five thousand years ago. The first industrial revolution started about two hundred years ago. During the cultural revolution men needed about two thousand years to take the step from the reversing plough – an invention of the ancient Romans – to the steam plough which was the great attraction at the World Fair in London in 1855. Just a few generations later agricultural production has become extensively mechanized. All of these developments took place over centuries, or at least some decades. Now we find ourselves already at the beginning of the third industrial revolution.

Today we are witnesses of a much faster transition than ever before. The industrialized countries find themselves at the epicenter of fundamental cultural shifts which manifest themselves in the form of ever accelerating dynamic structural changes. These all penetrating processes of change are of increasingly shorter durations, than a decade. And, we are observing, that structural changes exhibit rhythmic patterns as business cycles do. Similar to a business cycle's *waxing* (expansionary) and *waning* (contractionary) phases structural changes also occur in bursts.

Entrepreneurs and politicians need to be aware of this fact and take it into consideration in policy-making decisions. "A comparison between a rising and a declining structural change" as *Jenkis* calls this phenomenon, makes clear that with regard to the first case only very limited intervention as part of an industrial policy is needed whereas in the second instance greater intervention both, primarily by private institutionalized initiatives and by complementary public policy measures, may be called for – all within the framework of a market economy.

Many of the great inventions and innovations have taken place serendipitously, i.e. as unexpected discoveries during research or by pure accident in search for a new solution. For example, the German physicist Wilhelm Conrad *Röntgen,* accidently discovered in 1895 the hitherto unknown X-rays while experimenting with cathode rays. He became the first Nobel laureat in 1901 "in recognition of the extraordinary services he has rendered by the discovery of the remarkable rays subsequently named after him". The English bacteriologist Alexander *Fleming* incidently discovered in 1928 that the growth of bacteria was retarded by infection with mould fungi. He also was honoured with a Nobel prize "for the discovery of penicillin and its curative effect in various infectious diseases". The English physician Edward *Jenner* was told by a young farm girl, who had suffered from cow-pox that she never again had fallen ill from this disease. This information provided the stimulus for his small pox vaccination.

However, more is required to secure long lasting progress in advanced industrial economies under conditions of accelerating change. More systematic approaches, based on careful interpretations of the available signals indicative of future technological, social and economic developments are called for.

Disagreement between free market economists exists who are purists on the one hand and those who are willing to take in consideration changing conditions. However, those free marketeers who are willing to adapt the changing requirements of the times are growing in number. They are advocating adequate policy measures designed to strengthen market forces in the light of ongoing structural change.

As editor of this book and as organizer of the conference on "Industrial Policy in a Free Market Economy?", I would like to thank all contributors who made the symposium and this publication possible.

I am also very much obliged to donors who with their financial support made it possible to organize the symposium and this publication.

I am especially indebted to Dr. Otto G. *Mayer* of the HWWA-Institut für Wirtschaftsforschung, Hamburg, for accepting this volume as part of the Verlag Weltarchiv publications.

I am grateful to Mr. Ulrich *Drechsler* for compiling the index. The members of the Independent Institute for the Jurisprudential, Social and Economic Sciences desire to provide the readers with stimulating views of this controversial socio-economic policy issue. They would welcome comments or suggestions.

Grissenbach, 20th October 1985   Bodo B. Gemper

Address of the editor:
Professor Dr. Bodo B. Gemper
Grissenbach, Luisenstraße 11
D 5902 Netphen 3 (West Germany)

Contributors

Dr. Hilde *Behrend*
Professor of Economics, University of Edinburgh, Great Britain

Dr. Richard L. *Brinkman*
Professor of Economics, Portland State University, Portland, Oregon, USA

Dr. Tom *Cannon*
Professor of Economics, University of Stirling, Great Britain

Dr. Bodo B. *Gemper*
Professor of Economics, University of Siegen, Germany

Dr. Helmut W. *Jenkis*
Professor of Economics, Director of the Federation of Non-Profit Housing Societies in Lower Saxony and Bremen, Hannover, and Department of Physical Planning at the University of Dortmund, Germany

Dr. Siegfried G. *Karsten*
Professor of Economics, West Georgia College, Carrollton, Georgia, USA

Dr. Bernhard *Molitor*
Ministerialdirektor, Federal Ministry of Commerce, Bonn, Germany

Dr. Cedric *Pugh*
Senior Lecturer, Department of Economics, The South Australian Institute of Technology, Adelaide, Australia

Dr. Klaus Werner *Schatz*
Head of Department: Infrastructure in the World Economy, Institut für Weltwirtschaft, University of Kiel, Germany

Dr. Herbert *Schmidt*
Ministerialrat, German Federal Chancellery, Bonn, Germany

Dr. Egon *Schoneweg*
Chef de Cabinet du Président, Economic and Social Committee of the European Communities, Brussels, Belgium

Dr. Eberhard *Thiel*
Head of Department: Economic Structures and Economic Systems, HWWA – Institut für Wirtschaftsforschung, Hamburg, Germany

Dr. Nicolaas *van der Walt*
Professor of Economics, Rand Afrikaans University, Johannesburg, South Africa

Dr. Horst Friedrich *Wünsche*
Ludwig-Erhard-Stiftung, Bonn, Germany

Contents

Industrial Policy by Waxing and Waning Structural Change A Foreword by Bodo B. Gemper	V
Contributors	VIII

1. Preparing the Way for the Future: by Chance or by consciously Guided Industrial Progress?

Industrial Policy in a Free Market Economy: Slogan or Solution? by Bernhard Molitor	3
Industrial Policy in a Free Market Economy: A Matter of Conviction or Desperation? by Bodo B. Gemper	11
Democratic Planning in a Free Market Economy and Social Values by Richard L. Brinkman	21
Does Industrial Policy comply with Ludwig Erhard's Conception of the Social Market Economy? by Horst Friedrich Wünsche	37

2. Stabilization by Structural Change: Regional, Sectoral and Entrepreneurial Policies

Sectoral and Regional Elements of Industrial Policy by Eberhard Thiel	47
Stabilisation of the Social Structure versus Change of the Industrial Structure – The Case of the Ruhr District by Helmut W. Jenkis	57
The Contribution of Small and New Enterprise to Growth and Development by Klaus Werner Schatz	89

3. Improving Economic Performance: International Experience and Strategies

Industry Policy and Structural Change in Australia 107
by Cedric Pugh

The Contribution of New Enterprise to Economic Growth and Employment.
The Experience of the Scottish Enterprise Foundation 131
by Tom Cannon

The Envisaged Revised Industrial Development Strategy of South Africa 145
by Nicolaas van der Walt

The Meaning and Validity of a U.S. Industrial Policy 155
by Siegfried G. Karsten

4. Social and Industrial Relations Aspects

Views of Both Sides of Industry on an EEC Industrial Policy 167
by Egon Schoneweg

Some Reflections on Industrial Policies Based on British Experience 175
by Hilde Behrend

Labouroriented Managementpolicy in Industry within a
Social Market Economy 187
by Herbert Schmidt

Index of Names 201

Subject Index 205

1.

Preparing the Way for the Future:
by Chance or by consciously Guided Industrial Progress?

Industrial Policy in a Free Market Economy: Slogan or Solution?

Bernhard Molitor

In the 1984 report to President Ronald Reagan, the US Council of Economic Advisers under its chairman Martin Feldstein dedicated a special chapter to the issue whether the United States should formulate an industrial policy. I do not withhold the outcome of the Council's discussion. I quote: "The answer is 'no'. An industrial policy would not solve the problems faced by US industry and would create new problems. Industrial policy has a mixed record in Japan and has been unsuccessful in Europe."

This opinion has inter alia been confirmed by the conclusions reached by two journalists in Le Monde and Le Figaro for the country that is regarded as the main protagonist of industrial policy in Europe. The headlines speak for themselves: "Les entreprises francaises malades de la politique industrielle — French enterprises suffering from industrial policy", headline Jacqueline Grapin gave her article in Le Monde on March 24, 1980, that is at a time when M. Giscard d'Estaing was still president and "Politique industrielle: La dérive — Industrial Policy the road to ruin", headline of Annie Kriegel's article in Le Figaro of August 30, 1984, which refers to President Mitterrand's "new" policy.

Does this mean that Paul McCracken, who was the Chairman of the US Council of Economic Advisers from the beginning of 1969 till 1971, was right to compare, as he recently did, the demand for an industrial policy with the worldwide call for an incomes policy of the mid-1960s? Will industrial policy be just a reminiscence of a fashion trend in 15 to 20 years from now?

Although I feel strongly tempted to go along with what Paul McCracken and Martin Feldstein said, we should not evade a discussion of this problem which is so ardently debated worldwide. It should not escape our attention in this context that in the Anglo-Saxon languages the term "industry" has got a much wider meaning comprising services as well. On the European continent, on the other hand, this term only comprises manufacturing, mining, electricity generation and the building sector.

I should like to discuss the subject from three angles:
— Why is there a demand for an industrial policy?
— Why has industrial policy failed so far?
— What might be a viable way toward an efficient industrial policy?

I.

Why is there a demand for an industrial policy? I can visualize two main lines of argument why demands for an autonomous industrial policy have come up:

- The first is the historical philosophy that industrial and social development should not be left to be decided upon by entrepreneurs and the citizens, that is not by the market. Colbert, Karl Marx, Lasalle and others are the protagonists of this doctrine. It is their firm belief that government is not only more efficient, but also more equitable in respect of the planning, regulation and implementation of industrial activities. State planning and a centralized administration of these activities are both goals of this philosophy.
- The second is that many of the problems we face today hardly appear to be capable of being solved otherwise:
  - structural upheavals in industry,
  - the large number of unemployed,
  - the advent of new technologies which — contrary to the past — do no longer originate in Europe or, what matters more, are no longer translated into practical applications in Europe first,
  - large volumes of research spending under the US defence budgets,
  - industrial targeting in Japan,
  - keener international competition, not only on the part of the USA and Japan, but also of the Newly Industrialized Countries (NICs) as well as of less developed nations in traditional markets,
  - the impression that European companies are losing in competitiveness,
  - and, finally, growing fear that European nations are coping with major economic and social problems and in particular with positive adjustment much less well than others, e.g. the USA, Canada or Japan.

All this inspires not only those who — by the nature of their political philosophy — deem a planned economy best, but also socalled pragmaticians to be in favour of an "industrial policy from the top".

They often argue that for political or social reasons government intervenes in selected areas anyhow, e.g. in agriculture, residential constructions, shipbuilding and steel. This being so, an "industrial policy of one casting" would be precisely the thing that is needed in their opinion. This means that sinning against the principle of competition would become the rule. These socalled pragmaticians often defend their theory in the way army chiefs and their staff do: They demand and overall industrial policy strategy through which Europe can and must defend itself. In line with this military notion, they wish, first of all, to build up a Maginot line of protectionist measures behind which they want to organize a general mobilization of industrial forces and then develop a socalled forward strategy in the form of a comprehensive operation of attack on other nation's markets.

They ignore that, as a rule, the concept collapses in itself before phase 1, that is the Maginot line, is surpassed (please see the afore-mentioned French analyses).

What worries us is this military type of approach that does not fit into the economic landscape; for, in economics there is no zero-sum game in which one side gains what the other loses; on the contrary, either partner profits from the other's prosperity and either partner suffers if the other loses in prosperity as a result of recessionary trends. This precisely is the reason why we take such a keen interest in a better coordination of economic policies of industrial countries and in open markets in which competition works freely.

Moreover, experience has shown that governmental command structures lead to lethargy in industry and to a lack of awareness for cost trends and market requirements. This leads to a lack of Schumpeterian entrepreneurs or even Keynesian entrepreneurs but favours arsenal managers. It is true that arsenal managers have — on occasions — shown a high-standard technical performance, but, to my knowledge, they have never created a dynamic economy that responds to consumer wishes quickly. This is, in fact, the role Schumpeter's pioneering entrepreneurs are playing.

II.

Why have industrial policy notions failed so far? — "Industrial policy has a mixed record in Japan and has been unsuccessful in Europe". This conclusion by the Council of Economic Advisers is a shame for Europeans. It holds true not only for countries in which industrial policy plays a central role in government economic and social policy, but also for the European Coal and Steel Community and EURATOM (about which people talk so little) and in respect of more recent developments in the European Community as well.

What are the crucial problems involved in government-fixed and controlled industrial structures? — It appears to me first of all that the "feasibility" of efficient industrial patterns compatible with market requirements by central public bodies has been terribly overestimated. In this context, the protagonists mainly overlook the problems involved in central sectoral and corporate forecasts. In view of substantial gaps in information, of quickly changing demand patterns especially in highly developed and complex economies and of the European countries strong international economic integration, reliable ex-ante structural analyses for individual sectors and the innumerable products they make is not possible.

Who could have foreseen the 1973 and the 1979 oil price explosions, for instance?

Who was in a position to predict what chances European companies would have in OPEC markets and which companies would be in a particularly good position to find sales outlets for their products?

Who could tell beforehand which automobile producers in the USA oder in Europe would respond quickly with substantial investment programmes, new production technologies and new products?

Who could have foreseen the strong decline in specific energy consumption from the beginning of this decade (incidentally, one of the reasons underlying the expansion of nuclear generation capacity in France which — although right in concept — has been overdimensioned!).

Who knows what shares entrepreneurs of other industrial or developing countries will conquer for their products in our own markets?

If, in spite of all those unanswered questions, government takes action in this field nonetheless, it will have to take the blame for assessing matters wrongly.

And there will be an accumulation of management mistakes when entrepreneurs act as forecasted, which governments expect them to do. At this stage, government either must make good losses from tax money or from higher public debts or — since this can be done on a limited scale only — guard the corporate sector against foreign competition by protectionist measures.

This situation is worsened by sector-specific investment guidance. For, in the last analysis, this means selecting consumption patterns which substantially curtail the choice of consumer goods and favours the formation of grey and black markets. The competition among entrepreneurs in their decentralized search, at their own risk, for products, for which there is a market, would be deprived of its functioning ability. Such investment guidance would, especially in the case of homogenous mass items, make investors jump onto a quickly rotating merry-go-round very soon; they would start to set up capacities much too large for them so as to lay the basis for their claims to correspondingly large shares in future investment volumes; entrepreneurs will then see to it jointly that investment spending is kept to a minimum and that newcomers and foreign firms are denied access to the markets. From that stage, they need no longer minimize costs and apply new technological processes. Steel and coal offer good illustrative material for this.

Various advocates of industrial policy say that this is not what they have in mind; instead, they argue in favour of concerted action by government and individual industrial branches. As soon as such concerted action is successful, cartel managers can be heard knocking on the door. Competition bogs down. The existence of a decisive driving force for a dynamic innovation and investment behaviour is no longer guaranteed. This is at the expense of dynamic companies and, thus, of efficiency in the economy as a whole. It is to the detriment of small and medium-sized companies which, as a rule, find it much harder in policy-coordinating boards to win support for their own position compared to that of the big ones. One may call this the "law of attraction to cast decisions in favour of firms with a large investment and employment potential". On the other hand, small and medium-sized businesses in particular have shown entrepreneurial flexibility, creative initiative and a highly pronounced pioneering spirit to a special extent: All this would or could be lost.

Apart from this, structural guidance by means of investment and output quotas logically leads to a repartitioning of credit as well. And, strife for perfection would end up with centralized income and consumption planning and control. This reminds me of a remark by John Steinberg: "Today, a special licence is necessary to buy a watch with so and so many rubies and a second licence to wind the watch up". Howewer, what Steinberg did not realize at the time is that, in competition with others, entrepreneurs' capacity for innovation leads to the invention of the automatic digital watch and, in Switzerland, even to one that makes ticktack.

So far, this dilemma has often been circumvented by subsidies. I do not wish to condemn any kind of state aid right away, but it would most certainly be wrong to attempt to create highly efficient industrial structures by means of a system of extensive subsidies. Under whatever label subsidies are ultimately granted, they go to sub-marginal companies, as a rule. Efficient companies come to suffer from severe distortions of competition. Steel, textiles, shipbuilding and shipowners are telling examples in Europe.

It is a special matter of concern that problems – far from being solved – are not only prolonged, but even aggravated thereby. For instance, excessive amounts of subsidy paid to shipowners and shipyards have worsened the difficulties of large shipyards; for, the aid paid in previous years to preserve as many jobs as possible have favoured the setting-up of overcapacities in merchant fleets all over the world. Moreover, it should give us to think that assistance to shipowners and shipbuilders has been given in France for over 100 years (precisely since 1881). Adjustment aid would hardly be the proper name for such subsidies that testify to the political success of a powerful lobby and to generosity at the expense of tax payers as well as to the misallocation of enormous capital resources.

The more one studies the concept of an interventionist industrial policy – and on this occasion I have deliberately refrained from an in-depth analysis of the grave consequences of protectionism which is wanted or unwanted outcome of such a concept – the more I find that the Council of Economic Advisers is right.

But, the Japanese "industrial targeting", does it not contradict this experience? First let us listen to what the Council said on Japan's industrial targeting: "They have indeed picked some industries that turned out to be winners in part because of their efforts, but they also picked some industries that ended up as losers. They failed to pick some big winners and they also picked industries that would have become winners without help. The net effect of these policies on economic growth is not clear."

What is "industrial targeting" about?
The strategy jointly prepared by public authorities and private companies, is to focus innovation on specific sectors or products deliberately with the result that massive export capacities come into existence.

The outcome of such a policy is that individual countries pile up advantages for their industries in the markets for new technologies worldwide; such advantages are particularly great because companies may count on governmental protection and support, if the coordinated strategy turns out to be a failure. In my view, this exactly is the point why industries and industrial associations want government to come in to bear full co-responsibility. This is why I do not believe that the initiative in Japan has, as a rule, been taken by the Japanese Government and/or the MITI. Japan's industries are not less interested in such a coordinated strategy which allows them to go about their business knowing that it is for government to protect them against risks.

The Council of Economic Advisers is right in pointing to past and present failures: first the development of a "future-oriented" petro-chemical industry under state "guidance" now followed by a so-called "concerted" reduction of overcapacities, for example. The need for publicly promoted economic adjustment in Japan requiring structural crisis cartels and/or massive tax relief and credit support to shipbuilding, steel, fertilizer, chemical fibre and paper production or to the aluminium industry, speaks for itself.

Even more important from my point of view are disruptions in the world trade which is based on the principle of competition among enterprises, but not among states. Such disruptions give rise to demands for protection against imports or retaliatory action detrimental to everybody, as the discussion in the United States on Japan's industrial policy shows. Therefore, we have to regard "industrial targeting" as a large potential for major trade-policy conflicts involving substantial risks to investment and economic growth.

Schumpeter would then be right, though for a different reason: the breakdown of capitalism is imminent not because capitalism is so successful, but because entrepreneurs and government have formed an unholy alliance in favour of "industrial targeting" in major industrial countries. Against this background it may be historical dialectics that the origin of industrial targeting is in a country which has got a long tradition of seclusion permitting imports of three commodities only: books, drugs and sugar[1].

III.

What might be a viable way towards an efficient industrial policy?
The rejection of state planning and state control of industrial structures as a concept for industrial policy does not necessarily mean laissez faire. However, adjustment to changed market conditions must take place on the basis of decentralized management decisions and competition as the very foundations of a market-oriented industrial policy.

Adjustment is a task for business to accomplish. Industry itself has to give adequate answers to the new challenges of keener international competition, technological change and the translations of new technologies into practical applications. For this purpose, we need a clear distinguishing line between company and government responsibility. Weighing risks and opportunities of technological progress against each other and responding to market requirements are tasks for companies.

It is the responsibility of government to strengthen industry's capability and willingness to accept commercial risks through adequate market policies.

In view of the still severe employment problems the emphasis is on strengthening industry's capability and willingness to invest and to innovate, which will be of fundamental importance for the creation of new jobs in the coming years.

Keen national and international competition is the best motor for investment and innovation. For, investment and modernization are the only way to survive successfully in a world of competition. The best method enabling highly developed economies to live up to the challenges of new technologies is precisely the application of such technologies and structural adjustment by individual companies.

Government structural policy must aim at more flexibility and mobility of labour, capital and management as well as the removal of incrusted structures; this means first of all that

- earnings perspectives must allow the expectation that net returns on risky investments will be higher than net returns on long-term government bonds;
- public deficits must be reduced to give more room to private savings to finance business investment;
- taxes and fiscal charges must be curtailed;
- subsidies and tax relief which prevent private capital from being put to productive, job-creating uses must be gradually reduced;
- as a matter of principle, a time limit must be put on adjustment aid and such aid must be given on a declining scale;
- incrusted market structures must be dismantled and the creation of new ones by market-dominating enterprises, cartels and public procurement agencies must be prevented;
- government regulations posing major obstacles to the formation of more venture capital for the financing of innovative entrepreneurial activities, must be reviewed;
- government activities must be assigned to private individuals and private business which these can fulfill at least as effectively or even more effectively than government;
- regulations standing in the way towards more flexibility in the labour market and industrial employment must be abrogated;
- a more favourable research climate must be developed with technology being no longer an object of fear, but a challenge in international competition;
- new markets hitherto reserved to state monopolies, e.g. in the field of new communication technologies, or in overregulated fields, where private initiative has

not enough scope for development, e.g. residential construction, must be opened to private enterprise;

— the international European market must be accomplished;
— markets must be kept open and opened further to competitors from elsewhere, e.g. in the course of a new GATT round.

NOTE

[1] In a report of foreign trade Arai Hakuseki (1625–1725), poet, philosopher, historian, economist and political scientist recommended to the shogun in 1714 to restrict imports to Japan severely. Practically, this meant a ban on the importation of any product other than the three above mentioned ones. An expansion of exports was expressly rejected at the time.

Industrial Policy in a Free Market Economy: A Matter of Conviction or Desperation?

Bodo B. Gemper

I. The Present Situation

Economic Data

The cause for the ongoing debate over an "active" industrial policy in the 1980s is to be found in the acceleration of the scientific-technical evolution and its concomitant impact upon the socio-economic systems of the advanced industrialized countries.

Entire branches of trade and industry are dying out and old, established economic regions are substantively changing in structure. Although new industries come into being, modern production methods as well as the service sector require much less direct human effort, per unit of output, than has been customary. Moreover, as labor is becoming too expensive, entrepreneurs are forced to substitute capital for labor if they wish to remain competitive. This holds particularly true in world markets. The latter have undergone fundamental changes due to increased innovative competition from the United States and Japan as well as from the pressures of cheap supplies from the newly industrialized countries (NIC's).

The reason for these developments is that structural adjustment problems, which relate to labor as a factor of production, are no longer being settled in a perfectly competitive manner by the market. The facts are that, at the end of May of 1985, 2.2 million people or 8.9 per cent of the labor force were out of work in the Federal Republic of Germany. Over the last four years, West Germany experienced a declining trend in the level of employment, which just came to a halt. Therefore, it is not surprising that solutions, including that of an industrial policy, are proposed to resolve these problems.

What Needs to be Done?

One of the proposed solutions would be to follow an industrial policy which would bypass the market mechanism in the quest of society's goals. However, this approach is, at least presently, economically as well as politically unacceptable in a capitalist economy. An alternative presents itself in the pursuit of a market-oriented "active" industrial policy, which would accelerate the adjustment processes within the framework of a social market economy.

In principle, the demand to institute an industrial policy is in recognition of the fact that the consequences of rapidly occuring changes and the requisite processes of adjustment, as facilitated by an orthodox market economy, involve excessive sacrifices. Apart from social costs, the required structural changes also entail considerable economic losses. Socio-economic as well as political reality demands that the costs of adjustment be reduced to absolutely unavoidable magnitudes. This is only possible if the processes of structural change and adjustment, to new circumstances and requirements, are shortened, mitigated, and simultaneously steered in the desired direction.

However, this goal can only be achieved if policy makers adopt a far-sighted concept of an industrial policy, one which contains a vision of the future. In this context, industrial policy represents more than just a fashionable expression. It is destined to become a socio-economic as well as a political force behind fundamental issues. At stake are not only the survival of politicians and of the policies which they advocate, but, more importantly, our country's future role as one of the leading industrial economies.

The demand for a proper market-oriented industrial policy is linked, therefore, to the objective of keeping West Germany at the level of a first-rate industrial state. This new policy, designed to complement regional, sectoral, and industry-oriented industrial policies, aims at a future-oriented structural system which is conducive to progressive innovations.

Fundamental Controversies from the View of Ordnungspolitik

The questions which arise and which need to be clarified are whether industrial goals can be achieved within the setting of a free market economy; can they be realized under a free enterprise system? Often times, industrial policy is wrongly associated with interventionism in its ultimate form. A lack of clarity and understanding about the substance of this concept is, therefore, the reason why the term "industrial policy" arouses intense political emotions at many levels in West Germany:

1. It arouses distrust among the advocates of the competitive market system. They see the danger of this "active" policy as providing the promoters of a planned economy with instruments with which they can introduce elements of regimentation into the free market economy in order to overcome it (the Trojan horse theory).
2. The concept of an industrial policy also causes a conflict between conservatives and liberals on the one hand and socialists and communists on the other hand; it reflects the traditional controversy of freedom versus socialism.
3. The introduction of an industrial policy also is conducive to arouse controversial arguments among the supporters and opponents of an "active" industrial policy, affecting the whole socio-economic as well as political-party spectrum.

However, due to the fact that the dialogue on industrial policy is greatly influenced by factors of a political nature, it tends to overshadow factual arguments in favor of political convictions. This is, perhaps, the main reason underlying the controversial positions adopted toward this policy. Furthermore, negative experiences resulting from some rigid economic planning or from non-market based structural policies have led to the indiscriminate association of a market-oriented industrial policy with such attempts.

Past Mistakes make Cautious

The question which surfaces with regard to the applicability of an "active" industrial policy, within the framework of a price-regulated market economy, is similar to the one we faced in our discussion of a "structural policy". The resolution of this question is likewise influenced by political-structural considerations. The main reason for this development is that, as we have seen, the official public "structural policy" failed to be based on a goal-oriented conceptual framework of the industrial structure of the German economy. As a result, the officially pursued structural policy was negative in scope. Therefore, the processes of technological innovation were hindered rather than advanced.

The thus applied structural policy primarily served to maintain the existing structure instead to aid the adjustment process and to guide the direction of the processes of technological change and innovation. In other words, it proved to be a major obstacle for economic growth instead to invigorate it. The hope, at least to be able to preserve jobs, has not only proven to be false but the exact opposite occurred. Instead of slowing down and reducing the rate of discharge of workers, increasing unemployment was the outcome. The net result was a diminution of social welfare and a weakening of the social safety net in our society.

Through measures of public structural policies, which interfered counter-productively with the market mechanism, more work places were eliminated than would have been the case if the developing structural changes would not have been impeded by public measures, especially subsidies, to preserve the existing structure. A market-oriented solution, on the other hand, would have stimulated flexibility and mobility within the economy.

Reviewing the negative experiences with political-structural measures to solve the crises in the steel and shipbuilding industries, it is understandable that the concept of an industrial policy meets great scepticism. Also, no spontaneous concurrence is encountered when the adjectives market-oriented, innovative, or stimulative are added to the term.

The fact is that the attempts to avoid or at least to mitigate, to an absolute minimum, the consequences of regional and industrial crises with the aid of public structural policies, designed to "order" and to expedite the processes of change, proved to be unsuccessful. The reason for this failure is, in the final analysis, to be found in the lack of personal courage of politicians to assist the inevitable, market-determined adjustment processes with political thrust. Objectively oriented decisions are occasionally viewed as unpopular by the general public and, therefore, could negatively influence the voters.

For these reasons, policy decisions which affect the economy in general and industry in particular, should not be left primarily to politicians. Although the latter surround themselves with professional advisors and hold hearings to enhance their expertise, the final responsibilities for enterprises, for the invested capital, for the preservation of jobs, as well as for future-oriented investment decisions rest with businessmen and bankers. They are liable with their capital and with their reputation, which they risk, that the economic organism remains vigorous.

The carriers of entrepreneurial responsibility did not enjoy, so far, enough input and influence in economic and industrial-political decision-making processes. This is due to the fact that they themselves do not feel inclined to play a more active role in socio-economic decision making. Their extensive engagements with their enterprises and workers may not permit them to get more actively involved. However, it is they who possess the insight for the real dimensions of economic activity and who are able to judge and to evaluate what is possible and feasible. These traits are not typical of the average theoretician or politician. The former do not usually possess the requisite practical experience and are inclined to be more concerned with their scientific work and reputation. Politicians, on the other hand, tend to be more concerned with the protection of their political interests and mandates. This seems to be the case even if they had prior business experience and if they are personally convinced of the correctness of factual evaluations and policy recommendations. Concerns for reelection might prevent them from taking more objective action. Hence, experience proves that structural policy, which is to be associated with strategic objectives and which, therefore, requires far-sighted decisions, is in practice aligned with the preservation of existing structures. This is primarily due to political factors, exercised by administration officials at the federal and state levels. The regularly put forth argument that jobs were at stake and needed to be preserved found public approval. Due to lack of insight, the fact that government policies are not, as a rule, determined by the least costly alternative generally escapes the public. The costs, though hidden, are borne by the tax payers. An evaluation of benefits and costs for consumers and producers, and, most importantly, for taxpayers, and, therefore, for society, is missing, ex-ante as well as ex-post.

The fundamental cause for the almost indiscriminate rejection of an industrial policy in the Federal Republic of Germany is to be found in the apparent misinterpretation to view it exclusively as political policy. Its market orientation is totally overlooked.

According to widespread perception, public actions in the economic sphere are generally referred to as economic policy. As a result, any political policy measures with regard to the shaping of economic objectives is inappropriately generalized as being of the nature of public arrangement or accommodation. Hence, perceptions of what industrial policy is or could be has not been influenced by factual objectives but by the preconceived notion that it deals exclusively with governmental actions and policies. Gerhard Fels, for example, took this position only recently in two articles.[1]

It is in this manner that industrial policy was pushed into the shadow of interventionism. Consequently, one deprives oneself, without compelling reasons, of the opportunity to shape and to apply this policy within the framework of the market.

This one-dimensional view represents evidence that the prevailing interpretations and practices of a social market economy are no longer invigorated by the daring spirit of Ludwig Erhard. Structural theory is now imprinted by aging maturity. It is, therefore, neither conducive to absorb creative impulses nor to provide them. Structural theory of the social market economy, therefore, no longer makes contributions for constructive practical development. The restrained attitude toward an industrial policy proves this assertion. As a result, structural theory finds itself presently in a dormant state.

Solution to a Disruptive Misconception

The objective of political policy is, in the final analysis, the concern for a dignified life and for the development of man's potentials. Therefore, political policy cannot only be equated with governmental actions. Everyone, as a political creature, as a responsible citizen, and every institution, governmental as well as non-governmental, is obligated to pursue these goals.

Hence, one needs to distinguish three levels of political activity, of which the government is representative of one. For example, hardly anyone in the Federal Republic of Germany associates *Tarifpolitik* (wage settlements), the political, redistributional struggle between labor and management, with government action — simply because politics is contained in the term *Tarifpolitik*. Labor-management negotiations are assured autonomy by the constitution; the government has no right to intervene.

In a free socio-economic order, the state does not play the predominant role in freeing the forces of economic dynamics and of economic development. It is active citizens, i.e., labor and management, which keep the economic wheel in motion. The function of government is to oversee this process. It is to provide the economic framework by setting and enforcing rules of conduct, if the market itself does not already sanction, oversee, and enforce them if necessary.

II. The Fundamental Question

The fundamental question which now faces West Germany is whether she should employ more efficient instruments to eliminate the burdens of the past and the strains which might descend upon her. The reason is that we are not yet in a position to foresee whether we shall be able to continue to pursue our economic policy with familiar and proven instruments in a successful manner. In view of the new dimensions of economic challenges, can we, even with the greatest efforts in the most proficient handling of conventional instruments, sufficiently reduce political obstacles which interfered with the workings of a free market economy? Such a policy is likely to curtail the discretion and scope available to decision-makers.

We in West Germany quite rightly react to the continuous improvements in weapons technology by pondering more efficient defense concepts. At the same time, however, we are neglecting the need to think about how we can strengthen the "offensive power" of our free socio-economic system. The competitive system inherent in the social market economy not only fosters a high degree of economic efficiency, it also permits the country to afford its defense potential without forcing citizens to reduce their standard of living to any appreciable extent.

Just as national defense requires continuous adjustment in order to enhance defensive capacity, the socio-economic setting must also adapt to fundamentally changing conditions in technology, organization, and international trade. For example, workshop drawings become outdated in the course of time, necessitating new ones although the laws of statics and aerodynamics have not changed. Similarly, it is imperative for the human race, standing at the threshold of the 21st century, to reflect on new forms of socio-economic policy which not only accommodate change but also promote it.

We can only expect a pragmatic response to the question, as to whether industrial policy in a free market economy may be regarded as a helpful instrument of economic policy, if we succeed to separate it from its political encumbrances and base our judgment on purely objective criteria. This implies that our practice-oriented economic policy-makers should discard primarily tactical policies. They should adopt fundamental economic policies which are based on the principles of a market economy of the type which Ludwig Erhard developed and practiced with much success. The political parties should again free Erhard's concepts and this policy approach from electoral and tactical considerations.

III. What should an "active" Industrial Policy Achieve?

As the world stands at the threshold of the Third Industrial Revolution, the purpose of an active industrial policy, not only for economic and political decision-makers but also for the common man, is to improve the overall economic conditions. It is to facilitate future-oriented, far-sighted economic policies, which strengthen and enhance the potential of the economy.

A policy based on these objectives requires two essential elements, stabilization and development. In order to be able to realize its expectations, such a policy should consistently pursue a clear-cut concept and meet four conceptual requirements:
1. To follow an explicit definition.
2. To have an ascending order of objectives (hierarchy of objectives).
3. To provide information about steering methods.
4. To define a system, a set of measures, which facilitates efforts on a reasonable basis.

By offering an explicit definition, policy-makers could clearly express the fundamental idea which shapes their concept. By pursuing a clear set of goals, they could put the necessary discretionary decision-making process on an objective basis. Toward this end, they need to disclose the steering methods by which this policy realizes its stated objectives. For an active industrial policy to result in net economic benefits, it must be fundamentally future-oriented. It must take the offensive in the pursuit of its goals. Accordingly, it could be renamed an *offensive* rather than an *active* industrial policy. To the extent that such a policy is directed at the innovative capacity of the economy, it would be appropriate to speak of an *innovative* industrial policy.

IV. What can "active" Industrial Policy Achieve?

In keeping with the principles of a social market economy, an industrial policy can facilitate numerous functions, designed to improve the effective use of economic instruments in general and combinations of industrial policy in particular.

Under my concept, I draw a distinction between *classifying, orienting,* and *offensive* functions of an industrial policy. The primary responsibility for the development and implementation of a workable concept of an industrial policy, from which improved insights into factual connections may be derived, ought to rest with industry itself (primacy of industry). However, this does not rule out participation by the state. The latter's function should be to help to promote the concepts of industrial policy, by supporting its realization through the government's discretionary economic policy.

Within the framework of an *intermediary* move towards a solution which envisages cooperation between industry and state, as kind of a division of labor created by mutual consent, the state should only assume responsibility in a supporting role. Government should only intervene with regard to those tasks which the private sector cannot be expected to settle more proficiently or more rapidly (the principle of providing assistance for selfhelp).

A conceptual or innovative industrial policy, as part of the economic policy conducted by a sophisticated industrial society, has not only conceptual but also executive tasks to fulfil. It should provide help in the form of *starting-up assistance, adjustment assistance, reenforcement assistance, and breaking-up assistance.*

1. To provide *starting-up assistance* means to act as a promotor. This involves paving the way for entrepreneurial independence. It furnishes back-up support, by strengthening the market position of entrepreneurs of already established firms, which penetrate the market in an innovative manner.
2. To provide *adjustment assistance* implies to offer technical advice and managerial support to enterprises with a sound entrepreneurial structure which are (temporarily) not able to cope with the pressures of adjustment.
3. To offer *reenforcement assistance* aims to strengthen a provincially managed enterprise's adaptability to the accelerating speed of economic and technological progress, by reenforcing its ability to regain economic vigorous vitality, to become competitive again.
4. To provide *breaking-up assistance,* in extreme cases winding-up assistance, is aimed at shortening the liquidation process for those firms which are no longer competitive and which must, therefore, be taken out of the market as quickly as possible.

Under an industrial policy, starting-up assistance may be compared with the technical services furnished immediately before the take-off of a jumbo jet. Air is fed into the engines to permit the ignition to take place in the turbines. Or, if the air power unit has been switched off for technical reasons, the aircraft is connected to a source of energy on the ground. Economic start-up assistance should always be well prepared and only be granted for a relatively short period of time.

The purpose of official support for industry, during adjustment processes, is to protect the firms in question from losing their competitive position in the market. It is to help them — when they are themselves no longer able to do so — to carry out the requsite technical and organizational restructuring of the enterprise, at the speed required by competition.

It is also conceivable that firms, which have grown too rapidly or which have degenerated into unmanageable conglomerates, be broken up into efficiently manageable companies. An example of the latter is AEG of Germany. The idea is not to wait for a situation to develop which requires a "fire-brigade operation". It demands assistance measures which impose a high degree of responsibility on public authorities and on the private banking system alike. As a rule, the parts of a firm to be separated as independent units should be those which permit a sound detachment in the form of *buy-outs* or *spin-offs.*

With regard to winding-up assistance, this can noticeably speed up the removal of non-profitable production, provided that such help is furnished in an active manner. However, it could also take a passive form by depriving dying industries of customary benefits, i.e., benefits of a fiscal nature or those intended to maintain the structure of the industry in question. Of course, this approach also encourages the natural automatic process of structural adjustment to run its course.

V. Recommendation: Towards a Structural Industrial Policy

Our efforts should be directed to strengthen and to safeguard the efficiency of trade and industry. The focal point of this endeavor should be a regulative economic policy based on an active structural industrial policy, characterized by the following theses:

1. Industry is the core of a modern economy. Economic policy must, therefore, be primarily an industrial policy which accomodates and promotes structural change.
2. Ludwig Erhard developed the principles of a social market economy for a modern industrial state. It is essential, for our times, to reorient economic policy towards the thrust of Ludwig Erhard's ideas.
3. Ludwig Erhard's theory of the social market economy is the nucleus of a comprehensive economic *and* social system which ensures "public order in freedom" in a democratic state. The constituting elements of this theory are:
   a) Free competition as the key component in enhancing performance.
   b) Commitment of all individual groups to the common task of safeguarding the "wealth of nations" (Adam Smith).
   c) Full employment.
   d) Solidarity, provision of assistance for those who practice selfhelp, and the promotion of a "caring society".
4. The state must stipulate and guarantee the general institutional conditions for furnishing back-up support and to safeguard the maintenance of social peace.

The goals to be pursued under an offensive or innovative structural industrial policy can, however, only be achieved if we succeed in creating a synthesis which combines mutually complementary elements from competitive policy, structural policy, technological and research policy, als well as the integration of these elements into an innovative industrial policy.

An innovative structural policy should be based on a mechanism which sends warning signals about discernibly undesirable trends, particularly during phases of profound economic and technological change. This will permit a timely correction of course. An innovative structural industrial policy should eliminate the necessity of crisis management.

It should be pointed out, especially to the critics of an active structural industrial policy, that the risk of a relapse into a wait-and-see mentality in investment, due to inadequate orientation in industry, is greater and more dangerous than the pragmatic approach of an innovative industrial policy. The latter is compatible with the market economy; it strengthens the scope of the economy and, therefore, minimizes the risk of abuse by oderly administration.

The pursuit of an innovative structural industrial policy within the framework of a social market economy reflects reasonable people in pragmatic rationality. It paves the way to the future in the manner successfully demonstrated by Ludwig Erhard, in building the West Germany economy after World War II.

NOTE

[1] Gerhard Fels, „Industriepolitik, Instrument zur Förderung der internationalen Wettbewerbsfähigkeit?"; *Wirtschaftsdienst*, Nr. 5 (May 1975), pp. 233–37. – Gerhard Fels, „Im Wendekreis des Krebsens, Anmerkungen zur Industriepolitik", *Frankfurter Allgemeine Zeitung*, June 10, 1985, p. 13. – Gerhard Fels, „Im Wendekreis des Krebsens, Traktat über Politik und Wirtschaft", Cologne 1985, pp. 82–89.

Democratic Planning in a Market Economy and Social Values

Richard L. Brinkman

The Industrial Policy Debate

The science of economics, in its historical evolution, has always been concerned with economic policy in a general sense. Industrial policy, as such, has more limited meaning and constitutes a part but not the whole of economic policy. In the current debate, industrial policy appears as that part of overall economic policy more specifically related and relevant to the manufacturing or industrial sector of the economy. And while any culture in the stage of modern economic growth, in a sense, has an industrial policy, such policies were not usually delineated but rather were melted into the overall of economic policy. For example, one might argue that Japan has had an industrial policy dating back to the Meiji Restoration, and for the United States dating back to Alexander Hamilton's *Report on Manufactures*.[1] However, it has been the Japanese "economic miracle" of the post-World War II era which has produced a debate over the conceivable benefits to be derived from an industrial policy (Johnson, 1982, pp. 3–34).

But the exact meaning of industrial policy is subject to question; no agreed upon definition of industrial policy appears in the literature.[2] A conceptual clarification is difficult to achieve in that the substantive components of any given industrial policy are varied and complex. Even for a given nation, industrial policy is not fixed but evolves over time and is dependent on the era or stage of economic development.[3] And given the diversity of specific cultures what may be appropriate for a given nation, such as Japan or West Germany, may not be appropriate for the American economy and vice versa. In that conception and practice varies so much among nations, industrial policy, per se, is difficult to formulate for all times and all cultures. However, this does not preclude the identification of certain universal aspects of the current industrial policy debate which are cross-cultural and relevant.

The basic issues of the current debate relate primarily to the issues of economic productivity and international competitiveness. Since most economists recognize increased productivity and international competitiveness as being positive and benign, the debate really relates to the choice among alternative and concomitant social structures. Allowing for varying degrees of government intervention, the spectrum of choice concerns which institutional adjustment is best suited for amelioration. The polar positions concern deregulation or "privatization" on the one hand versus comprehensive plans for government cooperation and participation on the other.

Another important aspect of the debate relates not only to the clarification of the specifics of a given industrial policy, a difficult task, but how to indicate and measure its success. Economists engaged in the debate try to show, perhaps rationalize, how well a particular economy is doing. In this way economists substantiate and vindicate the wisdom and correctness of their particular prescription for industrial policy. Basically, those in support of institutional buttresses toward the polarity of deregulation point to the American economy as being successful and, consequently, the institutional model to follow. Success is frequently measured in terms of the capacity of the American economy, compared to the economies of Europe, to add more workers to the labor force. The success of the current American industrial policy is indicated by the fact that the employment growth for the American has been 2.4 per cent for the period 1970–1980, whereas the comparable figure for West Germany is −0.2 per cent.[4] As we will try to demonstrate below, simply adding more jobs is an argument relevant to the quantitative statics of economics growth; it is not relevant to the qualitative dynamics of economic development. However, it is the process of ongoing economic development and structural changes inherent in an advancing technology which relate to the productivity issue. To some the "more jobs added" argument represents an "absurdity" (Thurow, 1984, p. 25). To require more workers to produce relatively less, indicated by lower rates of productivity, is not indicative of economic health and well being but to the contrary represents a manifestation of economic malfunction and malady.[5]

Given their faith in the "Magic of the Market". Feldstein (1984) and Schultze (1984) both argue against the need for a new industrial policy.[6] Predictably, in view of their industrial policy perspective, Feldstein and Schultze (among many others) attempt to show and demonstrate why and how the Japanese and German economies have not really been that successful. And further, in that: "MITI is the primary Japanese government agency charged with the formation and execution of industrial policy", MITI is also viewed in the negative.[7] Is it quite correct to state: ". . . relative to the industries of other countries, American industry performed quite well by almost all standards."[8]

Among other indicators, critics of the current industrial policy being pursued in the United States turn to statistics dealing with economic productivity.[9] Data on economic productivity indicate a long-term decline for the American economy and especially in relative comparisons with that of Japan and West Germany, note Table I, "United States: Long-Term Economic Decline." "America has now had almost twenty years of declining productivity growth and five years of essentially no productivity growth" (Thurow, 1984, p. 17). Data on the American trade balance also indicate a faltering economy. Predating the culpability of Reaganomics, the international competitive position of the United States showed signs of weakness from the early 1970s forward. The strong, appreciated dollar of the current period is hardly indicative of an efficient or a more competitively favorable position of the American economy, as "dynamic comparative advantage."[10] The appreciated dollar rests on high interest rates and capital inflows and this of course generates problems for expanding U.S. exports in competitive world markets.

Is the portrayal of the American economy as one of long-term economic stagnation accurate and correct or simply a biased view and a way of justifying (rationalizing) a new industrial policy based upon, perhaps, other value principles? In our opinion, the prevailing view appearing in the literature presents the picture of long-

Table 1:

United States: Long-Term Economic Decline			
American Productivity Growth (per cent Change)			
– (A) –		– (B) –	
1948 – 1965	3.2	1947 – 1964	3.3
1965 – 1973	2.4	1965 – 1972	2.4
1973 – 1978	1.8	1972 – 1977	1.6
1978 – 1980	–0.8	1977 – 1980	0.2
Comparative Productivity Improvements (per cent Annual Av Increase)			
		(C) 1960 – 1973	(D) 1973 – 1979
Japan		9.9	3.8
W. Germany		5.4	5.0
U.K.		4.0	0.1
U.S.		2.8	0.9
Sources: (A) Magaziner and Reich, 1982, p. 31; (B) Thurow, 1984, p. 17; (C) & (D) Magaziner and Reich, 1982, p. 36.			

term U.S. economic decline and crisis.[11] For example, in the Wharton School study, hardly a citadel for an unwarranted or irresponsible critique, we find: "There is widespread agreement on the unsatisfactory perfomance of the U.S. economy and the need for a new industrial policy direction ... our shared belief is that America is over the hill" (Wachter and Wachter, 1984, pp. 2, 9). In June 1983, President Reagan established a Commission on Industrial Competitiveness which reported (1985): "Our ability to compete in world markets is eroding. Growth in U.S. productivity lags far behind that of our foreign competitors. Real hourly compensation of our work force is no longer improving. U.S. leadership in world trade is declining."[12] The recent upturn of the American economy has turned sluggish and has not alleviated the situation. As reported in *The Wall Street Journal,* recent data released by the Labor Department once again reveal ". . . a Decline in Productivity," ". . . Steepest Slide Since 1981."[13]

Consequently, the debate apparently is not over whether the American economic decline exists. The debate is over causation and which new industrial policy will rectify the long-term trend of relative economic stagnation. A new structure is being advocated in order to maintain the dynamics of long-term economic growth and development. But why is this so? Why does such a change in structure serve as a prerequisite for the ongoing dynamics and continuity of economic evolution?

The Paradigm and Dynamics of Economic Development

Economic evolution is comprised of the interaction between both economic growth as reproduction and replication and economic development as transformation. Though the two concepts are treated by mainstream economists as being synonymous, the two processes are different and conceptually distinct.[14] A problem arises when neoclassical and Keynesian economists apply their theories, essentially of economic growth, to analyze and prescribe policies relevant to the processes of economic development. The issue of institutional adjustment, the industrial policy debate, is really outside the paradigmatic boundaries of normal science in economics. The dynamic processes of technological change and institutional adjustment have historically been the *bete noire* of mainstream economic analysis.[15]

The Swedish Nobel laureate, Gunnar Myrdal, representing a heterodox view, conceptualizes economic development as the " ... *movement upward of the entire social system.*"[16] To our view, that "entire social system", from an holistic perspective, is best dealt with by the scientific conception of culture (Tylor, 1871) as "that complex whole". Culture in its material and nonmaterial components constitutes the substantive grist for the mill of the economic process.[17] Elsewhere, we have argued and at length for a general theory of economic development formulated in the matrix of culture evolution – the theory and methodology is called *Cultural Economics* (1981).

If a culture grows as indicated by an increase of GNP per capita, from that of zero (a free-good society) to that of approximately $ 15,000, is not such growth the equivalent of economic development? If so, why then engage the assumed-to-be-fuzzy and difficult areas of social and technological change? Why not resort to long-run Keynes in some form of a Harrod-Domar construct of economic growth? In the sphere of transportation, humankind has also experienced a similar type of growth. Growth in transportation, as measured in miles per hour has advanced along a steep exponential continuum from that of approximately four miles per hour (foot travel) to that of 20,000 (rockets).

The exponential growth curve was not achieved, however, by using more feet (replication) or by running faster, but rather was achieved through structural change inherent in the process of development. This entailed a series of *gestalt* switches from that of foot travel, to horses, to railroads, automobiles, aircraft and ultimately to rockets. If a specific technic of transportation only experienced growth, as more and more of the same, the end result would have been a growth curve in the form of the logistic or Gompertz as the typical "S" curve configuration. The avoidance of a ceiling and stagnation was achieved through a series of "logistic surges" in the changing of one structure of transportation to the next.[18] That ongoing growth requires continuous changes in structure is referred to in the literature as the "Principle of Similitude".[19] Consequently, humankind did not achieve the approximate $ 15,000 GNP per capita through a simple growth process as more and more bows and arrows. The high and sustained rates of economic growth, which characterize modern economic growth (Kuznets), were predicated on the transformation of culture via an industrial revolution. This is depicted in Figure I, "The Paradigm of Logistic Surges and the Stages of Economic Development".[20]

Figure 1:

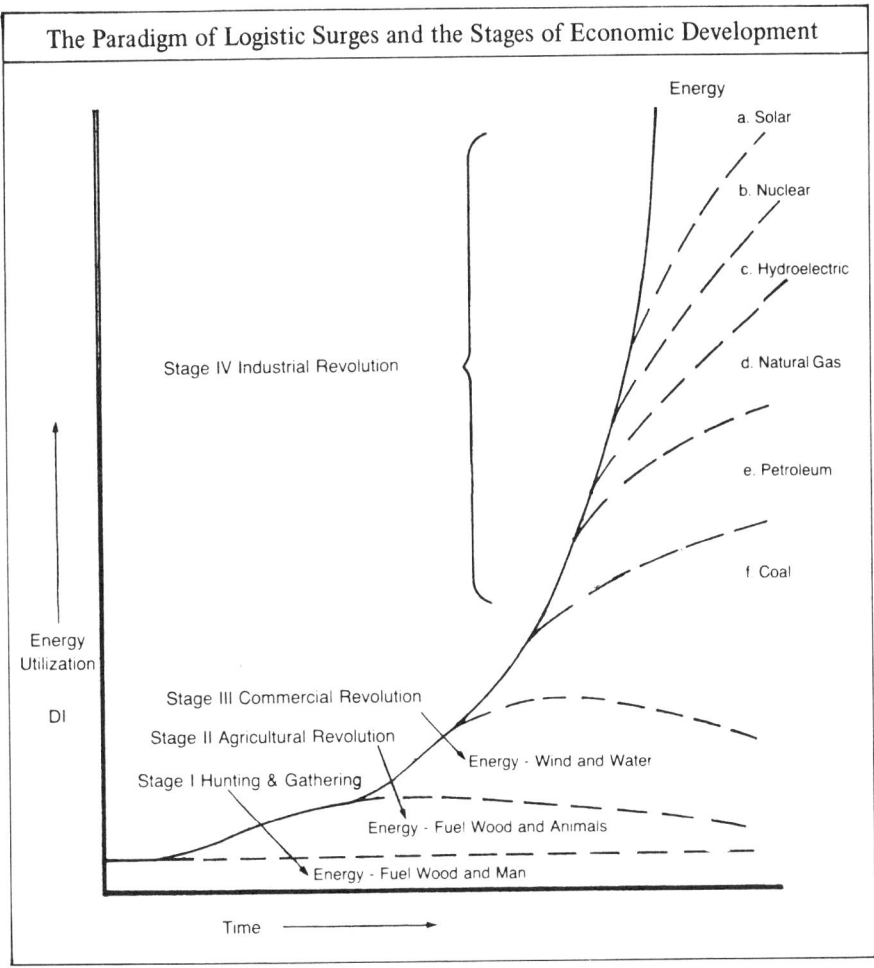

Many economists, however, tend to reject a stages methodology based upon what may be called the "unilinear" or "orthogenetic" fallacy. Karl Marx and Walt W. Rostow seem to infer that once started economic development, as a process of metamorphosis, is ongoing as in the world of biological development and evolution. The apparent assumption is that one stage or form leads inexorably and inevitably to the next. In that the global experience is one in which two-thirds of humankind have as yet to achieve modern economic growth, the stages approach as well as the concept of evolution tended to be discounted. Sahlins and Service have provided an answer with the very important conceptual distinction between specific and general evolution.[21] Specific evolution relates to a specific technic, such as propeller driven aircraft, or to a specific stage of economic development. General evolution refers to the transformation from one technic or stage of economic development to the next.

For the world as a whole, general culture evolution has indeed taken place and, in this context, the empirical evidence supports the stages of economic development. That is not to say that any specific or given culture will necessarily experience a similar transformation.[22] Many specific cultures have historically been in the vanguard of culture evolution only to ultimately stagnate and decay. This does not negate the fact that evolution, per se, and the stages of economic development have taken place for the earth as a whole. To our view, the stages methodology constitutes a necessary and integral part of any general theory of economic development and evolution.[23]

But to the point: if a nation wishes to engage economic growth on a long-term continuum, it must also invoke structural changes inherent in the process of economic development. The two concepts are not synonymous; economic growth by itself does not lead to transformation, but rather leads to an asymptotic ceiling of stagnation. But what causes the required structural changes of the economy and culture? Where is the locus of the evolutionary impulse?

Industrial Policy as Social Technology

The locus, it can be argued, resides in the mind of humankind and the capacity to symbol and abstract. The process basically concerns how humankind interacts with the environment comprised of culture and the physical universe to originate new knowledge. Such knowledge, when applied to problems of economic production and the concomitant social organization, is concreted into material and social technics. Such technics, as an integrated totality, comprise the overall *gestalt* of technology.[24] The technological advance so achieved represents the basic factor causing structural change as the dynamic force of ongoing culture evolution. This is not to endorse a simplistic technological determinism which assumes material technology to be a sui generis force of culture evolution.

While technological change serves as a necessary condition for structural change and ongoing culture evolution, that change is not always forthcoming or inevitable.

Technological change is related to a complex process of circular and cumulative causation and involves many variables, such as: the personality and innate capacity of the inventor and innovator; culture permeability and accumulation; as well as the physical composition of natural resources, among others. In such a circle of interaction, how can one delineate the specific point which serves as the starting point and, consequently, can be designated the causal factor above all others? Technological change in essence is predicated on a complex multivariate social process related to the advance of useful knowledge and science. Useful knowledge concreted into material and social technology constitutes the dynamics of the process of culture evolution.

But why does a change in technology lead to a change in the structure of culture? This is so because both technology and culture are made of the same substance; we speak here of knowledge.[25] Technology and culture represent opposite sides of the same coin, the coin of useful knowledge. On the one hand, in its application knowledge appears as technology and on the other hand, in its store as culture. To change one (technology) is to change the other (culture). If we change and transform the dough we transform the bread, in that the dough constitutes the substance of the bread.

Technology, as the dough of the bread of culture, appears in the form of material technics, such as automobiles, buildings and bridges. Technology is also of the form of concomitant social technics, such as the social institutions of the corporation, the trade union, government, and on. But such technics associated with the economic process also constitute the ingredients and substance of material and nonmaterial culture and function, therefore, also as a store of knowledge. Knowledge in its concretion is manifest in a dichotomy, with technology on the one hand and culture on the other. Consequently, by advancing and applying knowledge in the solution of the problems of economic production and social organization, humankind advances technology, but also in the process advances and transforms culture. This is so in that such technics constitute the substantive nature of culture. We speak here not of all of culture, but rather that the overall *gestalt* of technology constitutes the core of culture. It is consequently legitimate to describe culture evolution as a sequential pattern of the stages of economic development characterized by a given base of technology.[26]

The fountainhead and dynamics of the process reside in the accumulation and advance of knowledge. In that knowledge begets knowledge as a geometric progression, the overall growth path is exponential.[27] That this "mode of growth" is exponential is so pervasive and fundamental that Derek J. de Solla Price has ". . . no hesitation in suggesting it as the fundamental law of any analysis of science."[28] To others, it has been designated as a basic "Law of Progress".[29] If it is correct to assume that the path of knowledge is exponential and that culture substantively stores knowledge, how can it be explained that all specific cultures do not experience ongoing exponential evolution? The distinction between specific and general evolution is again relevant. Any given or fixed technic, such as propeller driven aircraft, will take on the path of a logistic growth curve and, ultimately, be limited by an asymptotic ceiling.

The Law of Diminishing Returns, as applied to knowledge, ultimately prevails in the perfection of a given technic. In 1903, two brothers, Orville and Wilbur Wright, set the groundwork for propeller driven aircraft in the form of a very rudimentary structure. At this stage (1903) a good deal of room existed for improvement. By World War II, however, the possibilities for improving upon propeller driven aircraft had run their course. By this time, though thousands of engineers were engaged in aircraft design and worked on the structure, further improvement, as measured in miles per hour, was difficult to achieve. Ongoing growth and the escape from the logistic ceiling was predicated on a *gestalt* switch from that of propellers on to jets. Again we invoke the process of general evolution and the paradigm of logistic surges. If transportation technology had remained locked into the fixed structure of propeller driven aircraft, humankind could never have broken the sound barrier.

Consequently, ongoing exponential growth, be it measured in miles per hour, BTU's of energy consumption, or GNP per capita, requires ongoing changes in technology as the dynamic process of general evolution. Specific evolution, as the perfection of a given technic or structure, results in ultimate stagnation as the levelling of the logistic.[30] In this context we argue that technological change be granted pride of place in any discussion of economic productivity. Indeed, many references could be provided in support of the contention that: "The most important source of productivity growth is technological change".[31] But if our conception and theory hold correct, a change in technology relates not only to material technics but social technics as well. The prerequisite institutional adjustment, in the form of a new industrial policy, would itself be an integral and functional part of the overall *gestalt* of technology.

The invention and innovation of a new industrial policy, itself, constitutes a change in technology and, ipso facto, also a change in culture. Social institutions do not only serve a static function as habituation. Social institutions in their genesis and function can also represent dynamic agents of culture evolution.[32] In fact one of the most dynamic technics ever conceived of by humankind is of the nature of a social institution. We speak here of the invention of the method of invention, the invention of science. Science is, also, a social institution.[33] A new structure of industrial policy appears in order. The next question becomes, how then to decide on the specifics of its composition? What structure of social organization will best serve to distinguish and innovate the sunrise industries over the sunset? In the harsh economic milieu of the late twentieth century, is the Schumpeterian risk taker and innovator, as entrepreneur, sufficient enough to provide for "creative destruction"?[34]

Cooperation and Consensus as Solution Toward Progress

The industrial policy debate essentially revolves around the issue of institutional adjustment and, consequently, can be analyzed in the framework of a classic cultural lag. Such a question is not raised in the matrix of neoclassical or Keynesian economics. Consequently, it is predictable that those economists operating within the paradigmatic boundaries of mainstream economics would settle for the remedies contained in conventional monetary and fiscal policy. Economists with such a predilection would eschew any ventures into "... any conceivable set of new industrial policies". According to Schultze, solutions to the current anomalies of the American economy, either in the form of a supply-side economics or industrial policy rest on "... theories originated outside the mainstream of professional economic thought."[35]

The problem is not that the current administration in Washington, D.C. does not have an industrial policy. The problem is rather that the current industrial policy directed toward the polarity of supply-side economics and nonintervention has not worked.[36] The direction of policy toward more and more of the same, as recommended by the President's Commission on Industrial Competitiveness, does not appear as a salubrious solution to the current anomalies characterizing the American economy. Also, and a rather obvious point, the current industrial policy being pursued in the United States is hardly devoid of government intervention. Given the astronomical deficits associated with Reaganomics, Keynesian economics is very much in evidence. Demand-side economics is manifest in unbelievably high levels of military spending. To break out of the current trend toward decline and stagnation requires a correct identification of the problem. Economists must address the issue of the need for ongoing institutional adjustment. Institutional evolution, as social technology, is necessary in order to organize and control the potential exponential advance of material technology and culture. Given the inherent paradigmatic blinders and predilections, orthodox theory does not allow for the correct identification of the problem and, consequently, cannot provide for an answer. To deny the social is to deny the solution.

Cooperation and consensus, rather than conflict and confrontation, are the desired objectives to integrate the interests of business, labor and government in the establishment and fulfillment of a rejuvenated national economy. In this discussion it is incorrect to conclude that those advocating greater governmental participation in the economic process are necessarily anti-market. "The goal is to set up a process in which government, labor, and management are encouraged to work together within a market framework to take actions to strengthen market outcomes. The state becomes not a centralized planner but a cooperative market player."[37] To raise the issue of the "free market" versus "national planning" therefore represents a false dichotomy (Reich, 1983, pp. 232, 235). "The issue is not one of state intervention in the economy. All states intervene in their economies for various reasons... The question is how the government intervenes and for what purposes."[38]

In theory and in practice, an unregulated market system is anachronistic to the needs of a modern industrial society. "But even the strongest proponents of free markets admit that the market does not always work perfectly in achieving either economic efficiency or other social goals set by society" (Palmer and Sawhill, 1984, p. 288). Market imperfections and failures relate to externalities, public goods and the overall issue of uncertainty, among others.[39] The necessary institutional adjustments to overcome such problems, requiring an analysis of social variables as well as the purely economic, cannot be derived from the application of mainstream economic science. In the United States, neoinstitutional economics appears most relevant to the problem at hand in that it includes the process of institutional adjustment within the matrix of theory. Institutional adjustment is relegated to choice and discretion. The process is subject to scientific inquiry and amenable to instrumental value principles.[40] In the United States, neoinstitutional economics is associated with some form of indicative or democratic planning.[41]

This is not to discount the positive attributes of the neoclassical synthesis or Keynesian economics, but rather that such a policy orientation does not go far enough. ". . . Keynes's interventionism is much less than the institutionalists' broader concept of indicative national economic planning" (Gruchy, 1984, p. 162; Tool, 1984, p. 180). To some, the term economic planning is best left out of economic discussions. But this is to invoke myth and to deny reality. "The enduring myth of the unmanaged market illustrates the power of ideology over reality" (Reich, 1983, p. 232). We speak here not only of the current magnitude of government intervention and management, which now exists, but also in relation to the economic planning actually taking place in the private sector itself. The issue is not over whether or not planning exists, but rather who plans and for which purpose. While the phenomenon of economic planning in the private sector has yet to penetrate basic textbook treatment, it has nonetheless taken over the economy.[42] The question then becomes, since we already have planning, why not make the instruments and mechanisms more democratic and in the process, perhaps, more closely aligned to the public purpose.

In part, resolution of the complex problems associated with a new industrial policy requires the advance and development of the science of economics, itself, to include social variables within the matrix of theory. "The central theme of this book is that in the emerging era of productivity, social justice is not incompatible with economic growth, but essential to it" (Reich, 1982, p. 20; Alinson, 1985, p. 138). Reich depicts this as a merger of the business and civic cultures, in theory and in practice, into an integrated whole, note Figure II, "The Path Toward Consensus and Progress". From this merger the objective is to then organize and integrate the interests of business, labor and government, with an ancillary buttress provided for by science, in order to formulate a sound and pragmatic basis for a new industrial policy.

Consequently, it is our conclusion that democratic planning is not incompatible or inconsistent with a market economy, but rather serves as a necessary condition for its continued evolution and development. "Only by acknowledging the powerful links between the social and economic dimensions of our national well-being can we forge a consensus for progress. And only through such a consensus can we craft rigourous institutions and forward looking strategies to accelerate economic evolution" (Reich, 1983, pp. 255 – 56).

Figure 2:

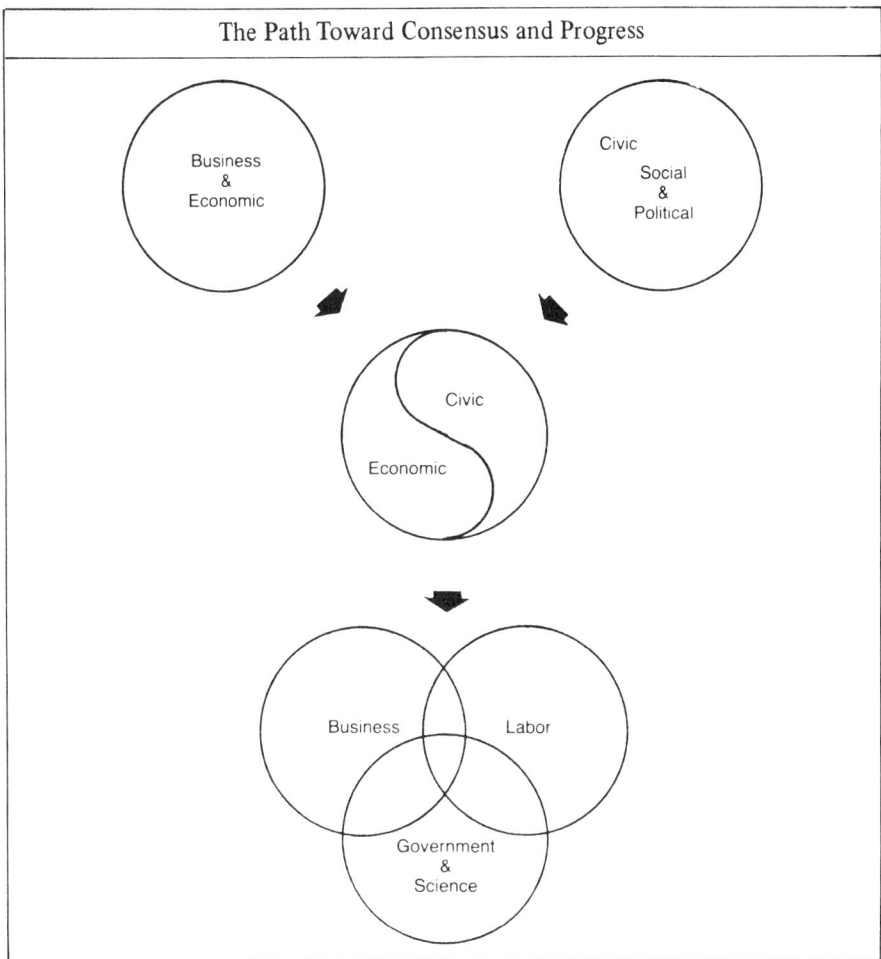

Leben und leben lassen

Current discussions of industrial policy, as necessary and as important as they are, tend to provide a myopic vision of the economic process and blur out a conception of the whole. The present debate focussing on industrial policy tends to obfuscate the fact that industrial policy is part but not the whole of economic policy. In the framework of circular and cumulative causation, it is the health and well-being of the economy, as a whole, which promotes the well-being of the industrial sector and, conversely, the health and well-being of the industrial sector in turn promotes the well-being of the overall economy as an organic whole.

Solving problems primarily in the areas of increased rates of economic productivity and international competitiveness, while necessary and important, obviously do not constitute the whole of the economic process and function. For it also can be argued that only in solving the problems of the economy as a whole will we be able to solve the problems of the parts. It is in this context that we have argued for an analysis of the economic process, and its concomitant parts, in the framework of general culture evolution.

The process of economic evolution, as measured in advances in economic production and higher levels of energy control, serves as a necessary but not sufficient condition for human progress. The *numeraire* or basic unit of account in assessing progress, to our view, should not simply be economic production but rather should focus on Homo sapiens, as humankind. How the economic process relates to the efficient production of more and more goods and services is only part of the problem. How all this promotes the cause of being human and further promotes human evolution and perfection is overriding and central. Human needs and the further perfectability of the specie do not reside simply in physical or economic needs, but go beyond.[44]

The objective rests with the full emancipation of each individual's genotype to its highest level of self-realization. Industrial policy, per se, conceivably could be a success, but in the last analysis such increased production may not trickle down to provide fulfillment or basic human needs. In the United States, would a successful industrial policy necessarily resolve the problems of poverty, unemployment, inequitable income distribution, increased hunger, poor health and education, pollution, the problems of the LDC world, the arms race and the nuclear build-up and beyond? The resolution of these problems will require the application of science not simply to economic production and social organization, but in addition and explicitly to the concept and theory of human development and evolution.[44] The basic issue is how then to apply science to the process of culture evolution in the ongoing advance and perfection of humankind. To our view such a policy objective is outside the market calculus and would require some form of democratic planning.

Admittedly, the innovation of such a social invention in the United States, as a policy objective, appears to lack the prerequisite base of political power. But all this is not pie-in-the-sky theorizing or analysis. For while the political realities in the United States are currently moving policy and economic theory in an opposite direction, it is also apparent that such policies will not alleviate, but rather will exacerbate, the long-term economic decline. Such a crucible of crisis and stagnation will nurture an environment for change and for a policy more oriented toward the humanistic and social dimensions of the economic process. In such a state of flux, the policy derivative may once again move in the democratic and emancipating tradition of the New Deal, to remove from humankind the historic bondage of poverty and ignorance. The forces which produced the proposed Humphrey-Javits Balanced Growth and Economic Planning Bill of 1975 are not dead in the United States. All this requires a new mood, a new public philosophy in the spirit of cooperation and consensus, the spirit of "Live and Let Live".⁴⁵

NOTES

¹ Johnson (1984), pp. 17–20, and for the basic and, perhaps, definitive analysis of the evolution of Japanese industrial policy, Johnson (1982).

² On this literature and the differing definitions note: Johnson (1984), p. 3–26, "... governments explicit attempts ... dynamic comparative advantage" p. 11; "... it is whatever the government does..." p. 48; "... a strategic consensus among government business and labor ..." Thurow (1984), p. 16; "The term industrial policy has many connotations ... the relationship between business and government on a micro-economic level ..." Wachter and Wachter (1981), p. 1.

³ "an elastic strategy evolving in response ..." Thurow (1954), p. 16; Johnson compares the evolution of industrial policy in terms of the Japanese "plan-rational state" to the "market-rational state" characteristic of the United States (1982), pp. 17–26, passim.

⁴ Magaziner and Reich (1982), pp. 38–39.

⁵ Report of President's Commission (1985), Vol. II, "The trend in real wage growth ... is particularly disturbing. Our American economy is not supporting an increasing standard of living for American workers.", p. 11.

⁶ On the "Magic of the Market" see W. Allen Wallis et al., (1984) that U.S. currently has an industrial policy, see Palmer and Sawhill (1984), pp. 19–21, 287–316.

⁷ While Johnson (1982), p. 17; Feldstein (1984), pp. 95–102; and Schultze (1984), pp. 6–7, Trezise (1984) ... etc. cast doubts, others are perhaps inclined to agree with Thurow: " I know of no serious scholar of Japanese economic success who thinks that their industrial policies have had a negative effect." (1984), p. 24. On the evidence plus additional references on the "Japanese 'Miracle'" note Johnson (1982), pp. 1–34.

⁸ Also, Feldstein (1984): "... there is no evidence ..." "... no such long-term decline ..." pp. 88, 109, in that Feldstein refers to overall manufacturing production he is perhaps correct. But this directs attention from the real issue which concerns economic productivity.

⁹ "The productivity with which a nation utilizes its human and capital resources plays the central role in its competitiveness." The President's Commission, Vol. II, p. 6.

¹⁰ Even during the earlier periods of a "weak dollar" the U.S. also experienced "weak exports". Note the President's Commission, Vol. II, pp. 7, 12–13, 175–177.

¹¹ The view: "Faced with a precipitous decline in its technological pre-eminence, with even basic industries in seeming danger of collapse, the United States needs a policy..." presented by Solo (1984), p. 713, also prevails in the literature.

¹² Volume I, p. 1 and passim. Vol. I & II.

¹³ *The Wall Street Journal*, May 30, 1985, p. 4, col. 2.

¹⁴ For a lengthy discussion of this distinction along the lines of holistic and interdisciplinary analysis, see *Cultural Economics* (1981).

¹⁵ Of the brave and the brainy who did so engage prior to World War II, the big three would be: Marx, Veblen and Schumpeter.

¹⁶ Myrdal (1974), p. 729. This conception is used elsewhere by Myrdal, the *Asian Drama*... etc.

¹⁷ The basic issue of the "Crucible and the Clay of Economic Development" of *Cultural Economics*, especially pp. 1–26.

¹⁸ The sociologists W. F. Ogburn and H. Hart provided for the analysis of the exponential and its underlying paradigm as "logistic surges".

¹⁹ Cf., D. Bell (1974), pp. 172–174.

²⁰ See *Cultural Economics* (1981), pp. 138–139 for empirical support and statistical quantification, the Entropy Law is relevant in this context and is integral to a general theory of economic development.

²¹ Sahlins and Service (1960): "Evolution: Specific and General", pp. 12–44.

²² Similarly, that the nautilus will not evolve into a mammal or Homo sapiens does not disprove the fact that general biological evolution has taken place.

²³ White (1947) makes the point that the concept of stages is relevant and essential to the concept of evolution.

²⁴ Such a "Wheel of Economic Development" incorporates the circular and cumulative causation associated with the work of Gunnar Myrdal, *Cultural Economics* (1981), pp. 198–236.

²⁵ Many social scientists have emphasized the primary role of knowledge and science, we speak here of: T. Veblen, W. F. Ogburn, K. Boulding, S. Kuznets, J. K. Galbraith, P. Drucker,... etc.

²⁶ Kuznets (1966), pp. 1–16, characterizes the basic "epochs" in terms of basic innovations.

²⁷ The dynamics of the economic process and culture evolution are consequently explained in the dynamics of the advance of knowledge.

²⁸ Price (1961), pp. 92–124; and (1963), pp. 4–5.

²⁹ Ayres (1962), pp. 119–121.

³⁰ The logistic or Gompertz configuration prevails for specific technics, such as: trade unions, business firms, railroads, canals, bridges and buildings as well as for a given stage of economic development.

³¹ Palmer and Sawhill (1984), p. 101; "The importance of technology was one of the central components of postwar Japanese industrial policy..." Johnson (1982), pp. 16–17.

³² Institutional adjustment, as a dynamic process, is subject to scientific inquiry, choise and discretion. Tool (1979).

³³ Whitehead (1925), p. 136 "... greatest invention of the nineteenth century..."; and that science is a social institution, Barnes (1972), p. 9–10.

[34] We do not advocate complete destruction, note Johnson (1984), p. 24 but that "... Japanese companies are willing to discard older technologies as fast as newer ones can be developed." Reich (1983), p. 261. Also we draw attention to the similarity to Schumpeter's creative destruction and the phenomenon of "logistic surges" and the "Principle of Similitude".

[35] Schultze (1983), p. 3; Basically, however, Schultze and Feldstein are not that far apart: "Most of the problems of U.S. industries can be solved with prudent monetary and fiscal policies." Feldstein (1984), p. 88.

[36] "Thus far, however, there is no clear evidence of overall favorable effects." Palmer and Sawhill (1984), pp. 21, 69–105.

[37] Thurow (1984), p. 17; and, "... well-designed adjustment policies – through which government seeks to *promote* market forces rather than supplant them..." Reich (1983), p. 234.

[38] Johnson (1982), pp. 17–18; and, "Laissez-faire, or a total absence of industrial policy, has never existed in the realm of ideological imagination." R. S. Ozaki in Johnson (1984), p. 49.

[39] Gruchy points to two basic problem areas in the context of uncertainty: 1st imperfect information and, 2nd technological change, (1984), p. 166.

[40] This constitutes a basic focus of neoinstitutional economics, note Tool (1979), and Stanfield (1984), also in Tool (1984), pp. 19–44, among others.

[41] Note Gruchy (1984); Gordon (1980); Dugger (1984); Stanfield (1979), among others.

[42] Note: Munkirs (1985); and Galbraith (1973).

[43] We refer here to the humanist psychologist A. Maslow and Wachtel (1983).

[44] Conceivably the next stage of culture evolution and designated as a "Human Revolution", cf. *Cultural Economics* (1981) especially pp. 391 ff.

[45] "The question is, can we find a new public philosophy that is at once adequate to reality and emotionally compelling?" Reich (1985), p. 79.

REFERENCES

Atkinson, Glen W. 1985. *"The Next American Frontier:* A Review." *The Social Science Journal.* 22 (January), pp. 138–140.

Ayres, Clarence E. 1962. *The Theory of Economic Progress.* New York: Schocken Books.

Barnes, Barry. ed. 1972. *Sociology of Science: Selected Readings.* Baltimore: Penguin Books.

Bell, Daniel. 1973. *The Coming Post-Industrial Society.* New York: Basic Books.

Brinkman, Richard L. 1981. *Cultural Economics.* Portland: The Hapi Press.

Dugger, William. 1984. *An Alternative to Economic Entrenchment.* New York: Petrocelli Books.

Feldstein, Martin. 1984. *The Annual Report of the Council of Economic Advisors.* Washington: U.S. Government Printing Office.

Galbraith, John K. 1973. *Economics and the Public Purpose.* Boston: Houghton Mifflin.

Gordon, Wendell. 1980. *Institutional Economics.* Austin: University of Texas Press.

Gruchy, Allen. 1984. "Uncertainty, Indicative Planning and Industrial Policy." *Journal of Economic Issues.* (March), pp. 159–180.

Johnson, Chalmers. ed. 1984. *The Industrial Policy Debate.* San Francisco: Institute for Contemporary Studies Press.
— 1982. *MITI and the Japanese Miracle.* Stanford: Stanford University Press.

Kuznets, Simon. 1966. *Modern Economic Growth.* New Haven: Yale University Press.

Magaziner, Ira and Reich, Robert. 1982. *Minding America's Business.* New York: Jovanovich Harcourt Brace.

Munkirs, John R. 1985. *The Transformation of American Capitalism: From Competitive Market Structures to Centralized Private Sector Planning.* New York: M. E. Sharpe.

Myrdal, Gunnar. 1974. "What is Development" *Journal of Economic Issues.* 8 (December), pp. 729–736.

Palmer, John L. and Isabel V. Sawhill. ed. 1984. *The Reagan Record.* Cambridge, Mass: Ballinger Publishing Co.

Price, Derek J. de Solla. 1961. *Science Since Babylon.* New Haven: Yale University Press.
— 1963. *Little Science, Big Science.* New York: Columbia University Press.

Reich, Robert. 1983. *The Next American Frontier.* New York: Times Books.
— 1985. "Toward a New Public Philosophy." *Atlantic Monthly* (May), pp. 68–79.

Sahlins, Marshall D. and Elman R. Service. 1960. *Evolution and Culture.* Ann Arbor: University of Michigan Press.

Schultze, Charles L. 1983. "Industrial Policy: A Dissent." *The Brookings Review.* 2 (Fall), pp. 3–12.

Solo, Robert. 1984. "Industrial Policy." *The Journal of Economic Issues.* 18 (September), pp. 697–714.

Stanfield, J. R. 1984. "Social Reform and Economic Policy." *Journal of Economic Issues.* 18 (March), pp. 19–44.
— 1979. *Economic Thought and Social Change.* Carbondale: Southern Illinois University Press.

The Report of the President's Commission on Industrial Competitiveness. 1985. *Global Competition: The New Reality.* 2 vols. Washington, D.C.: U.S. Government Printing Office.

Thurow, Lester. 1984. "Building a World-Class Economy." *Society* 22 (November/December), pp. 16–29.

Tool, Marc R. ed. 1984. *An Institutionalist Guide to Economics and Public Policy.* Armonk: M. E. Sharpe.
— 1979. *The Discretionary Economy: A Normative Theory of Political Economy.* Santa Monica: Goodyear.

Trezise, Philip H. 1984. "Japanese Miracles Revisited." *Society.* 22 (November/December), pp. 36–40.

Wachtel, Paul L. 1983. *The Poverty of Affluence.* New York: The Free Press.

Wachter, Michael L. and Susan M. Wachter, ed. 1981. *Toward a New U.S. Industrial Policy.* Philadelphia: University of Pennsylvania.

Wallis, W. Allen, et al. 1984. "The Magic of the Market." *Society.* 22 (November/December), pp. 7–15.

White, Leslie A. 1947. "Evolutionary Stages, Progress and the Evaluation of Cultures." *Southwestern Journal of Anthropology.* 3 (Autumn), pp. 165–192.

Whitehead, Alfred North. 1925. *Science and the Modern World.* New York: The Macmillan Co.

Does Industrial Policy comply with Ludwig Erhard's Conception of the Social Market Economy?

Horst Friedrich Wünsche

My subject is to clarify whether "industrial policy" is compatible with Ludwig Erhard's conception of the Social Market Economy. I have, in fact, been asked to draw up a comparison. And from all that I have heard so far, one expects me to proclaim the following reassuring message. If Ludwig Erhard were to re-appear in our world of today, he would come in order to achieve two things: firstly, to give a blessing to "his" industrial policy-makers; and, secondly, to purify the misjudged disciples of his ideas of the wicked suspicion that they are in reality pure interventionists and late-mercantilists who have vilely betrayed the teachings on a free market economy. Well then, let me see if I can meet these expectations in this respect.

My first point is this: I am very pleased about this opportunity to answer the questions as to what Erhard would say on modern industrial policy. Generally, one does not pose this question, because one is in search of contributions to a highly effective presentation of the given political goals and interests. One puts the question as academics and researchers. One asks about Ludwig Erhard's conception, because one has perceived in almost all industrial nations the existence of problems which can no longer be resolved with current economic recipes. These problems are: unemployment, inflation, economic stagnation despite large budgetary deficits and despite ruthless exploitation of our environment, awful manifestations of ruinous competition – national and international alike, and new kinds of class warfare. On the other hand, one sees that Ludwig Erhard faced similar problems to those of today and that he solved the problems. Ludwig Erhard's policy was marked by: full employment, low inflation rates, high growth rates, none of the regrettable or even catastrophic pollution of our time, social stability, and major contributions towards the liberalization of world trade. Admittedly, most people say not that precisely the same Erhard policy should be adopted as before. The conditions of the 1980s are quite different to those prevailing in the 1950s. Moreover, the achievements of the Fifties cannot be credited exclusively to the successful efforts of Ludwig Erhard. There existed a number of favorable factors which helped to shape the events of those times. Nevertheless, you assume in general that it would be a promising and meaningful policy – and perhaps even a necessary approach – to revive the principles underlying Erhard's policy. I can only concur wholeheartedly with this view. I also agree when one says: a revival of the Social Market Economy cannot take place simply by reviving the free-market doctrine. I agree. What we need is something wider-ranging. And your proposal is the adoption of a structural policy for industry oriented towards the market.

It is not easy to answer the question as to whether this market-oriented structural policy for industry really corresponds to Erhard's conception. Success springs from many sources. The successful concept of the Social Market Economy is said to have been created in a hundred different places: for example, in the South-West German town of Freiburg by a group of economists and jurists who called themselves "Ordo-liberals" and who included Franz Böhm and Walter Eucken; or by the internationally renowned Wilhelm Röpke, professor of economics in Geneva, author of "civitas humana" and "A Human Economy"; on the periphery of the Western world, by Alexander Rüstow in Ankara; by Alfred Müller and later Müller-Armack in the Westphalian town of Münster; and by Friedrich A. von Hayek in London, Chicago and Tokyo. If we trace these intellectual origins right back into former generations, then a number of powerful intellectual roots reveal themselves to our inquiring gaze. But a word of warning! In our pride about this tradition whose path no doubt leads right back to Adam Smith, we can easily overlook a researcher who perhaps thought longer than anyone else — from 1918 to 1948 — about the Social Market Economy and who then established, and then defended this system — and also this more and longer than anybody else: from 1948 to 1966. I am referring to a professor from Nuremberg called Ludwig Erhard. Clearly, Erhard is problematic inasmuch as it is difficult to classify him under any specific school of economic thought. For the systematic adherents of market-economy teachings, this is reason enough to incorporate his views within the chapter "free-market doctrine runable in practice" — overlooking that the Social Market Economy is *not* an interventionisticly qualified pure market economy — or on "miscellaneous theories and eclectic approaches". And there is another thing to bear in mind: Ludwig Erhard had studied Karl Marx's ostracized writings. Erhard's mind was influenced not only by Adam Smith but to an equal extent by Carl Rodbertus, who wrote a basic socialist text — entitled curiously enough „Das Kapital" — ten years before Karl Marx published the first book of his main work. Moreover, Friedrich List exercised a certain influence on Erhard. But above all, Erhard occupied himself intensively with the outsiders of political economy. I have to mention all these names, because without this background I am unable to answer the question as to whether the approach adopted under a modern industrial policy is compatible with Erhard's conception. Ludwig Erhard's academic preceptor was Franz Oppenheimer, a sociology professor in Frankfurt. As an ostensible socialist who defended the market economy as ardently as hardly anyone else in the Twenties, Oppenheimer also sharply castigated all liberal policies. He is said to be the man who aroused liberalism in Germany to fresh, militant life.

Erhard once said that his favorite teacher had been Wilhelm Rieger. We should remember in this context that, in Erhard's days, a teacher was somebody that pupils learned from: nowadays, a teacher is usually somebody who has to listen with great patience to his or her pupils' immature disquisitions. Meanwhile, we have all forgotten who this Rieger was. But Erhard learnt something important from him. Rieger's main interest in teaching was this: how can we manage to integrate an individual economic approach within the overall economic context? The "methodical individualism" espoused by so many people today is not without its problems. Erhard may perhaps have read about this in the works of Othmar Spann or those of other leading political economists such as Franz Eulenburg. But there is another point worth bearing in mind: It seems that this method to look at economic life has never gained genuine acceptance among economic researchers, although it does in fact contain the real legacy of the Austrian school of political economy. One has to say — as it does for example Walter E. Grinder from the New York University — that the subjectivism — the legacy embraces such scholars as Carl Menger and Eugen von Böhm-Bawerk down to Ludwig Mises, Ludwig M. Lachmann and Friedrich August von Hayek was never the heart of economic thinking in such a degree as it seems to be and as it should be, but more a convention without obligation. Our branch of science reveals many tragic fates, and numerous important economic works have failed to gain true appreciation. There is, for instance, the case of Professor Wilhelm Vershofen. Erhard worked together with him for no less than fourteen years. At first, Erhard was full of respect and commitment, but later he adopted a critical stance; and this led to sharp academic controversies — especially on issues of significance in industrial policy.

But why am I drawing your attention to this background? I am doing so simply on account of the contemporary trend to regard Ludwig Erhard as a mere subordinate of the liberal school of political economy, albeit with the rank of cabinet minister. Yet in point of fact, Erhard developed a completely original concept of his own and applied it in his economic policy. One cannot classify Erhard's complex image as a guiding light within the much simpler market-economy nexus of economic liberalism. This in turn renders it difficult to understand Erhard's image in full and thus also the foundations of his policy. Apparently, this thought has already occurred to you. When you invited me to speak at this symposium, you certainly did not expect me simply to appear as a protagonist of the free market economy. Instead, you no doubt expected me to draw a comparison between the true guiding image of Ludwig Erhard and the ideas on industrial policy. The image of Ludwig Erhard is not exactly what one normally discusses with regard to Erhard. But what, then, is the special conception of the Social Market Economy according to Ludwig Erhard?

Erhard's basic, guiding idea is the concept of an economic society centred round the market. What does this really signify?

a) Erhard's point of departure is his uncompromising support of a market-economy model. In other words, Erhard is a theoretically orientated political economist. An economist committed to historicism in political economy would base his dedication to the market economy to a system of this kind which had already been realized. But Erhard bases his conviction on a market model. Thus, he is a theoretician; and the Social Market Economy is therefore a theoretical draft designed for practical application, but not a draft to realize a pure market doctrine in practice. That is my first point — I hope, none without anything particularly exciting about it.

b) The choise of a model naturally leads us to the question as to how it operates in practice. Theories are, after all, theories and not necessarily good in practice. The step from market economy model to political economy is one exclusively manageable by seven-league boots omitting all virtual reason of economics. Moreover, the content of manuals on the market economy — such as how Robinson Crusoe manages to feed himself, how market-wide prices are determined on the stock exchanges and so forth — is not exactly of monumental importance for an individual's daily economic reality. It has been noted on several occasions that Erhard's view of a market economy differs from the theoretical concept set out in textbooks. Many people are afraid to voice this opinion. But that is surely a foolish attitude. Erhard was a realist. That is a simple fact, and it deserves to be stressed. He did not get bogged down in esoteric doctrines or theoretical models. Let us take a closer look at this from the standpoint of what might be important in regard to industrial policy.

Part of market-economy dogma includes the belief that private benefit is compatible with social benefit. Several Nobel Prizes have been awarded on this account to Samuelson, Arrow, Hicks and — more recently — to Debreu for the discovery, rediscovery and repeated delineation of this pretended reality. But the essence of this thesis has also always been re-affirmed, namely that it is only valid in pure theory or else in a world of pure exchange and extreme poverty. Böhm-Bawerk once made the following point: as soon as a point of time arrives when not everything produced is consumed and virtually snatched from the manufacturer's hands — or in other words as soon as unsold goods pile up and capital resources accumulate — then a worker's wife in more urgent need of a Sunday joint for her under-nourished children than her middle-class counterpart has few chances of actually obtaining such a meal. Erhard realized this nexus of connected facts very well. When Erhard took his university diploma examination in 1923, he faced an examination on the Knapp-Simmel theory of money; and we know how familiar he was with this approach. Our contemporary economic theories skate elegantly round these problems. Any interpersonal comparison of benefits is ruled out. The assumption remains that a dollar is a dollar for everyone. All right, people of good taste like to chat about theories. But the matter at stake here is something quite different: we want to realize a market economy in political terms. Anyone engaged in political economy cannot avoid facing the reality of any market economy, and this includes a policy of capital formation designed to prevent wealth from excessively distorting subjective estimates of the available benefits. The first book Erhard wrote was entitled: "Affluence for Everyone". It would be a misunderstanding to believe that his teaching in this book represented a socio-political remnant of the market economy, which must be respected in particular when the system's economic efficiency is great enough. But it is correct to say that a sound policy of capital accumulation forms an indispensable component of a Social Market Economy.

Without a wide spread of wealth, the model for a free-market system will unfortunately engender two consequences: the needs of the most indigent members of society are satisfied less than those of the better-off; and, secondly, there will not be any optimal use of economic resources among society as a whole. From this point follows as a conclusion: Erhard's concept cannot be compared with an industrial-policy approach simply on the basis of market-economy efficiency. If industrial policy helps to bring about an even spread of wealth, then it is compatible with Erhard's concept. If it does not do so, then it departs from Erhard's concept. What can we learn from the standard texts on industrial policy about this matter? The concepts of industrial policy are neutral in terms of capital formation. The view taken of the industrial policy is one-sided, namely from the production i.e. the supply side. We have to register this indifference to the demand side of an economy for the present. Furthermore:

The commitment by many people, including even a lot of liberals, to a market economy is fairly unenthusiastic. Yes, you heard me quite rightly! In point of fact, their commitment reads as follows: a market economy may well be an efficient tool, but let us not exaggerate – it cannot be a goal in itself. But Ludwig Erhard went a step further. He argued that the market economy must act as the guideline and goal of a social system under which we abolish all class differences and cast aside all inhuman personal links and opresive ties. Ludwig Erhard wanted his market economy, because the economy stands at the heart of social life and because only a market economy can make people mature and free and equal. In other words, such a system cannot be realized if there are differing degrees of membership of this society. Everyone must have an equal opportunity to achieve what he or she wants. Under a market economy based on a division of labour, the fundament of any demand is the possession of one's own supply. We do not live in the Middle Ages, but in a modern industrial society. Nobody must base his demands on presents from the rich members of society or on subsidies provided by the upper class or by government. The demand must be based on performance, on everyone's contribution to the standard of living of others' and the society as a whole. Hence, it must be possible for everybody to carry out a performance so as to be able to create a demand for something. This is why full employment is necessary in a Social Market Economy.

In the opinion of many men an women, a free-enterprise system and in particular the Social Market Economy can eliminate the shortage of jobs by means of unemployment insurance and by a redistribution of the available resources. But this is a short-sighted approach. The deprivation effects are not overcome by allocations. On the contrary! A market economy is doubly impaired by redistributions: confiscation weakens the will to work among those affected by it, whilst allocation weakens the will to work among recipients. No! Full employment is indispensable under the Social Market Economy.

Full employment ranks among the foremost aims of industrial policy. To that extent, one might believe that Erhard would at least amicably approve the goals pursued under industrial policy and simply lay the question of indifference towards a wealth policy to rest. But that would be an illusion. The texts on industrial policy affirm the intention of creating an economic growth calculated to mobilize employment by promoting technical innovations. Erhard was not keen on the idea of implementing economic measures to promote economic growth. But the papers on industrial policy speak in even more provoking terms of the "technological competitiveness of the economy" and of the need to enhance it. Erhard wanted to attain full employment from an economic standpoint, not from an technical one. The purpose of industrial policy is however to render the German economy for example more competitive in technological terms: Erhard was interested in the economic competitiveness of such trade and industry. That signifies a huge difference. In Erhard's opinion, the Federal Republic of Germany does not need to aspire to autarky in the supply of microchips and other modern techniques. Nor does she have to be present in all markets where innovations are traded. After all, it would be very uneconomic to compete in markets where others are better. It would make much more sense simply to buy the superior products which others manufacture. In this way, one can perhaps increase even more the competitiveness of those industries which already traditionally occupy the top ranks. Japanese computers with American software in German machine tools — this would probably represent Erhard's view of a technology based on economics. I have no intention at this point of setting out Ludwig Erhard's theories on employment policy. But let me just say this: the impact on employment remains the same, irrespective of whether new products or improved traditional products are manufactured.

The provisional outcome of my thoughts is as follows: Erhard's guiding concept of the Social Market Economy consists of three interconnected elements. He wanted to create a free market, but believed it could only function and be safeguarded in the long run if there was a wide spread of wealth and if full employment prevailed. Therefore the guiding concept of the Social Market Economy rests on three fundaments: free enterprise, wealth for all, and full employment.

— I have not examined industrial policy in terms of the market economy, but simply assumed that what has been written on this subject is correct, namely that industrial policy would be compatible with the market economy or can be made compatible with it, this is industrial policy would not be interventionist policy. Yet if industrial policy is really to be compatible with Ludwig Erhard's Social Market Policy, then the two other elements must be regarded as possessing equal importance as adherence to free enterprise. In Erhard's opinion, it is not possible to bring about a market economy without "affluence for all" and full employment. I have concentrated on these two elements.

— Industrial policy is, at most, neutral in terms of capital accumulation.

— With regard to employment policy, industrial policy differs fundamentally from Erhard's concept even if both these theories speak of the need for full employment. But let me say a few more explicit words about this decisive point from another angle, which held great importance for Erhard.

In line with Walter Eucken and other liberals, Erhard saw that it was not enough simply to introduce a Social Market Economy in which the three principles in question are translated into reality. Erhard insisted on the necessity of a constitutive policy as well as on a regulative policy. He developed several principles to back this policy. One of these amounts is to establishing a real consumer's autonomy. Apart from the manipulating of consumers by advertisements, demand for goods and services is regarded in all economies as a component of decisive importance. Accordingly, an attempt is made to stabilize the economy by artificially influencing demand i.e. by stimulating or damping it. A similar attempt is undertaken under supply-side economics insofar as the attempt is made to adapt consumers' claims to a given production capacity.

In respect of a normal economic process, i.e. one not disturbed by a world economic crisis, Erhard kept strictly to the principle that all economies have only one goal – the satisfaction of demand. When he spoke of demand, he meant genuine demand (and not artificial demand). An economist must regard the demand for a desirable social product as the primary goal. The economy must not be allowed to become an end in itself. However, the economy does become an end in itself if products are subsidized irrespective of demand and if competitiveness is promoted in markets where the person voicing the demand has no problems in meeting his requirements. But this is precisely what is intended under an infrastructural industrial policy oriented towards a market economy. The promotion of technology is to be directed towards markets where a keen competition for customers prevails. It is a competition which benefits the customers in these markets but which does not seem to industry as worthy of a commitment to invest and to provide new workshop places. With all this in mind, ladies and gentlemen, I must come to the following conclusion: even from the standpoint of the policy proceeding the practical economic procedure, industrial policy is not compatible with Ludwig Erhard's conception of the Social Market Economy. Even if industrial policy were compatible with market economy, it would fail to achieve the essence and the real aims of the Erhardian concept of Social Market Economy.

2.

Stabilization by Structural Change:
Regional, Sectoral and Entrepreneurial Policies

Sectoral and Regional Elements of Industrial Policy

Eberhard Thiel

I.

The last recession in the Federal Republic of Germany ended in the autumn of 1982; since then the rates of economic growth were positive again. They are smaller than they were before the oil crises, and they are still too small to reduce the high level of unemployment. Some condition for a faster growth improved: rather moderate wage increases, higher profits, progress in the consolidation of the public budget and increasing exports. But some other factors still seem to be less favourable: a high level of taxation and regulation, insufficient differences between wages for different qualifications and regions, fear of protectionism, uncertain expectations about the social acceptance of technical progress, a defensive rather than offensive strategy in investment behaviour, and an insufficient volume of innovations. In periods of intensified competition between the European countries, the USA, and South East Asia faster structural changes should be expected. This country still suffers from too slow structural change.[1]

Experience shows that a higher rate of economic growth is accompanied by faster structural change. But it is also evident that faster structural change is also a precondition for any progress in real income; without structural adjustments the growth of real income and the employment situation will hardly be improved.

This problem of inadequate adjustment is not only important for an intersectoral approach, but also for the development of the various regions of this country. During periods of high growth rates the disparity of incomes between the regions became smaller, during recessions and stagnations this gap widens. This cannot be observed only with regard to the Bundesländer, but also between Northern and Southern Germany, and between agglomerated and rural areas. Many factors determine such unequal paths of regional development: the advantages of an early start, geographical location, available raw materials, differences between the special regional policies and the development of social and economic structures.[2]

So the hope seems to be idle, that a quicker growth of incomes, increasing employment, and a reduction of the regional gaps could be achieved without a fundamental adjustment to the changed economic and social situation. The direction and the speed of sectoral and regional changes are determined by a large number of factors. Therefore, it is necessary to look for restrictions and obstacles which slow down that needed adjustment. The question has to be answered, whether a new or an alternative industrial policy could be helpful. In the following only some of those state interventions which belong to the complex of industrial policy will be discussed.

II.

Within the system of a market economy the decisions pertaining to the supply of goods and, thus, the decisions about maintaining or changing the regional or sectoral structures are left to private entrepreneurs. Therefore, the discussions about industrial or structural policy contain nothing but the question: Under what conditions and in what way should the public authorities influence that private decision making? This is one of the classical cases of choice between the private and the public sector. In general one could come to the conclusion, that under market aspects any industrial policy should be abolished, when analysing the targets of industrial policy, – for example the targets of regional and sectoral subsidies. But structural policies in different forms and intensities are executed worldwide, also in those countries which are proudly claiming, that they are practising a market economy. In reality neither the supply of subsidies nor the demand for subsidies has been declining.[3] Considering the economic situation interest should focus upon the way industrial policy finds its concepts, upon the way it is executed, and upon its results.

Though in the following not all the targets and instruments of industrial policy can be analysed, some of the main problems will become obvious, when presenting empirical findings on typical state interventions. In the Federal Republic of Germany the subsidies summed up to DM 80 billion per year in the beginning of the eighties.[4] Included are tax concessions, grants, interest-subsidised loans, some special transfers to private households, and payments by the EEC. Because of incomplete statistics this sum does not contain all subsidies; but these DM 80 billion alone mean 5 per cent of the gross national product (Other researchers estimate sums of about DM 100 billion). More than 75 per cent of those DM 80 billion flow into four sectors (housing, agriculture, transportation, coal-mining). To a certain degree this kind of industrial policy isolated these sectors from the market. The highest amount of the subsidies does not flow into fast growing sectors, but into sectors with decreasing shares in the country's production and employment. Since these sectors were subsidised already for long periods, these interventions do not represent examples of positive adjustment, but of conservation.

Most branches of manufacturing industry showed low rates of subsidy (subsidies in per cent of gross value added); the shipbuilding and the aircraft/aerospace-industries form important exceptions. The shipyards in the Federal Republic have received grants and aids in different forms for a long period. But the present situation could not be prevented: surplus capacities, declining employment, demand for more subsidies. With some exceptions the shipbuilding industry is no longer competitive compared with those low cost yards in Asia. The subsidies were not properly used for adjusting production to changing conditions. The reduction of capacities and shifting to other productions was delayed.[5] The aircraft/aerospace-industries in the Federal Republic belong to the fast growing sectors. But the policy of industrial targeting was not yet able to make that sector more independent of the public research and development programmes or of public securities for the production costs.[6]

Though the acceptance of public aid in the form of subsidies is voluntary, the grants are combined with the public expectation that the receiver behaves in a certain way. In most cases this expected behaviour will be different from that without state intervention: Prices and costs will be changed, the discrimination of those firms, branches, regions without subsidies will lead to changed income- and price-relations; the danger of misallocations of the factors is great, and the distribution of risks between the private and public sectors is no longer evident, and backward and forward linkages will be disturbed. Besides, long lasting public intervention lessens the private efforts and the ability to react properly without public help. In total, the subsidies affect the allocation of factors and prevent structural change from following economical paths; the chances of increasing real incomes therefore are reduced.[7]

Against these negative judgements a lot of justifications were brought forward — with great success as the effective development of subsidies indicates.

III.

For the purpose of evaluating this kind of industrial policy it is necessary to analyse some of the justifications and aims which are discussed when these subsidies are introduced into the political arena. The catalogue of justifications is great, demonstrating that interventions into the market system need many, good arguments against the negative judgement brought forward against them under the criterions of the market economy. A lot is done to find good reasons to identify these public activities as being of public interest.[8]

In the cases of old industries the argument is often used, that national production is necessary to secure the supply of certain goods in critical and in uncertain times; but mostly it would suffice if stocks could be prepared. The justification used most refers to the fact that other countries also grant subsidies. At first sight this does not seem to be a valid argument, because it might be favourable to exploit the foreign tax-payer by buying their products. But under certain circumstances the risks of stopping the inland production might to be too high.

During periods of high unemployment the danger of destroying jobs by decreasing subsidies quickly occupies the political interest. But if this employment argument were accepted, this policy would quickly lead to a public guarantee of employment even for companies which have not been competitive for long periods.

If subsidies are granted for a short period, if they are gradually declining, or if they are granted for resettlements or for retraining programmes they could be justified to avoid greater social losses — but always as exceptions. In the case of new industries the infant industries argument is often discussed; subsidies should help new productions or products against foreign competitors until they can hold their own. But for sure, not all products have to be produced in each industrialised country. Even if these are products which are also of high importance for the production of other industries, it should be carefully discussed, whether it is not a private task to take these risks. In the cases of intensive state intervention via defence expenditures in other countries similar considerations have to be given to the calculations of external effects. Thus, the theoretical discussions, and the experiences with state interventions seem not to be a very stable ground for arguments in favour of industrial policies, especially not for sector-specific interventions.

IV.

As for the regional type of structural or industrial policy the argument for interventions mostly run along this line: There are political, social or ecological reasons why the migration of relevant parts of one region's population could not be tolerated. Though the amount of agglomeration costs is not known, the public authorities on the other hand try to prevent too intensive agglomerations. The standard of supplies with infrastructure and the chances for earning income should therefore be improved especially in comparatively low developed areas of the country. That means that market results have to be corrected.

Those elements of regional policy which tried to improve the infrastructure in economically weak regions were rather successful in this country. Regional policy was unable to prevent the existing and enlarged income disparities, and the great differences in employment.[9] Beside fiscal equalisations a lot of programmes supported the public sectors in those assisted regions.

The main instrument to help the private sector is the Joint Task between Bund and Länder for improving the regional structure; grants for investments are the main instruments. Under this programme especially worthwhile promoting from a general economic point of view are those firms which sell their products outside the region – a condition referring to the export-base-theory. The selection of the regions mainly depends on criteria such as standards of income, unemployment, and infrastructure. The areas to be promoted are selected in a highly sophisticated manner; a lot of ideas are discussed to improve that.

It is obvious that this kind of regional policy cannot be justified under aspects of the market economy (with the exception of the existence of external effects). Regional policy discriminates between regions and – to a certain degree only – between sectors. Actually it is discussed to include other branches than the export-oriented sectors into that programme; this idea should not be favoured for fiscal reasons and because of the fear that only a few additional jobs could be created. All these are important factors for the receivers of grants and also for the government and the parliament, when demonstrating their care for these regions.

Market economists prefer programmes without sector-specific selections. So regional policy activities often have a rather good standing. The share of investment in these assisted regions of all investments in the Federal Republic shrank during recent years. This is an indicator that the chances for creating new jobs in the assisted regions declined relatively. If one distinguishes between those industries with growth rates above the average of the total industrial sector and those industries with lower rates, the result is even worse: The relation between the investments in fast growing sectors in the assisted regions and the investments in these sectors in the Federal Republic as a whole decreased during the last ten years. Thus, the programmes were not successful in creating jobs in fast growing sectors. Additionally the relations between the investments in low rate sectors in assisted regions and the investments in these sectors in the Federal Republic as a whole increased.[10]

Of course, it is obvious that the ex post fast growing sectors must not be the winners in the future. Besides, the regional statistics do not allow a satisfying disaggregation of production or investment figures. Nevertheless, it would make better sense to introduce a moderate sectoral selection to avoid maintaining or creating unsuccessful structures. Under new special programmes for Bremen and the steel-regions it is now possible for companies to get grants only, if they do not investments in shipyards or in the steel-industry; this seems to be a first step in the right direction.[11] The critique about this kind of sectoral selection within the regional policy has a rather small weight in view of the comparably greater amounts flowing into the regions under sectoral programmes. Those not regionally specified aids for numerous sectors and functions mostly have greater regional effects than the regional policy activities. The already mentioned Joint Task programme has a volume of about DM 1.4 billion a year, this is less than 2 per cent of all granted subsidies.

The selection of tomorrow's winners is almost impossible; the selection of today's losers also has traps – especially when complete sectors have to be identified. But if branches or productions for a long time are not competitive or show surplus capacities, or can pay their wages only by collecting subsidies, then this kind of negative selection seems to be adequate in the view of the aim of regional policies: to create or maintain long-lasting jobs.[12]

This proposal to introduce a more effective sectoral selection into regional policy – and by that a concentration of the available funds – could be a counterposition to those critics who believe that the incentives of investment grants are rather small and that these subsidies are only taken along by most of the companies.

The actual development shows, that beside the traditionally weak regions along the eastern and western border of the Federal Republic more and more old industrialised areas tend to join the group of assisted regions. Perhaps in the future also old and unadjusted service centres will wish to be assisted.

V.

The discussion of these aspects shows that the sectoral and regional structural policies – under the aspect of the market economy – have a lot of weak points. The example of the regional policy gives the impression, that not only economic growth, but also equalisation belongs to the targets. Nevertheless, it might be predicted that the market for subsidies will continue to flourish; the economist has the task to prevent greater losses, – but how could that be achieved?

This question could lead to an attempt to create a conception for an industrial policy aiming to influence the structure of important parts or of the entire economy of this country. The concept of the market economy does not contain such a state plan for an optimal sectoral or regional structure. The history of what one may call the industrial policy of the Federal Republic of Germany also does not show a comprehensive concept. Most of the sectoral aids have been the answer to special situations, and have to be called a series of ad-hoc policies.

Thus, the subsidisation of housing results from the situation after the First and the Second World Wars, combined with a concept of tolerable rents. – The subsidies for the agricultural sectors are a mixture of regional income policy and a sort of fee for membership of the EEC. – Though the aids for the shipbuilding industries have existed for a far longer period, not even for this sector is a concept available. In the absence of a comprehensive concept for an industrial policy and of consistent concepts for many individual sectors it is all the more necessary to ask for a very intensive discussion of the aims of each subsidy or of each other programme aiming at influencing market processes or market structures.

It should not suffice to claim an advantage for one sector or region without analysing the effects on this sector and on those sectors which do not participate in this advantage. The decision of the state to grant subsidies for one sector, region or function simultaneously means a disadvantage for others. Therefore, the political decision that a certain structural policy corresponds with the public interest, should be a decision, that the discrimination of other sectors, regions or functions meets the public interest, too.

It is rather easy to formulate such requests, that the state has to consider all the consequences, but it is rather difficult for the executive and the parliament to fulfil this demand. But a rational policy needs clear aims for justifying the policy, for selecting the proper instruments, and for the necessary ex-post control.[13] Referring to the mentioned justifications it is possible to formulate aims of policy more exactly than it is practised today. The more exact the targets are formulated, the greater are the chances for a successful activity; but the greater are also the chances that this policy will not be executed at all; because the targets and the possible effects might become too transparent with the possible consequence, that the public interest could no longer be demonstrated in a convincing way.

Industrial policy means selection. The ability of the state authorities to select tomorrow's winners will hardly be greater than the ability of a private entrepreneur. The difference is that the private entrepreneur bears the risks for himself, and the state transfers the burden to the society. In the past, the state often failed to select the winners, with the consequence that subsidies had to be paid for a long period. Many old industries get their subsidies for decades, often because no precautions were taken for incentives to adjustment.

The success of an industrial policy depends on the proper choice of instruments. The concept of the market economy forbids too compelling conditions for private activities. On the other hand, the public interests have to be observed too. Even if indirect instruments (i.e. aids for R&D in general and less for special products) and more the help for entire sectors (instead of helping one company only) are favoured, the instruments have to be controlled and have possibly after short periods to be altered. To find out an optimal set of instruments and to have the opportunity to control the effects, it is necessary to get proper methods for evaluation. Neither economic policy nor economic theory so far have been able to develop satisfying methods for measuring the effects of the subsidies. They cannot identify the opportunity costs, and the production functions, the cost and demand curves, the reactions of the receivers of subsidies and the behaviour of the discriminated companies remain unknown; and it is difficult to estimate the effects of changes in forward and backward linkages. In many cases there are only rough estimates to give a picture about what will happen with this or that sectoral or regional activity or about what would have happened without it.[14] For want of better information and transparency this is far from being satisfying. These deficits indicate, that relevant preconditions for setting up a concept of industrial policy do not exist.

Beside the problems of identifying targets, instruments, and effects the coordination of different programmes marks another set of difficulties. The individual activities at least should be harmonised to prevent conflicts between different programmes. Within a federal system the coordination of industrial policies is rather difficult. The Federal and the Länder governments, and even the local communities have their own targets and instruments; often contradictions between the individual programmes occur; now and then the end of a federal programme is answered by creating new Länder activities.

The question has to be answered, who should do this coordination. Proposals are made to create a new council for subsidies or to pass a bill with exact criteria for granting subsidies. There are doubts whether a council would be helpful, if it has no power to prevent new programmes; a law with criteria for granting subsidies will sooner or later become a law for claiming subsidies.[15] The parliament — though often playing an active role in increasing subsidies — should discuss the constitutive elements of each subsidy in public; only the public debate about the state's interest in introducing grants and aids, and in the promotion of the receivers, and in the discrimination of the other parts of the society seems to give a chance for evaluating contradictions and perhaps for stopping the expansion of these public activities.

VI.

After discussing several sectoral and regional elements of industrial policy some results should be mentioned:

— Under the critical aspects of the market economy hardly any justification for subsidies can be accepted; exceptions refer to external effects, and to less selective programmes for short periods.

- Nevertheless, industrial policy will exist in the future; the more it is necessary to discuss the targets, to analyse the effects of discriminatory activities, and to discuss the social costs and benefits.
- But even if such discussions could be conducted, the chances to close the market for subsidies cannot be judged with great optimism, as long as the description of policy targets is not exact enough, the evaluations suffer from a lack of transparency and from not yet sufficient methods to measure the effects of industrial policies and as long as the existence of these deficits show no substantial consequences.
- Therefore, recommendations in favour of increasing industrial policy activities should only be discussed, if there is a chance of avoiding these deficiencies, and at the same time of avoiding the suspicion of being carefree or arbitrary.
- These remarks should not be interpreted as the opinions of a purist, — just on the contrary: Knowing that for many reasons (social, defence, foreign policy) industrial policies in the future will exist, it should be self-evident, that the expenditure of 5 per cent of GNP must be more carefully watched.

NOTES

[1] HWWA-Institut für Wirtschaftsforschung-Hamburg; Analyse der strukturellen Entwicklung der deutschen Wirtschaft – Strukturbericht 1983 –, Hamburg 1984, pp. 15.

[2] W. Crinius, R. Richert, H. Tesch, E. Thiel; Analyse und Bedeutung raumwirksamer Faktoren in Norddeutschland, Teil II: Demographische und ökonomische Entwicklungen, in: Akademie für Raumforschung und Landesplanung, Arbeitsmaterial Nr. 73, Hannover 1984.

[3] K. Borchert; Protektionismus im historischen Überblick, in: A. Gutowski (Hrsg.): Der neue Protektionismus, Hamburg 1984, pp. 17.

[4] A. Gutowski, E. Thiel, M. Weilepp; Analyse der Subventionspolitik – das Beispiel der Schiffbau-, Luft- und Raumfahrtindustrie (Ergänzungsband 4 zum HWWA-Strukturbericht 1983); Hamburg 1984, pp. 13.

[5] A. Gutowski, E. Thiel, M. Weilepp, op.cit., pp. 19.

[6] A. Gutowski, E. Thiel, M. Weilepp, op.cit., pp. 49.

[7] A. Gutowski, E. Thiel, Subventionen in der Marktwirtschaft, in: Deutscher Juristentag (Hrsg.), Verhandlungen des 55. Deutschen Juristentages, Band II, München 1985, pp. M 45.

[8] A. Gutowski, E. Thiel, M. Weilepp, op.cit. pp. 86.

[9] E. Thiel; Stärkung der Regionalpolitik, in: Wirtschaftsdienst, Nr. 3/1985, pp. 106.

[10] R. Richert, H. Tesch; Investitionsförderung und das Süd-Nord-Gefälle, in: Niedersächsisches Institut für Wirtschaftsforschung (Hrsg.): Süd-Nord-Gefälle in der Bundesrepublik?, Hannover 1984, pp. 59.

[11] E. Thiel; Bewegung in der Regionalpolitik, in: Wirtschaftsdienst Nr. 11/1984, p. 520.

[12] E. Thiel; Stärkung der Regionalpolitik, in: Wirtschaftsdienst Nr. 3/1985, pp. 106.

[13] E. Thiel; Möglichkeiten zur Konkretisierung von Subventionszielen als Grundlage für eine Erfolgskontrolle – Hinweise auf Notwendigkeiten und Grenzen, in: Erfolg und Mißerfolg sektoraler Strukturpolitik, Beihefte der Konjunkturpolitik, Heft 31, Berlin 1985, pp. 51.

[14] A. Peacock, The Political Economy of Strukturpolitik, in: Zeitschrift für die gesamte Staatswissenschaft, Band 140, 1984, pp. 364.

[15] A. Gutowski, E. Thiel, op.cit., pp. M 45.

Stabilisation of the Social Structure versus Change of the Industrial Structure
The Case of the Ruhr District

Helmut W. Jenkis

I. Introduction

It seems relevant for the treatment of this topic to start with two introductory questions: firstly, why is it necessary in the market economy to have an industrial policy and secondly, can the use of an industrial policy be reconciled with the concept of a social market economy?

In my view, definitions of the term "industrial policy" should not have the aim of solving a problem but should spell out which problem areas are not relevant. The task therefore is to outline the limits of the adopted frame of reference while acknowledging at the same time that a shift of emphasis involves the introduction of additional questions and affects the interpretation of the topic and of the proposals for action as regards both aims and means. The setting of these limits involves normative judgements – whether consciously or unconsciously. Such judgements are also necessary when constraints exist which mean that only some aspects of the whole topic can be dealt with.

Why have an industrial policy in a market economy?

If one accepts the arguments of the self-regulating market mechanism, that is, the premise that this mechanism automatically produces better results than any government policies, this means that not only economic policy interventions but also industrial policy interventions must be rejected. Among representatives of this school of thought were the "Harmonisten", who argued that the natural laws of economic life provide positive effects for the community as well as for individual interests as long as economic freedom is not subject to restriction. One advocate of the concept of harmony was the Frenchman Frédéric Bastiat (1801–1850). One look at the history of the economy in Germany shows that the state in modern times not only set economic political goals during nearly all the different historical stages but also pursued them and if necessary even imposed and enforced them. This is particularly true with regard to the "absolutist" state. Only during the liberal periods of the 19th century did the state (often referred to in German as the "nightwatchman state") hold back. In doing so it created the mistaken impression an economic or industrial policy is incompatible with a free market economy. This is also illustrated by the fact that economic and industrial policies have been in the past and right up to the present time, part of a power and armaments policy.

In German speaking countries the use of the concept of "industrial policy" has undergone changes[1]. Originally one spoke of a "policy for craftsmen"; later of a policy for "crafts and trades" and eventually industrial policy. Nowadays industrial policy is looked at as part of a sectional economic policy which comprises an organisation and process policy, competition and structural and regional policy.

If one's starting point is that of the concept of harmony, every government intervention – including therefore industrial policy – is considered unnecessary or even damaging. However, at the latest since the world economic recession, this idea of harmony or a "pre-established harmony" (as the philosopher Leibniz called it) does not exist any more; correcting government interventions have become inevitable, particularly at the present time. Government economic policies therefore are the consequence of the inadequacies which arise in a self-regulating economy.

While parliament regulates the institutional frames of reference, general economic policies have as their aim the objective of influencing the ups and downs in the trade cycle in the shorter run. By contrast, the task of structural, regional and industrial policies is that of securing longer term regional economic growth, a task in which external and internal problems arise; for instance, problems arising from rapidly changing technology, demographic changes, foreign trade factors and so on must be tackled or at least ameliorated by normative judgements. Thus, for example, the different assets of particular sectors have to adjust to technical progress, to distortions which do not merely hamper growth but can at the same time give rise to social problems in some industries and/or regions. Industrial policy can therefore be defined as that part of sectorial economic policy which is concerned with the attainment of prescribed structural norms which are determined by normative objectives and the use of government measures within the market economy. This type of industrial policy supplements the market mechanism; it influences what happens in certain regions (and may thus be referred to as regional policy); it influences industrial structure (hence may be referred to as structural policy); it influences the trade cycle (hence trade cycle policies) and in addition it has social consequences hence involves social policy. According to the emphasis given to one or other of these components industrial policy can be a structural, regional, trade cycle and a social policy.

What is worth noting with regard to the Federal Republic of Germany is that the country has not got a Department of Industry and therefore no explicit industrial policy; the topic is part of the sphere of the Federal Economic Ministry and of its sectorial economic policy.

The Social Market Economy

The image of the social market economy – interpreted and used in different ways – has dominated economic policy in the Federal Republic since 1948. Ludwig Erhard, the Federal Economics Minister and later Chancellor, is often referred to as the "father" of the social market economy. It is true that he introduced the concept after the currency reform on the 20th June 1948 and established it in the face of opposition, but the intellectual father was Alfred Müller-Armack.[2]

Müller-Armack — who later became an important colleague of Ludwig Erhard — defined the concept of the social market economy as follows: "its purpose is to combine the free initiative which is based on competition in a market economy with assured social progress through the efficient operation of the market economy".[3]

The market stands in the forefront of this economic system and fulfils social tasks through competition. The competition must be supplemented by government intervention, because the market economy is merely a formal and neutral steering mechanism which has no specific moral convictions as a frame of reference. It was a momentous error of 19th Century thought that it postulated that the market mechanism represented an adequate regulator of life. In the long run the market economy cannot survive without adapting to the pressure of moral values. These include the concept of freedom, but also that of harmonious social order[4], that is, that certain social political advantages result from the market economy but that others can only be achieved through the regulation of the market mechanism. Müller-Armack[5] outlines the limits of the free market economy as follows:

> While it is necessary to understand and secure the interconnected wholeness of the market economy, it is equally necessary to be aware of the technical and specific character of the market economy. The latter is merely a purposeful mechanism but nothing more; and it would be a disastrous error to expect that the self-regulating mechanism of the market could fulfil the task of creating an acceptable valid social order and could pay attention to the needs of public and cultural life. What is required is a conscious orientation which accepts that the market mechanism encroaches on the organisation of human life and which accomplishes the necessary corrections and supplementations to the purely technical course of the production of goods. Liberalist philosophy overlooked the need for taking over this extended task.

These two quotes indicate that even the intellectual father of the concept of the social market economy, Müller-Armack, did not envisage an economic order or economic policy in which the state merely backs a free market economy. His thesis demands, by contrast, that the state should be actively involved and not merely take on the role of the "nightwatchman state" of the 19th century. However Müller-Armack did not spell out in concrete terms when and where state intervention is necessary, nor in what form and to what extent it should intervene to safeguard the social component of a market economy.

Since the social aspect has not been clearly defined by the economic literature a look at the constitutional law of the Federal Republic may close the gap. According to Article 20(1) of the German Federal Constitution for which the German term is GG (Grundgesetz) "the Federal Republic of Germany is a democratic and social constitutional state" and Article 28(1) GG lays down that "the constitutional order in the 'Länder' must be in accordance with the republican, democratic and social constitutional state in the sense of the Grundgesetz".

These clauses have led to lively discussions, as to whether they mean that a blank cheque for action or a concrete task has been given to the state.[6] After lengthy discussion it seems that at present the predominant opinion among states and constitutional lawyers is that the word social used in the Grundgesetz "is not used as a decorative ornament without a normative force behind it, but a basic constitutional concept, on a par with concepts such as 'republican' and 'democratic' and that it determines together with these the basic structure of the relation between the Federal Republic and the 'Länder' (its constituents)"[7] This makes it clear, that the social state obligation is not just a vague prescription but one which demands that there must be special social legislation which defines this goal against the liberal outlook of past governments.

The expert in constitutional law, Ernst Rudolf Huber[8] has stressed the relation between the state and its citizens; the *social state* is the product of the relation between the state and industrial society. The concept of the "social state", however, must not be equated with the concept of the "welfare-state" – that is with a comprehensive welfare services policy; the concept of the social state must be seen as the product of the contrast between past government traditions and the social structure in an industrialised era; the concept of the social state, therefore, is a product of the industrial revolution. This means according to Huber[9] that: *"The middle-class society"* is a society based on freedom of state intervention. *"The social state"* is a state which copes adequately with the problems of the industrial era through social intervention. The social state, however, is neither a social service nor a welfare state but a state for social integration. This means that: "The social state is the state of the modern industrialised society which tries to overcome the conflict between traditional functions of the state and an industrial class society through social integration"[10]. This legal interpretation of the German social state clause is acceptable. At the same time, however, one must ask the question how this postulate[11] should be applied in a specific case; to this question there is no clear answer. The same judgement also applies extensively to decisions made in the German Federal Constitutional Court[12].

In the decision related to the Investitionshilfegesetz (statute related to investment help) BVerfGE 4,7 the Federal Constitutional Court developed the thesis of the *economic political neutrality of the Grundgesetz*. The wording of the judgement[13] was:

> The Grundgesetz guarantees neither the economic political neutrality of the government or the legislators nor a 'social market economy' which is regulated solely by market forces. The 'economic political neutrality' of the Grundgesetz simply means that the founders of the constitution did not make an explicit decision in support of a particular economic system. This would enable the legislators to pursue appropriate economic policies in the light of available knowledge at any given time, as long as he takes account of the Grundgesetz. The present economic and social order is *one* such possible order under the Grundgesetz, but by no means the only possible one. It rests on an economic and social political decision based on the will of the legislator which can be replaced or altered by another decision.

This interpretation of the Federal Constitutional Court has been accepted; namely, that the legislator can pursue at any given time what appears to be an appropriate economic policy. This means that there is ample scope for interpretation and action which lies between the concept of the liberal market policy of the 19th century and that of a totally planned economy. This interpretation of the social state principle made by the Federal Constitutional Court has the great advantage that it is neither rigid nor dogmatic; in this, however also arises the disadvantage that successive cases can be interpreted differently and applied differently. In the end it is a question of political decision.

This point illustrates that economic policy in general, and industrial policy in particular, depends on political outlook and willingness and is therefore not based solely on economic principles. This is true and particularly so for the Ruhr district. The political attitudes, that is, the judgements by the highest judicial interpretations of the constitution merely provide a framework but do not provide answers applicable to concrete situations.

II. Industrial and Social Policy Contradictions – The Example of the Ruhr District

The introduction has shown that industrial policy has come to the fore because of the inability of creating an economic market process which leads to harmony. This consideration applies even more in a market economy which is meant to be and must also be a social market one, i.e. one which has a political objective and a constitutional task. The problem of pursuing simultaneously industrial as well as social political aims are illustrated by the example of what happened in the Ruhr district. This will also show that political aspects must often be taken into account.

The Ruhr District as an Economic Region[14]

Among the new conurbations in the German Federal Republic the Rhine-Ruhr district is the largest. A population of about 11 million inhabitants live in an area of 10,700 square kilometers. This part of the Ruhr district (popularly referred to as "Revier" or "coal chimney") is 130 km long and the average width amounts to 35 kilometers. This space corresponds to the area of the Housing Association of the Ruhr coal district. (Siedlungsverband Ruhrkohlenbezirk SVR)[15]. The Ruhr district is the greatest conurbation in Europe.

The Ruhr district commands excellent transport facilities. In the east-west direction the Hellweg[16], in the north-south direction the Rhine with its tributaries and with access to Rotterdam, one of the major seaports of the world; transport facilities have been improved through numerous canals; 1914 the Rhein-Herne-Kanal; 1931 the Lippe-Seiten-Kanal. Duisburg has the greatest inland port of the world and Hamm houses a great railway junction. A close railway network has been built up which was started in 1847; it has been supplemented in the last decades by a quick intercity network and two motorways.

Coalmining of Steinkohle (hard coal) began in the middle ages at the frontier of the Ruhr valley and expanded to the north, east and west during the first 30 years of the 19th Century. The mining of iron which was developed between 1850 and 1912 provided a second base, side by side with coal, for the development of the Ruhr district with its production of iron and steel. Three centres emerged: the western Ruhr district with Duisburg and Oberhausen, the middle region with Hattingen, Bochum, Essen and Gelsenkirchen as well as the eastern Ruhr district with Hagen and Dortmund. Continuous changes in the industrial structure led to changes in the geographical location. Stimulated by favourable transport facilities – the so called "Rheinschiene" (Rhine rail) has given rise to a concentration of industry in the western Ruhr district.

The following table presents an overview of the population changes in a number of towns in the Rhine-Ruhr district.

Changes in the Population of the Rhine-Ruhr District[17]					
– in 1 000 –					
Town	1819	1871	1905	1962	Percentage of employees on the secondary sector 1961
Bochum	2	21	119	368	60,6
Castrop	1	3	22	89	71,4
Datteln	1	3	5	30	73,4
Dortmund	5	44	176	647	58,3
Duisburg	5	33	260	506	58,5
Düsseldorf	24	69	287	703	47,6
Essen	5	52	231	734	56,0
Gelsenkirchen	1	8	147	389	64,6
Hattingen	3	6	10	29	51,5
Köln	55	129	440	809	46,6
Marl	1	2	3	73	79,6
Moers	2	3	6	47	45,8
Mülheim	6	14	94	188	60,8
Oberhausen	–	13	52	261	67,1
Wattenscheid	1	5	24	80	63,0
Witten	2	15	36	97	64,8

Division of the economy into three sectors; Primary sector = agriculture forestry and fisheries; Secondary sector = manufacturing, mining and industry; tertiary sector = services, trade and transport.

This table indicates that not only urbanisation increased between 1871 and 1905 but also that industrialisation increased considerably because the two processes are interrelated. It is true that the size of the population has increased till 1962 but this has only fortified the growth of industrialisation. Particularly noteworthy is the high share of the secondary sector in 1961 which comprises the mining and steel industry.

The Rhine-Ruhr district (particularly the real Ruhr district) has made a major contribution to the industrialisation of Germany. This industrialisation did not only give rise to a high standard of living in the whole of the German Federal Republic but also attracted workers from East Germany and from Poland. The Ruhr district is therefore not merely an industrial region but also a demographic melting pot.

The Ruhr district however was not merely an expression of economic growth but also Germany's armaments factory, that is, it was of primary importance in the first and second world war for the armament industry. This did not merely lead to much destruction during the second world war, but also provided a special position within the policy of the British Control Commission after the war.

The problems of the Ruhr district after 1945

The Ruhr district – particularly the coalmining district – was of great and decisive importance both politically and economically for the Federal Republic of Germany. The British Control Commission sequestrated the coalmines on the 22nd December 1945 and handed over the administration to the North German Coal Control (NGCC) which they had established in August 1945. In doing so the British took over a branch of the economy which was of decisive importance for the war economy as well as for the peace economy and for reconstruction.

On the face of it the coalmines had suffered little destruction; in reality, however, their productive capacity had deteriorated during the rearmament period and, in particular, during the second world war. This applied not merely to the technical running of the mines but also to the age structure of the miners. What was found therefore was not so much war damage as economic destruction through "Raubbau" (literally translated as "robbery production") i.e. excessive exploitation of the resources.

With the sequestration of the coalmines the British Military Government reached the political purpose of fending off more far-reaching influences – that is international control through the Allies; for instance, the closure of pits in the spirit of Morgenthau. This shows that the British recognised the importance of the Ruhr district very quickly, particularly the role of coal production for reconstruction in the western countries and in Germany. From the economic point of view sequestration was also justified because the pits had incurred heavy losses (728 million reichsmark between October 1944 and the end of August 1945). In addition there was the close interrelation between the coalmines and the iron and steel industry. The sequestration was not necessarily carried out as a nationalisation project; this purpose was first voiced in the House of Commons, by Bevin, the British Foreign Minister, on the 22nd October 1946. But this first step in that direction led immediately to differences of opinion within the Berlin Control Commission, which were reinforced by internal competence conflicts and further differences of opinion. The USA was a firm opponent of nationalisation.

As far as the Germans were concerned there was a high degree of agreement for nationalising the coalmines and other key industries, as regarded both the Social Democrats and the Christian Democrats. The Landtag (parliament) of North Rhine Westphalia passed a decision in which the abolition of the sequestration order of the pits and the take-over of the coal industry by the community was announced. However, the Military Government declared that the Landtag had no right to make such a decision. It expressed the view that such an important decision would have to wait until it could be made by a future German government. This reply may be seen at the same time as an admission that the nationalisation plans had failed.

The Americans provided material help, in spite of their opposition to nationalisation, on condition that the help would be used for reconstruction and would further the American stabilisation policy. Because the sequestration of the pits had not produced the desired output targets, there was opposition to the nationalisation argument for pragmatic reasons. General Lucius D. Clay adopted a defensive preventative strategy, particularly after the setting up of a bi-zonal British and American Control Commission on 1st January 1947. At the Anglo-American coal conference (held in Washington from the 12th August to the 10th September 1947) the US put pressure on Britain to find a solution for increasing coal production. Through the newly formed Bipartite Economic Control Group the Americans acquired the right to take part in the running of the Ruhr coalmines which meant that they controlled the newly formed Deutsche Kohlenbergbauleitung (DKBL German Coalmining Management) jointly with the British. This did not solve the question of ownership; the first priority was to increase production because coal was the main source of energy available for reconstruction.

The growth of production depended more on problems of providing adequate food supplies for the miners than on an answer to the question of the ownership of the mines. Because the special rations for miners had been abolished at the end of the war, their physical fitness was too low to enable them to produce more. Living conditions too were bad; in Bochum for instance only 5.65 square meters per person were available and the situation deteriorated till the end of 1947 when it was 4.13 square meters per inhabitant. In this situation the British Military Government recognised the need to grant special treatment for the miners. Food rations were raised, wage rates were improved and pensions were guaranteed once more. A period of material priviledges for miners began with these measures. While this did not increase productivity in the short run, it brought new workers to the Ruhr district. The incentive measures changed the living conditions of the miners decisively, that is, the food question was no longer a major problem.

Coal production was the critical factor for economic growth which means that the whole economic policy focused on output growth and the just distribution of coal. While other economic sectors were affected by Allied dismantling measures, coalmining was treated as an exception. This illustrates that the industrial coal policy did not simply deal with an economic problem but also with a political and social problem.

In 1936 the monthly average output of Steinkohle amounted to 353,000 tons, in 1945 to 110,000 tons, in 1946 to 166,000 tons, 1947 to 219,000 tons and in 1948 to 265,000 tons. With this increase in production the volume of output began to catch up with pre-war standards. It is true that a sizeable part of the coal production was exported as reparations and that there were also transport problems. However, the supply situation was improving visibly and not only for private consumption but also for industry. The bottleneck of low coal supplies which had affected nearly all sectors of the economy and of the reconstruction work up to July 1947 began to be increasingly overcome. The coal and with it the energy problem, lost its all pervading economic dimension.

It is an open question whether one can say that what was done during the first years after 1945 can be described as an industrial policy in the modern sense of the word. Nevertheless the following trends which have been present later partly existed then, as we can see, and partly with opposite omens:

1. Modern industry relies on an adequate energy supply and the production of energy assumes top priority when there is a shortage. After 1945 the supply of coal for industry and for private households was the most important provider of energy in West Germany.
2. For this reason the Allies sequestrated the coalmines and toyed with the idea of nationalisation, without bringing it about, because a change from private to public ownership would not have increased production. Nor was there any dismantling.
3. To further coal production and at the same time to improve the supply of energy material incentives were introduced (better food, clothes, housing as well as financial incentives, that is, higher wages). Coal production rose and provided the base for the growth of industrial production and for the improvement of domestic coal supplies. At the end of 1947 the position became less critical.

This post-war example shows that the objectives of increased productivity and output through social and political measures — better food, better provision of clothes and housing, were in step with the economic objectives. This means that there was no contradiction between the industrial and social policy. As will be shown below, a completely different situation arises, when overproduction and/or structural change exists which lead to retrenchments and create, in turn, social problems.

The political aspect of coalmining[18]

I shall only refer briefly here to the question of ownership. The ownership question was given low priority; in its place incentive measures for increasing production were introduced and the introduction of nationalisation became less and less probable. The first step in transferring responsibility to the Germans was the establishment of the Deutsche Kohlenbergbauleitung (DKBL) ond the 19th November 1947. The Allies — and by then the Americans played a decisive role — wanted to avoid an excessive concentration and capacity for carrying out a war. The Allies felt that the final decision about the ownership of the coalmines as well as of the iron and steel industry should rest with the new German government.

According to the Ruhr statute of 28th April 1948 between the USA, Great Britain, France and Benelux countries the international Ruhr Behörde (Ruhr Office) was set up; it was given the task of allocating the output of coal, coke and steel in the Ruhr district in the German and international market and at the same time the task of avoiding an excessive economic concentration. From the Petersberg agreement of 1949 onwards the Federal Republic of Germany was also represented in the Ruhr Office. In 1953, after the establishment of the Umbrella Organisation of the European Coal and Steel Community the Ruhr Office was closed. This measure shows up again in the political relevance of the industrial coal policy.

In the spring of 1949 the Allied Combined Coal Control Group (CCCG) put forward a new plan which envisaged the division of the areas into ten mining groups and, in addition, the termination of the association for coal and iron. This proposal was received with great scepticism. On the 15th September 1950 the General Secretariate of the Deutsche Kohlenbergbauleitung put forward a new plan, which took account of the relation of coalmines with the steel industry and the chemical as well as the electricity industry. This new organisation plan arrived too late; because the Allied High Commission had changed the legal framework related to disaffiliation measures in May 1950. The proposal of the DKBL failed and the new Allied organisation measures were passed; 23 autonomous coalmining companies were created which were disaffiliated from the rest of the coal enterprises — the total number of mining companies before this was 80. This measure was in line with the American advisers of the CCCG, but was rather artificial, because it was still based on the assumption that there was a scarcity situation and did not take into account increased competition from other energy providers. In the middle of 1953 the DKBL was wound up; the greater part of its tasks had been taken over already in 1952 by the newly set up Unternehmensverband Ruhrbergbau (UVR) (Association of Ruhr-mining Companies).

Ideological questions also played a major role in the attitudes of employees. As the chances of nationalisation, briefly envisaged in 1947/48 began to evaporate, the employees began to focus their attention on the objective of co-determination. The mining industry co-determination agreement which came into force on the 21st May 1951 had its origin in the iron and steel industry where close cooperation had been developed between the management and the employee representatives (Betriebsräte) from 1945 onwards. This had as its main aim the prevention of dismantling plants. The organisational changes which were announced in December 1948 by the British Control Commission North German Iron and Steel Control (NGISC) was introduced in the spring of 1947. In this context the employers offered far-reaching participation rights for employees to the trade unions. Without a formal contract but in complete concensus between employers and trade unions co-determination had begun to become a practical reality.

At the end of 1950, in the context of the negotiations to set up a Western European Coal Union, the Schumann Plan (Montanunion), the handing over of the German coalmines by the Allied Administration, to the German Federal Republic was under discussion. At the same time a conflict about co-determination developed between the trade unions and the Federal Ministry of Economics. Against a background of acute coal and steel shortage and a difficult domestic and foreign political situation it was important that the Federal Government should avoid a strike in the coal-mining and steel industry. The trade unions considered that co-determination in the coal industry was merely a first step towards a qualified co-determination policy for the whole industrial sector. Chancellor Adenauer, however, was successful in limiting the application of co-determination to the coal and steel industry; the Federal Parliament accepted this on the 21st May 1951. The new statute corresponded with existing co-determination customs and practice in the independent companies of the iron and steel industry.

At the end of the 1950s qualified co-determination in the coal enterprises was held to be one of the most successful innovations which the re-organisation of the postwar period had brought to this mining area.

This brief summary shows clearly that the economy in general and industrial policy in particular cannot be separated from politics. Industrial policy, therefore, is not merely an economic question but also a social policy one and above all also a highly political one. Any study which ignores these factors leads to mistaken assessments and judgements.

The Energy Crisis of 1950/1951

The currency reform of 20th June 1948 created the preconditions for German reconstruction. The new organisation of the Ruhrbergbau increased the severity of the investment problem so that the international competitiveness of the Ruhr coal-mining industry declined. Most of the West European Steinkohle districts had either reached or surpassed the pre-war shiftwork output standards at the time of the beginning of the Korea crisis. However, compared with 1938 the Ruhr district produced, only 72.3 per cent of the 1938 output in 1950. The Federal government as well as the steel industry had tried (and succeeded) to get into the armament market; however, in doing so they increased the coal shortage. When the Allies abolished the steel quota in August 1951 the preconditions for industrial expansion were provided and the world wide rearmament boom could spread without hindrance to the Federal Republic which was still working below full capacity and could therefore increase the strategic potential of the West quickly and with a lasting effect.

In 1952 an energy crisis in the Federal Republic led to a measure passed on the 23rd December which requested that two hours of electricity and gas should be saved by domestic consumers between the hours of 6 a.m. and 8 p.m. and that electric advertisements and shop window lights should be switched off and enterprises with a high consumption of electricity were asked to reduce this by 25 per cent on the 15th January 1951. In addition railways restricted holiday traffic from 10 January 1951. Fears that industry might collapse did not prove warranted in spite of the fact that the industrial sector received 50 per cent less coal in the third than in the second quarter of 1951.

The Federal Republic experienced a "coal miracle" because there was evidently a black market which bypassed the official steering system. Moreover it became apparent that the distribution of scarce coal which was based on directions from the state was not sufficiently effective to close the gap in the provision of supplies. Numerous unofficial energy sources appeared, such as poor quality fuels and coal from the occupation force; in addition black market coal was bought in Yugoslavia and Czechoslovakia in exchange for scarce dollars. The result was an export deficit so that the European Currency Union was threatened. Faced with this situation John McCloy, the High Commissioner and Special Envoy of the administration of the Marshall Plan demanded that there should be a "significant modification of the free market economy", that is, there should be direct government economic intervention measures, namely price and foreign exchange controls, production priorities and planning organisations. This intervention by the occupation force authorities gave rise to a two-way split in the Federal Government, and the position of the liberal wing under Ludwig Erhard was weakened. In this situation the industrial associations (Fachverbände) offered their help to Chancellor Adenauer.

In the spring of 1951 the energy crisis reached its peak. Because indigenous coal production remained a bottleneck, an extensive assistance programme for the Ruhr district was worked out which involved major changes.[19]

A whole series of proposals were put forward to find a way out of the economic political crisis. The most important problem was that of building up capital for the necessary investment programme. On 28th March 1951 the Bundesverband der Deutschen Industrie (BDI, Federal Association of German Industry) published a memorandum evaluating the economic situation of the Federal Republic of Germany in which it came to the conclusion that the safeguarding of the supply of coal as a raw material must receive top priority from the economic and social point of view as well as from the political one. The necessary investment volume would have to be created by redirecting money going into consumption through appropriate private measures. Investment by the state was ruled out by this proposal.

The decision which was reached was that of "investment help", that is, a voluntary assessment in the business sector and the money thus obtained would be given to the bottleneck sectors through the "investment help law" of 7th January 1952. On 24th February 1955 this law was terminated together with the investment terminal law. Thus an active industrial policy provided the missing capital through private self help activity. From a collection of nearly 12,000 million DM 42.5 per cent was given to the electricity, gas and water supply, 29.7 per cent to the Grundstoff industry, 22.8 per cent to mining and 5 per cent to transport. In addition the mining industry was supported by special collections which provided 850 million DM for investment purposes.

The energy crisis lasted throughout 1951 and the situation only began to improve a little in 1952 because of sizeable imports. Nevertheless prices were increased to cover costs; the coal price index rose from 100 in 1950 to 155 in 1955, and that for iron and steel to 177. These positive factors were accompanied by negative ones. It was a widely held view that coal alone would not cover future energy needs and that the Organisation des Ruhrbergbaus (Organisation of the Ruhr mining industry) as well as the sale of Ruhr coal had not created sufficient competition to solve the problems.

Oil imports for heating purposes began during the energy crisis in 1950; however, only 530,000 tons of heating oil were used in 1950 whereas in Britain the consumption already amounted to 5.3 million tons. This situation contained the seed of a new – completely different kind of crisis; in spite of this new pits were opened up till 1957; rationalisation was also increased and the miners reached the top of the wages league. The years 1956 and 1957 represented the peak of the development of coalmining in the Ruhr district. All the experts shared the view that coalmining would retain its unique importance with regard to energy supply. But already on the 25th February of 1958 did short time working lead to a cutback of 16,000 working shifts. The coal crisis – with the opposite omen – began.

The Coal Crisis as a Product of Structural Change

Certain trade cycle movements had already taken place in the postwar period, for instance, in the middle of 1954. However, this time it was the expression of important structural changes.

The change in demand came quite unexpectedly. Neither the mining industry nor the public were prepared for it; thus, after 1956, the top management of the European Coal and Steel Community (ECSC) had demanded that there should be sales plans to ensure the just distribution of scarce coal. People were concerned about scarce energy supplies rather than about excess capacity. In response to this situation the Federal Government abolished tariffs for heating oil and extended the duration of import contracts for United States coal and heating oil for three years. Ludwig Erhard considered that this measure would provide a fundamental solution for future energy needs. Given this state of affairs the West German coalpits greatly increased their prices, this meant that the price mechanism provided a favourable opening for oil and United States coal. The prices for oil fell drastically in the period 1957 to 1960. The price for heavy oil (paid by industry) fell from 142 DM to 60; for light heating oil (used by private households) it fell from 242 DM to 125. In addition, the import of United States coal was favourably affected by a fall in transport costs so that imported coal was more favourably priced than the Ruhr coal. If one takes account of the quality of heating fuel, the light fuel oil had a price advantage of 45 to 80 DMs in the Ruhr district and in South Germany. This landslide made a considerable impact on the structure of energy consumption; it meant that the Federal Republic of Germany became an energy importer (See table "Structural Change ...").

Structural Change of the Energy Economy in the Federal Republic of Germany 1956–1969 (in million tons)							
	German Coal			Production and Import of oil			
Year	Output of hard coal	Sales(a)	Stocks(b)	Imports of Coal	Output of crude oil	Crude oil imports	Imports of mineral oil products
1957	149,4	148,5	0,8	21,7	4,0	8,2	5,6
1958	148,8	136,2	13,8	16,2	4,4	10,8	5,8
1959	141,7	137,9	17,6	8,5	5,1	16,7	5,7
1960	142,3	148,7	11,2	7,3	5,5	23,3	7,8
1961	142,7	142,2	11,7	7,3	6,2	29,7	8,7
1962	141,1	143,2	9,6	8,0	6,8	33,3	13,2
1963	142,1	147,9	3,8	8,7	7,4	40,4	17,5
1964	142,2	138,2	7,8	7,7	7,7	51,7	15,7
1965	135,1	126,6	15,4	8,0	7,9	59,1	17,0
1966	126,0	117,9	20,4	7,5	7,9	67,7	18,6
1967	112,0	114,6	17,8	7,4	7,9	72,0	19,3
1968	112,0	120,3	9,5	6,2	8,0	84,1	20,5
1969	111,6	120,2	2,6	7,5	7,9	89,6	25,5

(a) Output figures ± stocks at pits and stocks at the Notgemeinschaft Deutscher Kohlenbergbau GmbH.
(b) Figures excluding stocks held by the Notgemeinschaft.

Source: Stat. Jb. für die BRD; Statistik der Kohlenwirtschaft e.V., Daten zur Entwicklung der Energiewirtschaft der Bundesrepublik Deutschland, hrsg. v. BMW, Ausg. 1972.

This change from being an exporting country to becoming an importing one was encouraged by the price advantages, that is, the imported US coal was very much cheaper than the Ruhr coal and so was heating oil. The attraction of oil, however was not based simply on a price advantage; it was also affected by the competition of new suppliers (outsiders) and by the fall in transport costs. While the United States, Great Britain and France introduced quotas for oil imports the Federal Republic of Germany did not do this because they gave a higher priority to free trade.

At the same time it was thought important that the monopoly position of coal should be restricted so that favourable energy prices could be procured for the West German economy. The coalmining enterprises raised no objections to this development.

The miners and trade unions were the first to notice the approach of a structural crisis when the first redundancies took place in the coal mines at the end of 1958 and when idle shifts reduced the number of shifts worked by 3 million. These developments were judged in different ways by members of the Federal Government. While Adenauer did not want to see coalmining exposed to the whims of competition from heating oil, Economics Minister Erhard saw it as a natural development and was against directional intervention; as a temporary observation he considered it an energy gap.

In a memorandum of 13th November 1958, the Association of Ruhrmining Companies advised the Federal Chancellor that between 1958 and 1963 there would be an excess supply of energy produced by the standard energy sources of 15 to 25 million tons of hard coal units (SKE). It further stated that the over-supply was a result of increased mineral oil production. Federal Economic Minister Erhard declared before the Federal Parliament on 29th January 1959 "that the coalmining industry must be kept alive and remain an essential part of our energy supply, that the employment of miners must be safeguarded and as far as possible of a uniform nature". The oil-cartel, founded in 1958 was given notice of termination by the Mineral Oil Industry as early as 1959, however.

At the end of 1959, the Employers' Association of the Ruhrmining Companies warned against false hopes that by a stoppage of 10 to 14 million tons of annual mining capacity, the preservation of the coal-mining industry could be achieved. In a programme presented to the Federal Chancellor on 23rd January 1960, it was explained – inter alia – that despite strong efforts the coal-mining industry would not be in a position to compete with the fuel oil industry. The Employers' Association demanded that a series of government action be implemented in order to effectively influence the energy market and to avoid further crises. The question of an effective energy policy remained unresolved by the Federal Government. On 16th May 1962, during a debate on energy policy before the Federal Parliament, the Federal Economics Minister declared that the mining industry could rely on two things:

„Firstly: The federal government will not permit a fragmentory development as a result of a forging ahead of other energy carriers.

Secondly: The federal government will support all efforts of adaptation on part of the mining industry as effectively as possible."

Despite his efforts, the Federal Economics Minister was unable to motivate the Mineral Oil Companies to reduce their capacity. They expanded their refineries and continued their liberal import of mineral oils. In addition to an increase of output per shift (from 1,600 kg per man/shift in 1957 to 2,400 kg in 1962), the coal companies concentrated on productive beds. The negative rationalization resulted in a certain mine "robbing" of the richer beds.

Pursuant to the law on rationalization of the coal-mining industry, which was passed on 29th July 1963, the Rationalization Association of Coal-Mining Enterprises was established in order to increase the competitiveness of the German coal-mining industry. The Rationalization Association had considerable funds at its disposal in order to promote the process of concentration; that is, the closure of unprofitable mines. The bonuses for the mine closures, however, were not subject to any conditions in order to improve the structure of the Ruhr district. Since 1957/58 (the beginning of the coal crises) until 1964, 37 large mines with an output of approx. 18 million tons (of these, 27 mines were located in the Ruhr district with an output of 14 million tons) and another 131 smaller mines with an output of 6.5 million tons had already been closed-down. Effective 31st October 1964 another 31 large and 20 smaller mines with a total capacity of approx. 26 million tons gave notice of closure. The rationalization measures effected some 73,000 jobs, 53,000 of which were location in the Ruhr district. During the same period, 48 smaller pits were converted into 25 large pits. The Rationalization Association was the first economic instrument to contribute to a shrinking of the output of German coal, which at the time was seen merely as rationalization measure.

An extraordinary cold spell during the winter of 1962/63 caused a temporary exhaustion of the dumps, but in 1964 dump stocks grew again. At the beginning of 1964, the Federal Economics Minister made a statement during a forecast to the effect that supply-and-demand will remain in balance for the foreseeable future. "It was concluded from this assumption that economic and political measures were no longer necessary."[20] Following talks between the Ruhrmining Employers' Association, the Federal Chancellor and the Federal Economics Minister on 6th November 1964, assurances were given in a press release that annual sales of a 140 million tons as well as a productive German Coal-Mining Industry should be preserved. But as early as 1965, the dump stocks as well as unworked shifts increased; attempt of harmonization between the coal-mining industry and the mineral oil industry did not show any practical results.

Erroneous assessments of the future prospects of coal were widespread and there was no concept as how to overcome the crises. Because of different production and profit structures among the mining enterprises, there was no uniform and strong representation of their interests on part of the Ruhrkohle Employers' Association. The Coalmining Industrial Union (Industriegewerkschaft Bergbau) by contrast demanded that there should be a strategy for overcoming the coal crisis; for instance, by consolidating mining companies into a unified enterprise; that is, by nationalization. Without public ownership of the coal-mines – according to the trade union – there couldn't be any "coal-policy" – neither on an economic nor a socio-political level. Only by following along the above lines, the establishment of optimal-size enterprises was feasible. All efforts however proved to be politically unacceptable; so was the proposal to set up an economic council.

No basic consensus could be reached on the future political development of energy. The trade unions pleaded for extensive conservation of mining capacity; the Federal Economics Minister was in favour of cheaper energy to further economic growth; the Employers' Association Ruhrkohle was unable to define its own position. Even the European Coal and Steel Community – whose concept was based on a energy shortage and not on excess capacity – was not, or only in a limited way, able to act because of a conflict of interests of member states at the level of the Council of Ministers. Not till spring of 1959 did the European Coal and Steel Community put forward a crisis plan, which was to guarantee output, control of imports of solid fuels, the freezing of stocks of coal and, finally, a minimum wage for miners. The top management was defeated by vote of the advisory committee as well as the Council of Ministers. It emerged that the agreement with respect to the European Coal and Steel Committee had guaranteed the Western Partner States access to the German coal market, but it did not manage to bring the sales crisis. Finding a solution was therefore the responsibility of the national governments.

The provision of cheap energy, that is, of oil, was of major importance to the Federal Republic of Germany, affecting its economic and political interests. Ludwig Erhard recognized the structural changes and believed that coal would be driven out of business by the cheap oil prices. Coal and oil imports created problems only to the extent as it affected the job situation for redundant miners; that is, new jobs had to be found. Despite an increase in fuel oil tax, the decline of the coal-mining industry could not and was not being avoided. During talks between the Federal Economics Minister and the Minister-President of Land Northrhine-Westphalia on 22nd November 1965, the output goal of 140 million tons per annum — maintained for many years — was officially stopped. This was the *turning-point* in energy-policy; the motive for this action was not explained. The turn was obviously an expression of economic principles of market-policy; that is; priority was given to cheaper energy — namely oil.

The Coal-Mining Industry was therefore compelled to draw its consequences from the newly-developed situation: At the beginning of 1966 it became evident that another 30 to 35 million tons of annual capacity had to be relinquished. No legal instruments were available, however, to implement the stoppage, neither were reliable data. Thus the coal crisis rapidly approached a new climax in 1966.

The different economic and socio-political concepts with respect to the coal crisis, dating back as far as 1957/58, became clear:

1. *Trade Unions:* The trade unions realized that the coal — as one of the most important sources of energy — could no longer maintain its domineering position of the postwar era, but urged a gradual capacity reduction, a rationing (quota-fixing) of oil imports, and in particular stressed the safeguarding of jobs. One could term the above industrial policy as being socially-oriented.

2. *Ludwig Erhard:* The Federal Economics Minister not only recognized the bottleneck in the coal field, but also realized that the oil prices were more economical. He considered oil imports as an important factor in breaking the coal monopoly in order to strengthen and safeguard economic growth. Erhard proceeded on the assumption that in a growing economy, the redundant workers in the coal mining industry would find new employment opportunities. Consequently he restricted his interventions with the energy market to specific issues and left the adjustment largely up to the market itself. One could term this as a free-enterprise system in industrial policy.

3. *Coalmining Industry:* The Ruhrmining Employers' Assoc. did not have a convincing concept with which to overcome the crisis. Interventions with the Federal Government were primarily aimed at procuring a *production guarantee* in order to safeguard mining sales as well as the national energy supply.

In view of the diverging attitudes, an industrial-(coal)-policy could not be achieved. The mine closures had by now reached a most critical stage which exceeded the Government's expectations by far; they threatened to upset the entire Ruhr district. The Federal Government now made a serious effort to get the oil situation under control. The restrictive measures came too late for the year 1965, however, the coal production continued its downward trend. In anticipation of the closure-programme, the output capacity was reduced by another 8 million tons. In comparison to this tremendous drainage of working places, there were hardly any new jobs since there was no settlement of industry in the Ruhr district to speak of. Furthermore, the mining companies controlled large areas of land and were thus in a position to discourage industrial settlements by "blocking" land. For instance, due to the non-availability of land in the Ruhr district, the Ford Factory was compelled to move to the Belgian City of Gent as an alternative measure.

The collapse of mine capacity made numerous workers redundant. The *monostructured economy* of the Ruhr district was not prepared to absorb them due to a lack of an active industrial policy; also, the market mechanism by itself could not handle the adjustment process. The question was not planning or controlled economy, but how to channel the unavoidable change in structure and to absorb the unemployed in new jobs.

The political dimensions of the coal crisis

Ever since the onset of the coal-crisis in 1957/58, it had never merely been a question of energy policy but also to an extent of regional policy and finally also of *politics*. The miners not only were peak wage earners because of the hard and dangerous work they were doing, but also because coal was scarce. If they insisted on remaining at the top of the pay scale, they would support the shrinking process while at the same time the profits were diminishing. If the peak wages were lowered, however, an exodus of young and skilled miners was inevitable. This particular situation created a special social partnership between the Employers and the Labour Unions, which received further support by the co-determination of the Coal, Steel and Iron Community (Montan). Despite political differences of opinion, it was agreed that the financial and social situation of the miners must be safeguarded.

The Labour Union focussed its politics on a reduction in working hours and on the conservation of social policies[21] because 1958/59 the number of miners was reduced by 61,000. Large demonstrations took place in several cities of the Ruhr district and on 26th September 1959 as many as 60,000 miners took part in the

"MARCH TO BONN": They demanded co-determination regarding closure policies, working places for dismissed miners, indemnification for loss of earnings, and a reduction in age limit for miners working underground to 60 years. At the beginning of the Sixties, the Labour Union achieved certain benefits such as hardship allowance and wage increases partially by demonstrations. After 1965 there was a tight network of social benefits provided through federal and state budgets as well as by the Coal, Iron and Steel Community (Montan). The grants for the social safeguarding of the adjustment processes increased from 1.5 million in 1959 to 29.6 million in 1960, dropped to 8.2 million in 1965 and reached 44.4 million in 1967, 49.1 million in 1968; during 1971 and 1976 they dropped to 6.8–19.5 million annually. The purpose of the grants was to promote the mobility through re-training, separation allowance, reimbursement of moving costs, etc. The *socially*-oriented measures prevented the redundant miners from having to relinquish their social positions and thus becoming radicals. Due to the remarkable economic growth until 1960, the majority of miners were able to find jobs in other branches of industry.

In 1965/66 the Federal Republic experienced its first recession; the Ruhr district found itself in a whirlpool of an overall economic development thus causing a cumulation of economic and structural effects. In May of 1962 the Federal Government had granted an output guarantee of 140 million tons per annum, which it reconfirmed in 1965, but at this point in time the guarantee was not redeemable. In these days of looming crises, the Employers' Association of Ruhrmining Industries and the Labour Union urged the federal government to intervene. The latter, however, was obviously not inclined to do so.

In the spring of 1966 the situation in the Ruhr coal-basin became more and more critical: Negotiations failed, more than 90 per cent of the Labour Union members were in favour of work stoppage/strike, the federal government increased its adjustment grants.

On 10th July 1966, the CDU Minister-President Franz Meyers emerged from State Parliament elections with a weakened coalition majority. Protests in form of demonstrations and church rogation services increased, and the Employers' Assoc. turned to the Federal Minister of the Interior for help as public law and order were in acute danger; previous policies were declared as having been inadequate and a market guarantee of 117 million tons per annum demanded. Finally, the Employers asked for a decision as to an unrestrained development of the mineral oil industry and a reasonable conservation of the Coal-mining industry. Although Federal Economics Minister Kurt Schmücker appreciated the difficulties, he rejected protective (coal-) measures for reasons of overall economic considerations. Shortly before the overthrow of Chancellor Ludwig Erhard's government on 1st December 1966, the Government was willing to revise its measure – *not* its goals – with respect to coal policies. This change in attitude however came too late for the Erhard government.

The market economy-oriented crisis policy had contributed to the weakening of the CDU majority in Northrhine-Westphalia and finally to the overthrow of Chancellor Erhard. The dramatic developments in the coal industry – which in particular affected the Ruhr coal district — had by now reached political dimensions: During the State Parliament elections on 10th July 1966, the SPD obtained 49.5 per cent of votes casted; the CDU-FDP coalition a majority of only 1 vote. After the FDP left government on 27th October 1966 (on 1st December 1966 Chancellor Erhard resigned from Office)[22] the coalition in Düsseldorf fell apart and was replaced by a center-left-coalition under Minister-President Heinz Kühn (since then Northrhine-Westphalia has had an SPD government; on 12th May 1985 it achieved an absolute majority).

The foundation of Ruhrkohle AG

The new State Government of Northrhine-Westphalia under Heinz Kühn made an earnest effort to solve the coal crisis. It focussed on industrial settlements in the Ruhr region and finally set up the so-called "Ruhr Development Programme" which — for the first time — defined the goals of regional and state (Land) planning as well as long-range infrastructure measures. The overall programme allocation amounted to 17 billion Deutschmark; for the coal-mine industry alone, Land Northrhine-Westphalia made available a total of 3.9 billion DM for the decade 1966–1976. The utilization of the funds makes clear that the *social* components received priority:

Financial Measures taken by Northrhine-Westphalia for the Benefit of the Coalmining Industry for period 1966 to 1976[23]	
Measures	Total Million DM
1. Social benefits for miners	325.6
2. Measures with respect to the social field through the employers	472.0
3. Aid for mine closures	570.8
4. Marketing aid	1,205.8
5. Structural aid	777.3
6. Measures in support of Ruhrkohle AG	225.9
7. Research, technical development and studies	213.1
8. Miscellaneous promotion measures	93.0
Total:	3,883.5

Approximately DM 800 million were allotted to social benefits, closure aid; almost DM 1.8 billion went for marketing aid; to research and technical aid only DM 213 million. The above figures are an indication that Land Northrhine-Westphalia placed particular emphasis on social components.

The Employers also underwent changes; that is, they were striving for structural changes of the Ruhr region and for a concentration of the coalmining industry. On one hand, trade and industry was interested in cheap energy (oil), on the other hand in a lowest bid regarding domestic coal production. The "Joint Venture Group of German Coal-Mining Regions" (ADS) financed until the end of 1968 a total of 17 mine closures with an annual capacity of 16.8 million tons of hard coal; it also acquired power of disposition for real estate and was thus able to influence industrial settlement. Numerous proposals and plans were submitted in order to revive the Ruhrmining industry. The new Federal Economics Minister of the Great Coalition (as of 1st December 1966 Prof. Karl Schiller) announced a new energy programme on 8th November 1967, which was to end the coal crisis for once and for all by the end of 1970. This was the moment of transition to an *active* industrial(coal-)policy.

The essential points of Karl Schiller's concept were[24]:
1. the foundation of a unified enterprise for the Ruhrmining Industry;
2. the compilation of a central adjustment plan;
3. the compilation of an overall social plan for miners affected by the closures.

Schiller set-up a so-called "Concerted (Coal)Action Group" comprised of government representatives, the labour union, employers and associations, in order to achieve a harmonization of interests. The Trade Union Mining and Energy Industries now were in full agreement with the reform of free enterprise, and the Employers likewise with a unified enterprise. An adjustment and restoration of the Coal-Mining Industry was to be accomplished in three phases:
1. a preparatory phase to be concluded by the end of 1967;
2. an adjustment phase till the beginning of 1969; and
3. a stabilization phase during the period 1969–70.

After more than one year of consultations, the ground was prepared for a cooperative harmonization of interests. On 15th May 1968, the so-called "Coal-Act" (i.e. legislation on an adjustment and restoration of the German Coal-Mining Industry and Coal-Mining Regions) was adopted, its aim being the strict adherence to the government's policy of curtailing energy supply from domestic sources. The above law envisioned the installation of a Federal Commissioner with full powers for the Coal-Mining Industry as well as the Coal-Mining regions.

Great pressure was exerted on the Mining Industries with a view to consolidation in order to form an optimal-size enterprise. In late 1968 the foundation of a unified enterprise emerged and on 27th November 1968 *RUHRKOHLE, INC. (RAG) was founded.* It was not until 1969 when the last mining companies finally joined the Corporation. The above unified enterprise controlled 52 coal-pits with an annual output of 85 million tons of hard coal, 20 coking plants with an annual capacity of 26 million tons of coke, and 5 briquette plants with an annual production of 200 million tons of hard-coal briquettes; the enterprise employed 186,000 workers. Special agreements were concluded between the Ruhrminging Corp. on the one hand and the steel industry as well as the electric power industry on the other hand for the duration of 20 years, which stipulated the terms of sales.

During the years subsequent to the foundation of Ruhrkohle, Inc. the coal-mining output dropped continuously; in 1973 it dropped by 97.6 millions thus falling below the 100-million-ton mark for the first time.

The foundation of unified enterprises — despite numerous setbacks — were based on the following reasons:

1. It had become obvious that the structural change of the energy market, that is, the advancement of oil, could not be stopped. Neither an output guarantee nor the "Verstromungsgesetz" (law regulating the share of domestic coal in the production of electricity; that is, 50 per cent of domestic coal was to be used for the production of electricity).

2. Previous market-economic measures had been inadequate in solving the problems on hand, all the more since beyond economic components, social and political elements were added. The Employers as well as the Labour Unions relinquished their dogmatic positions; that is, the labour union agreed to a reform of free enterprise and the employers to the foundation of a unified enterprise.

3. A new economic concept was established under the Great Coalition and the Federal Economics Minister Prof. Karl Schiller: The liberal market mechanism was replaced by the guiding principle of global control and a harmonization of interests within the framework of concerted action. Whilst observing the market economy as a ruling principle, changes were taking place which not only allowed the State to concretely influence the economic process; they also commanded action on part of the State.

Thus a coal-crisis that had lasted for 10 years had come to an end. Not all problems had been solved; however, under the circumstances reasonable solutions had been found.

The Consolidation and Adjustment Process

The goal of the newly-founded unified enterprises was the consolidation and adjustment of the Coal-Mining Industry of the Ruhr region:

From 1958 until 1968 a total of 15.1 billion DM were poured into the Coal-mining industry, of which 10.1 billion alone went to the Ruhr district without, however, having brought the coal crisis under control. With the foundation of Ruhrkohle, Inc. the intention was made clear *not* to relinquish the German Coalmining Industry, but to maintain a limited output for political and economic reasons. The 1968 coal legislation was considered as being the appropriate framework. The Federal Commissioner for the Coal-Mining Industry and Coal-Mining Region (as of 15th May 1968) not only had to take into account matters of overall economic concern, but also social and regional economic conditions; that is, he not only was responsible for the adjustment plan of the unified enterprises, but also for the preparation and observance of the social- and structure plan. The "Coal-Act" provided for a binding *"overall social plan"* by which socio-political special terms were created which protected against the adjustment measures; analoguous to the closure bonuses for the employers, workers were paid indemnification money. The above social plan was augmented by the "structure plan" for the settlement of new industry; that is, tax deductions were granted for new investments and property was being procured.

Until the end of 1970, Ruhrkohle, Inc. was to submit an "overall adjustment plan"; instead, it only provided a basic plan as the difficulties were more complex than originally assumed. One of the problems was that insufficient investments had been made during the crisis phase, so that Ruhrkohle AG were forced to obtain loans and thus had to accept losses. The burden was such that during 1972–73 the coal-industry was heading towards a new crisis. The closures of unprofitable mines (with an annual tonnage of 13–14 million and 20,400 employees) achieved certain costs reliefs; at the same time, however, there was a need for capital expenditure for the period 1971–1975 in the amount of DM 2.15 billion. Public authorities as well as Ruhrkohle stockholders granted financial aid. During 1969 and 1972 profits gained amounted to DM 28 billion as compared to DM 30 billion expenditures incurred.

The 1973 energy crises as well as increased prices for energy once again made the Ruhr-coal seem attractive. Nevertheless, at the end of 1974 financial concessions of DM 840 million by the public authorities and shareholders became necessary in order to consolidate Ruhrkohle AG (during the first 5 years funds provided for Ruhrkohle AG amounted to close to DM 3.3 billion). Favoured by the energy crises and a steel boom, coal sales increased and the prices climbed. One talked about a renaissance of coal. But only one year later there was a reversal of the situation and the state/public authorities had to "help out" again: a "10 million ton *national coal reserve*" was established; annual investment aids to Ruhrkohle AG during 1978–1981 amounted to DM 450 million; the tax payers and energy consumers brought another DM 9.6 billion between 1970 and 1978; a grant for coke-coal came to DM 2.7 billion (price reductions to adapt to the international market level) and, finally, the sum of DM 6.9 billion was expanded for "Verstromungs"-Aid (Verstromung = regulates the share of domestic coal in the production of electricity).

A decisive factor was that these financial sacrifices were counterbalanced by the adjustment achievements; thus there were no losses of subsidies (see Table page 80: ,,Development of Ruhrkohle, Inc.").

An uncalculable and uncontrolled decline of the Ruhr-coal and thus of the entire Ruhr district was now being replaced by unified control measures of the coal-district. These measures not only are conducive to rationalization, but also allow for an orderly process of adjustment, which equally consider the political, economic and social aspects. For instance, over 50,000 were affected by redundancies without causing radicalism.

With the foundation of RUHRKOHLE, Inc. there was a transition to an *active industrial policy,* which combined regional- and social policy at the same time.

Development of RUHRKOHLE, Inc.[25]				
	1969	1973	1978	1982
Number of Mining Companies	7	6	3	3
Mines	52	38	28	24
Number of production facilities	390	252	180	155
Coke-plants	29	22	14	13
Personnel *)	182,700	157,223	136,503	134,479
Corporate turnover (mil/DM)	5,827	7,806	12,488	17,595
Output per coal-pit	660	7,289	9,000	10,500
Shift performance under ground (kg/MS)	3,781	4,143	3,966	3,975
Overall output (mil tons)	85	74.2	61.2	63.2
*) at the end of the year				

Source: RAG, Essen

Coal policy as a tension factor in international and national politics

Industrial policy comprises several aspects: Initially it is a coal policy which concerns mining enterprises. At the same time, however, it is social policy since those who work in the mining industry are affected by the overall development. These two aspects combined will result in a trade structure policy which — in turn — will touch on regional policy as the Ruhr region is involved. This makes the complexity of industrial policy evident. The various components of industrial policy may be reconciled provided the economy as a whole and/or a branch of the economy in particular (e.g. the mining industry) is in a process of growth so that there are no problems as far as sales, employment and income are concerned. As soon as there is a structural breakage as well as shrinkage, there will be tension. These tensions will lead to a conflict between the economic necessities and socio-political interests, which in the last analysis affect political decisions.

With respect to coal policy and/or the Ruhr district, a relatively accurate determination of the "breaking point" can be made:[26]

Listing of Coal Production/Consumption in the Federal Republic of Germany for the Period 1950–1980						
— 1,000 t SKE = coal unit —						
Year	Coal Output[1]	Hard-Coal		Changes in Stock[3]	National Consumption
		Import[2]	Export[2]		
1950	126 224	1 429	30 567	− 1 577	98 663
1951	136 204	6 870	30 231	+ 1 521	111 322
1952	141 037	8 982	28 680	+ 2 900	118 439
1953	142 070	6 384	29 519	+ 4 919	114 016
1954	145 890	5 476	33 131	− 1 973	120 208
1955	149 142	12 659	30 763	− 450	131 488
1956	152 705	16 277	29 241	+ 1 851	137 890
1957	150 839	19 231	28 817	+ 4 198	137 055
1958	150 005	14 130	26 326	+13 135	124 674
1959	142 698	7 884	27 752	+ 1 036	121 794
1960	143 255	7 876	29 688	− 6 909	128 352
1961	143 615	7 738	28 797	− 853	123 409
1962	141 899	9 525	29 321	− 3 092	125 195
1963	142 786	10 363	29 742	− 3 459	126 866
1964	142 704	9 558	26 204	+ 4 253	121 805
1965	135 464	9 789	23 930	+ 6 882	114 441
1966	126 290	8 776	24 979	+ 7 880	102 207
1967	112 294	8 861	26 419	− 1 906	96 642
1968	112 165	7 754	30 472	− 8 598	98 045
1969	111 780	9 249	28 707	− 9 368	101 690
1970	111 443	11 083	26 898	− 1 220	96 848
1971	111 053	9 128	24 188	+ 5 676	90 317
1972	102 707	9 106	22 935	+ 5 452	83 426
1973	97 599	9 447	24 912	− 2 033	84 167
1974	95 226	8 232	31 497	−10 714	82 675
1975	92 790	8 694	22 890	+12 063	66 531
1976	89 598	8 533	20 956	+ 6 465	70 710
1977	86 536	7 908	21 516	+ 5 969	66 959
1978	85 139	8 073	28 426	− 4 444	69 232
1979	87 528	9 625	27 190	− 5 877	75 840
1980	88 200	10 800	20 500	+ 1 500	77 000

[1] incl. small pits
[2] hard-coal, hard-coal briquettes, hard-coal coke (not converted to coal)
[3] total stocks of manufacturers, consumers and Notgemeinschaft Deutscher Kohlenbergbau (coke not converted to coal)

Source: Energiebilanzen, published by: Arbeitsgemeinschaft Energiebilanzen

The breaking point is the year 1957/58 when a peak in coal output and national consumption was achieved. This was followed by a continuous decrease. The change in structure will even become more evident if one uses the primary energy consumption as a criterion:

Primary Energy Consumption in the Federal Republic of Germany

Year	Hard-Coal	Brown-Coal	TOTAL Coal	Mineral Oil	Natural Gas	Water Power	Nuclear Energy	Misc.	TOTAL
				– Million tons Coal-Unit –					
1957	137,1	28,9	166,0	21,6	0,6	5,5	–	2,4	196,1
1960	128,4	29,2	157,6	44,4	0,9	6,6	–	2,0	211,5
1965	114,4	30,0	144,4	108,0	3,5	6,8	–	1,9	264,6
1967	96,7	27,3	124,0	127,2	5,6	7,9	0,4	1,7	266,8
1969	101,7	29,9	131,6	160,4	13,1	6,6	1,7	1,6	315,0
1971	90,3	29,3	119,6	185,7	24,0	6,4	2,0	1,7	339,4
1972	83,4	31,0	114,4	196,4	30,6	8,1	3,1	1,7	354,3
1973	84,2	33,1	117,3	208,9	38,6	8,2	3,9	1,6	378,5
1974	82,7	35,2	117,9	188,3	46,5	8,2	4,1	1,7	365,9
1975	66,5	34,4	100,9	181,0	49,2	7,4	7,1	1,7	347,7
1976	70,7	37,6	108,3	195,9	52,0	7,8	7,9	1,7	370,3
1977	67,0	35,1	102,1	193,9	55,5	4,5	11,8	1,7	372,3
1978	69,2	35,9	105,1	203,3	60,4	7,3	11,8	1,8	389,0
1979	75,8	38,1	113,9	206,8	66,0	6,6	13,9	1,8	408,2
1980	77,0	38,5	115,5	187,0	65,2	5,8	14,0	1,8	391,0
				– Total consumption in per cent –					
1957	69,9	14,8	84,7	11,0	0,3	2,8	–	1,2	100,0
1960	60,8	13,8	74,6	21,0	0,4	3,1	–	0,9	100,0
1965	43,3	11,3	54,6	40,8	1,3	2,6	–	0,7	100,0
1967	36,3	10,2	46,5	47,7	2,1	3,0	0,1	0,6	100,0
1969	32,3	9,5	41,8	50,9	4,2	2,1	0,5	0,5	100,0
1971	26,6	8,6	35,2	54,7	7,1	1,9	0,6	0,5	100,0
1972	23,5	8,8	32,3	55,4	8,6	2,3	0,9	0,5	100,0
1973	22,2	8,8	31,0	55,2	10,2	2,2	1,0	0,4	100,0
1974	22,6	9,6	32,2	51,5	12,7	2,0	1,1	0,5	100,0
1975	19,1	9,9	29,0	52,1	14,2	2,2	2,0	0,5	100,0
1976	19,1	10,2	29,3	52,9	14,0	1,2	2,1	0,5	100,0
1977	18,0	9,4	27,4	52,0	14,9	2,0	3,2	0,5	100,0
1978	17,8	9,2	27,0	52,3	15,5	1,7	3,0	0,5	100,0
1979	18,6	9,3	27,9	50,7	16,1	1,4	3,4	0,5	100,0
1980	19,7	9,9	29,6	47,8	16,6	1,9	3,6	0,5	100,0

Whereas both the hardcoal and brown coal in 1957 still maintained a proportional share of 85.7 per cent and mineral oil merely 11 per cent, the coal proportion had shrunk to 29.6 per cent by 1980 while the mineral oil increased to 47.8 per cent; as early as 1967 — within just one decade — a semi-balance had been achieved of the two types of energy. Despite this rapid change there was no comprehensive industrial-(coal-)policy until the end of the Sixties, an extensive energy programme was not developed until 1973.

Immediately prior to the 1973/74 mineral oil crisis the Federal Government for the first time provided a complete energy programme: The Federal Government assumed that the primary energy consumption would increase from 354.5 million SKE (coal units) during 1972 and 1985 to 610 million SKE's while at the same time the share of hardcoal would drop and the nuclear energy share increase. Although the mineral oil continued to be a "favourite", the dependency on imports was being realized; but it was viewed as a balance-of-payments problem. Moreover, one was not yet aware of the internal-policy problems in connection with nuclear energy.

The concept of a far-sighted industrial-(coal-)policy was being upset by the OPEC-generated oil crisis in 1973/74; i.e. it became apparent that a solely nationally-oriented industrial policy was not realistic as it was also being influenced by *international factors*. The "oil shock" was followed by an updating of the energy programme based on the assumption that there would be no further shrinkage but a stabilization of coal output; that is, an approx. tonnage of 94 million. The stabilization was to be achieved by three so-called "Verstromungsgesetze" (= law regulating the share of domestic coal in the production of electricity) which were passed in 1965, 1966 and 1974 respectively, according to which power stations were directed to utilize domestic coal for the production of electricity. Another factor considered beneficial to the stabilization was the grant for coal-coke (Kohlenkoksbeihilfe) for steel production (coke supply was accomplished on the basis of the world-market price level). The sales of hardcoal to power stations as well as the steel industries did indeed achieve a stabilization, the recession took place in industry (excluding power and steel), on the trade sector and in households.

In December 1977 a second updating of the energy programme was being accomplished. An escalation of energy prices in 1979/80 lead to a general political consensus to maintain the still available output capacity of the German Coalmining Industry. From 1957 to 1980 the output capacity dropped from 150 million tons to approx. 80 million and manpower was being reduced during the same period from 600,000 to approx. 180,000.

With the help of the energy programme an attempt was made to avert *political influences* and to decrease the dependence on non-influential factors. The attitude displayed by OPEC left no doubt that all the industrial countries were dependent on the quantity- and price-policy of oil-producing countries. Protests against an expansion of nuclear energy — in particular on part of the younger generation — set the *political limits* of industrial-(coal-)policy. The Federal Republic as energy consumer was thus subjected to double political pressure: The dependence on OPEC grew internationally, on a national basis Germany was confronted with radical elements trying to stop nuclear expansion by violence; the installation of nuclear power plants were stopped — or at least delayed — by judicial decision.

Taking the above into account it becomes clear that industrial policy is not merely an economic and social question, but also a problem of foreign and domestic policy. The inclusion of these aspects not only increase the complexity of the problems but clearly indicate that a solution on an exclusively economic basis is doomed from the outset.

III. Lessons Learned

It is exceptionally difficult to try to learn a lesson from the developments in the Ruhr district — and in particular with respect to the Coalmining industry. One can justifiably argue that this particular region is not comparable to any other industrial regions. One can also argue that at the time there was an entirely different starting point — namely the postwar era — which resulted in a development which was more or less inevitable; moreover, it would be correct to say that a one-time situation cannot be generalized or lessons learnt from it. All these objections are acceptable. If despite of the above lessons are going to be learned, then the reasons are as follows:

In the last analysis all historial phenomena of a technical, economic, social and political nature are unique, so that there cannot be any generalization. Despite the uniqueness of each particular situation one cannot help but recognizing certain tendencies as being repeatable or being of a similar nature, so that one can draw lessons from it with respect to related situations. Of course, one should be careful not to apply too restricted a criterion or to establish "laws" from which to deduce (scientific) regularities. If at all, one can only deduct tendencies which, in similar situations, might recur.

The following could be viewed as a guiding principle with respect to the experience gained in the Ruhr district in terms of industrial policy or (sectoral) economic-policy:

1. Industrial Policy cannot be separated from Politics

Successful industrial policy must be imbedded into a general, similarly aligned (national) policy, as such a policy — as mentioned previously — is not automatically generated by the market. Since the market does not establish norms and also is socially "blind", it demands intentional corrective measures. This again requires the setting of political norms as well as action. It is important, however, that no significant deviations exist between a general setting of norms and the concept of industrial policy; otherwise there will not be a realization of goals. If for example (national) policy requires a restructuring of a certain region (for example, the Ruhr district) by virtue of law, industrial policy develops the required programmes, but the Minister of Finance does not provide the necessary funds or the legislature does not pass the legal instruments for the expropriation of land, then industrial policy cannot succed.

Industrial policy is thus an integral part of general politics. In terms of democracies this means that it has to have a majority in order to succeed. Majorities however may only be obtained from a broad populace, but not from powerful economic but, in terms of figures, small groups.

2. Industrial policy during a rising and declining structural change

The example of the Ruhr district — and in particular with respect to coal — makes clear that a consensus between general politics, social politics and industrial policy can be reached without much difficulty, provided the entire economy — or at least a certain branch of trade — is in the process of development. This I would term as a *rising* structural change.

This applied to the Ruhr region prior to 1914 and also after 1945: Coal was the most important energy source and steel the most important product for the industrialization. Given this situation, private initiative needs to be augmented by national corrective measures only minimally; that means, the market mechanism is dominant. A growing and flourishing industry attracts manpower; prospects of profitable investments increase — mostly voluntarily — the standards of living and the social benefits. National interventions occur only with respect to marginal sectors; they are comparable to traffic regulations which are merely intended for maintaining and accelerating the flow of traffic.

We have an entirely different situation, however, if a given industry or region is in the process of stagnation; this I call a *declining* structural change: A structural shrinking process not only destroys capital (e.g. closures of mines or steel factories), it also causes workers to become redundant. If it involves key industries, it will in turn affect other branches of trade and thus include them into the shrinking process (declining structural change), as there are not enough substitute jobs. This will lead to social problems which we do not have in cases of rising structural changes. Provided a state does not consider itself a "nightwatchman" State reminiscent of the 19th century, and instead sees itself as a *socially-oriented* constitutional state (comparable to the FRG), an active industrial policy will simultaneously contain elements of an active social policy. Subsidies and social benefits will become inadmissible. A decisive factor is whether the state pursues a policy of preservation or one of adjustment:

If the state pursues a *policy of preservation,* it will more or less neglect the forces governing market trends in order to preserve a certain branch of trade, or region, by subsidies — either for social reasons (safeguarding jobs) or for supra-regional political reasons (securing an energy basis for emergency cases). If the latter apply, the marketing machinery will purposely be rendered ineffective and losses in growth will be accepted. A *policy of adjustment* does not envision rendering the market forces ineffective, but strives to alleviate the effects in order to compensate for social hardships. For instance, public funds are being used for retraining and resettlement of unemployed workers, or funds will be made available for settlement of new industry.

A comparison between a rising and a declining structural change makes clear that in respect of the first case a limited state intervention as part of industrial policy is taking place whereas in the latter case such an intervention may attain great intensity — also with respect to the ruling principle of market economy — and in certain circumstances ignore these principles.

3. Tasks and Constraints of Industrial Policy

The task of industrial policy — in particular in terms of a declining structural change — is to supplement and/or correct an inadequate adjustment mechanism of the market and particularly to compensate its social "blindness". The function of industrial policy is thus of a *corrective nature*. The course and scope are being determined in a western democracy by a parliamentary majority.

The *constraints* of industrial policy become visible when in a descending structural change social frictions occur which transgress into the political domain; that is, a shifting in majority rule during parliamentary elections takes place, which signals changes in industrial policy followed thus far. An example were the election results in Northrhine-Westphalia and the replacement of the CDU majority in Federal Parliament by the Great Coalition in 1966, which was followed by the social-liberal coalition who determined domestic and foreign policy in this country for over a decade. There might not be a causal connection between the Coal/Ruhr-crisis and the changes in the political majority, its influence is nevertheless unmistakable. This however means that an industrial policy, which deliberately and systematically pursues a policy of adjustment (to the market), cannot ignore the socio-political aspects — if a parliamentary majority must be safeguarded or obtained.

Economists, who view industrial policy on a solitary basis and under exclusively economic aspects, seem to have the notion that a (sectoral) industry policy takes place in a vacuum. Only during a rising structural change in the 19th century was the State in a position to restrict itself to making merely minor corrections of conditions within the scope of the law. In a parliamentary democracy, which is confronted with rapid technological and economic structural changes, the State cannot leave the adjustment process up to the marketing machinery, but must actively intervene in order to avoid a social degradation and political radicalism (an example for such social and political radicalism is the Miners' Strike in Great Britain).

Industrial policy should not be understood as an economic model but as a conflict of interest and power in a given political environment; it requires political components which, under certain circumstances, may violate the rules of a purely economic theory in order to preserve the social and political order in its entirety. In this sense, industrial policy is more than merely economic policy.

NOTES

[1] See Helmuth St. Seidenfuß: Sektorale Wirtschaftspolitik, in: Kompendium der Volkswirtschaftslehre, Bd. II, 4. Aufl., Göttingen 1975, pp. 206 – 274, Viktor Guttmann: Industriepolitik, (I): Theorie, in: Handwörterbuch der Sozialwissenschaften, Bd. V, Stuttgart-Tübingen-Göttingen 1956, pp. 272 – 276; Herbert v. Beckerath: Industriepolitik, (II): Epochen und Bereiche, ibid., pp. 276 – 281; Walter Hamm: Strukturpolitik, sektorale, in: Handwörterbuch der Wirtschaftswissenschaft, Bd. VII, Stuttgart-New York-Tübingen-Göttingen-Zürich 1977, pp. 479 – 491.

[2] Alfred Müller-Armack: Wirtschaftslenkung und Marktwirtschaft, Hamburg.

[3] Alfred Müller-Armack: Soziale Marktwirtschaft, in: Handwörterbuch der Sozialwissenschaften, Stuttgart-Tübingen-Göttingen 1956, Bd. IX, pp. 390 – 392, quoted p. 390.

[4] Müller-Armack: Wirtschaftslenkung, pp. 103 – 106.

[5] Ibid, p. 85.

[6] Ernst Forsthoff (ed.): Rechtsstaatlichkeit und Sozialstaatlichkeit, Darmstadt 1968.

[7] So Hans Gerbert: Die Sozialstaatsklausel des Grundgesetzes, in: Rechtsstaatlichkeit und Sozialstaatlichkeit, pp. 340 – 410, quoted p. 408.

[8] Ernst Rudolf Huber: Rechtsstaat und Sozialstaat in der modernen Industriegesellschaft, in: Rechtsstaatlichkeit und Sozialstaatlichkeit, pp. 589 – 618.

[9] Ibid, p. 599.

[10] Ibid, p. 600.

[11] See Hans-Hermann Hartwich: Sozialstaatspostulat und gesellschaftlicher status quo, 3. Aufl., Opladen 1978.

[12] Wolfgang Bohling (ed.): Wirtschaftsordnung und Grundgesetz (Uni-Taschenbücher, Bd.1118), Stuttgart-New-York 1981.

[13] Ibid, p. 5.

[14] See Achim Ragsch/Lore Ponthöfer: Wirtschaftsraum Ruhrgebiet, 1986.

[15] The SVR was founded as early as 1920. It is an office of public law and has the function of a community planning association which takes part in the planning of building programmes and

is involved in plans which represent important projects leading beyond the frontiers of the district. The SVR has a high reputation and has been a pathbreake for planning in the whole of West Germany and abroad.

[16] "Hellweg" is a widely used term for long distance transport routes. In the Middle Ages the Hellweg in Northrhine-Westphalia was a route for the salt trade which was a part of the foreign trade route which led from Flanders and the Netherlands to East Germany and East Europe. Towns grew up at the cross-roads with North-South routes. The Ruhrschnellweg of to-day corresponds to a large extent to the Hellweg.

[17] Ragsch/Ponthöfer, p. 18.

[18] Helmuth Burckhardt: Deutscher Steinkohlenbergbau im Spannungsfeld zwischen Politik und Wirtschaft – Eine Dokumentation, Köln 1968 (Burckhardt was the chairman of the Association of Ruhrmining Enterprises).

[19] Heiner R. Adamsen: Investitionshilfe für die Ruhr – Wiederaufbau, Verbände und soziale Marktwirtschaft 1948–1952, Düsseldorfer Schriften zur Neueren Landesgeschichte und zur Geschichte Nordrhein-Westfalens, Bd. 4, Wuppertal 1981.

[20] Burckhardt, p. 18.

[21] Walter Arendt: The social programme for the mining industry in a structural crisis, in: R. Bartholomäi/W. Bodenbender/H. Henkel/R. Hüttel (Publisher): Social policies after 1945 – history and analysis, Bonn-Bad Godesberg 1977, pp. 239–249 (From 64 to 69 Arendt was Chairman of the Miners Union, subsequently Federal Minister for Labour and Social Affairs).

[22] On 1st December 1966 Kurt Georg Kiesinger was elected as Federal Chancellor of the Great Coalition (CDU and SPD). On 21st October 1969 he was replaced by Willy Brandt as Chancellor of a social-liberal coalition (SPD and FDP) which remained in Office until 17th September 1982. On 1st October 1982 Helmut Kohl (CDU) was elected as new Federal Chancellor. The coal crisis although not exclusively may be contributed to continuous changes in domestic policy in the FRG.

[23] Abelshauser: Der Ruhrkohlenbergbau seit 1945, München 1984, p. 198.

[24] Burckhardt, p. 23.

[25] Abelshauser, p. 161.

[26] The following two tables are contained in: Burckhardt, p. 62 etc.

The Contribution of Small and New Enterprise to Growth and Employment

Klaus-Werner Schatz

Introduction

In Europe, millions of new jobs would have to be created in order to reduce unemployment to previous or tolerable levels, and to provide jobs to those who will be set off by the decline of many industries or because of the substitution of capital for labor which the emergence of new technologies seems to induce. For these reasons, it need not wonder that economic policy makers have devoted much effort to generating new jobs. In Germany, as well as in all other European countries, they have created numerous programs by which subsidies of various sorts are channelled to private job-promising-activities. In addition, governments have tried to expand employment by expenditures on public demand, or by using state owned enterprise for the creation of jobs. As empirical evidence reveals, lasting success has not been achieved.

With regard to company size, for long governments have set hopes above all on larger units to overcome economic difficulties. In the UK, for instance, specific incentives were granted to private enterprise for merging, as the government thought that too small company size was one major obstacle towards faster growth and higher degrees of employment. Or in Germany, in a number of cases subsidies to industry have been provided under the condition only that companies merge; examples at hand are pit coal mining or the aerospace and aircraft industry. Similar observations apply for other countries, too[1]. More recently, governments have rediscovered small and new enterprises as sources for structural change, growth and employment, and consequently, they have paid more attention to them, i.e., they have channelled more subsidies to the emergence and the cultivation of them. In general, however, not all new and small enterprises enjoy the same care. Preference is given to them, if they are engaged in high-tech industries, in the so-called future growth industries, and particularly important on this side of the Atlantic, if they promise contributing to the closure of the technological gap between Europe and the US (or Japan), e.g., in information technologies and industries.

In my paper, I shall first shortly deal with some basic considerations on the positive role assigned to small and new enterprise in economic development[2]. Next, I shall try to analyse whether the arguments which can be put forward supporting the role of these enterprises, hold to empirical scrutiny. I shall begin investigating into the contribution which they may have made to employment, and I shall analyse thereon, what they have contributed to growth, competitiveness and innovation. I shall end with some economic policy implications.

Why Small and New Enterprises are Assigned Positive Contributions to Economic Development

In the past, the positive contribution of small and new enterprise to economic development has mostly been discussed under the heading "competition". The role assigned to them was to provide fresh wind to the market, and in particular to prevent that old enterprise, from well established market positions, could quasi levy taxes on consumers, instead of competing for consumers' money. Additionally, it was argued, that small and new corporations were a locomotive for technological progress, because only by being innovative they could attain market shares and defend them in competition with older and bigger corporations. Together, both arguments mean that it are in particular such new and small enterprises which contribute to the change of economic and technical structures and, hence, to improving welfare and to economic growth; in this way, they also help stabilising the capitalist economic system, to which private property of production means and competition are constituent. The notion stabilising the system, however, does not imply that the system develops in equilibrium. In contrast, disequilibria are characteristic for a climate which is conducive to new and small enterprises, as they typically destroy old, inherited production structures in an unforeseen manner, ending up with new structures and supplies of goods and services which had not been anticipated by others. It is for this simultaneous process of destruction and creation that one can assign particularly fruitful contributions to change and development to new and small enterprise. This assessment of their role can be found in the writing of Joseph Schumpeter, to whom we owe deeper insights into our understanding of the capitalist economy than to presumably any other economist. Schumpeter did nothing less than define competitive capitalism by the very fact that new corporations can be established and grow, and that they can decline and go bankrupt, too, after having become big. He identified enterprise with entrepreneur who takes risks establishing the supremacy of capitalism over other economic systems.

"All this is different in 'trustified' capitalism", Schumpeter stated (Schumpeter, 1951, p. 707 sqq.). In trustified capitalism, growth and change go on with less friction in the individual case. They are both a matter for big enterprises which are owned by numerous shareholders, and individual entrepreneurs owing own corporations are neither important nor is there scope for their spontaneous activities. Innovation is no more typically bound to the emergence of new enterprises, but springs off from thoroughly planned investment in research and development, guided by specialists caring for its organisation and financing. Because the trustified and well organised capitalism lacks outsider competition, development is more smoothly than in competitive capitalism, but innovation, structural change and growth slacken. With the erosion of the role of entrepreneurs which such capitalism implies, the capitalist system itself becomes obsolete. The order is outdated which was necessary to allow for entrepreneurship. Capitalism can be replaced by other organisational principles. In Schumpeter's view, in the United States capitalism was highly trustified in the 1920s already (ibid, p. 48). While — different to Karl Marx — no believing in historically unavoidable developments, he thought that much evidence was at hand allowing for the conclusion that capitalism would be replaced by socialism, not through spectacular action or through spectacular policy changes, but by and by, and marching into socialism stepwise (Schumpeter, 1950). At the final end, trustified capitalism does hardly differ from socialism. "It will be merely matter of taste and terminology to call (it; the author) socialism or not" (Schumpeter, 1951, p. 72).

For these reasons, one can regard it as a symptom of economic sclerosis, if the number of small and newly established enterprises declines. In recent years, these enterprises have not only been paid increasing attention because it is hoped that they intensify competition, stimulate innovation and induce faster growth, but employment aspects have substantially gained momentum. Under employment aspects, the interest in small and new Enterprise rests above all on the consideration that they should be particularly able to discover market niches which are neglected by bigger enterprises and, hence, to provide new and additional supply of goods and services which by creating its own demand would then lead to new and additional jobs. Given the arguments supporting the positive role of them, it seems to be plausible that above all in Europe, where unemployment is high, growth weak and innovation apparently insufficient, governments are undertaking strong efforts granting help to new and small enterprises.

The Contribution of New and Small Enterprise to Employment

In the United States, in the 1970s, roughly 21 mill. additional jobs have been created, and including 1985, more than 7 mill. further jobs will have been made available. This contrasts completely to the developments in the EC where from the mid 1970s to 1985 approximately 2 mill. jobs will have been lost. In consequence, in the US employment is 35 per cent higher than it was in 1970, and unemployment will be down from its 1982 peak of 9.6 per cent of the labor force to 7 per cent in 1985; in Europe, employment was reduced by 2 per cent, and unemployment rates have steadily increased from 2 per cent (1970) to 11.5 per cent in 1985[3]. Asking the question "Who creates jobs?", David Birch ended up with the result that in the period 1969 to 1976, two thirds of all new jobs had been created by enterprises which at the beginning of that period were very small, employing twenty and less persons (Birch, 1981). More than three quarters of the jobs were supplied by enterprises with fifty and less employees. Moreover, the enterprises which turned out to be the most significant source of the employment increase in the US, were not only small but also new. For, four fifth of the jobs were created by enterprises existing less than five years. In manufacturing, such very new enterprises were a bit less important for job creation than in the economy as a whole, but referring to enterprises aged 8 years and younger instead to 4 years and younger, it was shown that they created approximately the same share of jobs in manufacturing than in other parts of the economy, namely roughly 85 to 90 per cent (Birch, 1984, p. 7, table 3).

The results of Birch were felt sensational, as they contradicted completely the then ruling perception that in the US job creation could be expected above all from big and old enterprise – a perception which Schumpeter presumably would have maintained with regard to trustified capitalism which according to many observers is typical for the US economy today, and which Schumpeter observed for large parts of the US as early as in the 1920s. Therefore, Birch's results provoked much critique concerning his methods, his data base and the time period of investigation which many thought to be unrepresentative for later years. Further research by Birch (1984) and others which concerned the recent past, too, (Harris, 1983; Harris, without year) came to slightly different results, but basically it supported Birch's earlier conclusions concerning the overwhelming importance of small and new enterprises for job creation in the United States.

It has often been argued that in Europe such enterprises are far less important, and that despite the role which can be assigned to them for contributing to increasing employment on theoretical grounds, they actually have contributed little. Such arguments are broadly shared in the Federal Republic of Germany, for instance. In this context, reference is mostly made to census figures which usually show that the absolute number of small enterprises declines as well as the absolute number of persons employed by them and their share in total employment. While in Germany these trends are clearly evident from census figures for the 1950s and the 1960s, in the recent past, however, the downward movement seems to have come to a halt, or it may even have been replaced by an upward movement. As the last census in Germany dates back to 1970, investigating the question in what direction the number of small enterprises moves, one must take recourse to other sources. One of these sources are labor force statistics. They reveal that the number of self-employed persons and persons working on own account which has heavily decreased in the 1950s and in the 1960s, since the mid 1970s is slightly increasing (excluding farming; Schatz, 1984). If past trends would have continued, their number would have been 12 per cent or by 225.000 persons lower in 1983. In manufacturing, even 25 per cent more persons were self-employed in 1983 than could have been expected from past trends. In the 1950s and in the 1960s, the number of self-employed persons and persons working on own account was very closely correlated to the number of enterprises. Taking into consideration that the bulk of all enterprises – 98.0 per cent according to the 1961 census, and 97.7 per cent according to the census of 1970 – are small (less than 50 employees), and that as a rule small enterprises are owned by one person only (identity between enterprise and entrepreneur), this close correlation becomes plausible. If past correlations have held for subsequent periods which can be assumed without running much danger of error, since the mid 1970s, the number of small enterprises must have declined far less than in the 1950s and in the 1960s, or even increased. These presumptions are supported by other research based on the number of enterprises registered by chambers of trade and commerce, which comes to the end that in the whole 1970s, the number of enterprises decreased by 0.3 per cent annually only, compared to 1.5 per cent between 1961 and 1970 (Schmidt et al., 1984; Schatz, 1984), and that after 1976, for the first time in post war German history, the number of enterprises has increased (Szyperski, Kirschbaum, 1981).

As interesting and important these observations may be as such which contradict the commonly shared opinion that the number of small and new enterprises continues to decrease at past trends, they can hardly help shedding light on the role which such enterprises play for the creation of jobs. What is measured by census figures or figures on the number of self-employed or on the number of enterprises registered by chambers of commerce and trade is the stock of persons or enterprises. But, stock figures and even their changes may disguise very dynamic changes by entries to and exits from the stock. For instance, if the number of newly established enterprises is high and equals the number of enterprises which are closed down, stock figures will remain constant; but they remain constant, too, in a situation, where entry and exit figures are low and, hence, where is little movement behind the stock figures. If in both situations each new enterprise may create a same number of jobs; together, new firms are obviously more important for employment creation in the first case, however.

For these reasons, it is important to refer to gross figures, to figures on entry and exit to the stock, instead of using stock figures themselves, if one wants to adequately deal with the question who creates jobs. Moreover, one must also estimate from micro data on individual firms. In the US, the share of new and small enterprise in total employment has remained fairly constant over time, contradicting Birch's results at the first glance. But the stability of the shares over time is due to the fact that new and small enterprises while increasing their employment will sooner or later be classified as bigger or even large enterprises. As the number of enterprises moving upwards in the size hierarchy and the number of those moving downwards because of decreasing employment was approximately the same in the US, the shares of new and small and big enterprises remained stable, too. Therefore, it is essential to ask how many jobs have been created by enterprises belonging at the beginning of the time period under investigation to the various size categories. This can be done only, if micro data for individual enterprises are available, and this was the way in which Birch arrived at his results.

While Birch and others had access to such data for the US, comparable figures are not available in Germany [4]. Some rough estimates for the importance of new and small enterprises for employment creation in Germany can be made. It has been estimated that in the US, the entry or birth rate of new enterprises was 8.2 per cent annually in the 1970s, and the death rate was 7.5 per cent; both rates calculated on the stock of firms existing at the beginning of the 1970s (Birch, 1981; 1984). In Germany, based on data for the registration of new enterprises and date for the extinction of old ones at chambers of commerce, birth rates have been estimated by one investigation to have been 8.0 per cent annually in the average of the 1970s, and death rates 7.5 per cent (for details see the sources mentioned in: Schatz, 1984). In accordance with the upward movement of the number of self-employed persons and persons working on own account, another investigation came to the result that the birth rate has increased in the second half on the 1970s to 9.6 per cent. While the death rate also increased to 9.1 per cent, different to the first half of the 1970s, it was lower than the birth rate. These rates are approximately comparable to those for the US, and they signalise that the number of enterprises is increasing in Germany, too, though because of smaller differences between birth rates and death rates not at the same speed than in the US. The German death rate of 9.1 per cent means that of the number of enterprises initially existing, within a time period of, e.g., five years, roughly 55 per cent will be closed down; and a birth rate of 9.6 per cent means that over five years the number of newly estabilshed enterprises makes up for about 58 per cent of the initially existing stock of enterprises.

Presumably, more than 95 per cent of all German enterprises are small, employing less than 50 persons, which is the definition chosen here meeting one definition used by Birch[5]. Accordingly, birth and death concern above all small enterprises. As they provide 7 to 8 mill. jobs in Germany, it follows that within five years about 3 to 4 mill. jobs are lost by the closing down and some hundred thousand more jobs gained by the establishment of small enterprises. Most likely, the number of jobs created by them is even substantially larger, because it has not been taken into consideration that new and small firms may expand employment over time; also, the number of jobs lost by them may be overestimated in relation to the number of jobs newly created. For, exit concerns both smaller and bigger companies, while companies which are newly established mostly are small at the beginning. However, what matters for the argument which I am going to put forward, are not the precise figures, but the order of them. This order is big enough allowing for the conclusion that, similar to the US, new and small enterprises are the most important source for new jobs in Germany and presumably in other European countries, too. There is, of course, one important difference between the US and Germany. In the US, new and small firms have created a large number not only of new, but also of additional jobs; in Germany, employment has significantly decreased by trend. But this difference cannot be assigned to a lower job creation potential of these firms in Germany, but must rather be assigned to an economic climate and to institutional provisions which are less conducive to the creation of employment.

Aspects of Growth, Competitiveness and Innovation

It has often been argued that scepticism should be at hand with regard to employment as created in the US by new and small enterprise, and with regard to their contribution to jobs on the German labor market. For one, it is pointed out that the bulk of new and small enterprises remains small, often offering but a job for their owner only. As a matter of fact, roughly 60 per cent of all new enterprises in Germany are established in "Trade" and in "Other Services" where the average size of enterprise, as measured by employment, is very small, and where bigger enterprises are an exception. Similar observations apply for the US, where the largest part of them is established in "Trade" and "Other Services", too. And while most of them remain small, it is only 12 to 15 per cent of all (originally) small enterprises which make up for the largest part of the jobs created by the group together (Birch, 1984, p. 10). However, what matters only is whether the number of newly or additionally created jobs remains permanently higher if the number of newly established firms is higher than the number of firms which close. In this sense, the evidence from the US tells a story of very success on the labor as attributable to new and small firms. Whether this is a real success is doubted, for another, arguing that the quality of the jobs created is poor, and that they concern to a large extent but part time work (DIW, 1984). Such arguments disregard that many persons are relatively unqualified, indeed, or are looking for part time jobs. Therefore, it is a great achievement, if unqualified jobs are supplied to unqualified persons and part time jobs to part time job seekers, as was the case in the US. Accordingly, not the US labor market, but the German labor market performed poorly, because in Germany less qualified and part time workers are remaining unemployed to a higher extent.

In addition, research for the US has revealed that new and small enterprises are by no means restricted to stagnating or declining industries; in contrast, they often are engaged in growth industries (and, e.g., services in general; Armington, 1983; Armington et al., 1983). It seems inconsistent, however, with these observations and with the increasing contribution of new and small enterprises to jobs that they have apparently become less important for overall economic growth in the US. This observation has been made by the US Small Business Administration (1981, p. III) arguing that their contribution to Gross Domestic Product is declining substantially, and that in particular the very small, very dynamic and very innovative enterprises are running danger to be outcompeted by big enterprises — obviously a process as described by Schumpeter for trustified capitalism. Again, however, one must take into consideration that small companies while growing will be classified bigger and, hence, their contribution to GDP is underestimated as is their contribution to employment. Nevertheless, the fact remains that the share of enterprises classified small is apparently constant in employment, while their contribution to GDP decreases.

In this context, I should like to argue that both observations do neither contradict each other nor that they indicate undesirable developments. In the US, real wages are flexible downwards, at least compared to Europe, because the dregree of unionisation is lower than in Europe, and because wages cannot be declared compulsory for non-partisans, as they can be in Europe. Together, this means, among others, that the many new and small enterprises in the US, while neither belonging to a bargaining employers association nor concluding bargains themselves, can contract with workers at freely agreed conditions[6]. Under these conditions, it becomes plausible that the share of small enterprises in employment has remained constant, while their contribution to GDP decreased. For, new and small enterprises can then employ labor at lower wages than big enterprises. It becomes worthwhile to employ marginal labor, and to undertake entrepreneurial activities which would not be profitable if wages would be higher, for instance, in the service sector. In consequence, because of the lower productivity of labor which can be engaged at lower wage rates and because of activities which become profitable at lower wages only, value added per employee will be lower in newly established or small enterprises. It may be nothing else than this which the observation of the US Small Business Administration means. Seen in this way, the observation only suggests that new and small enterprises have been particularly successful contributing to the reduction of US wages to levels which are consistent with higher degrees of employment, and faster growth.

The argument remains that new and small enterprises may be relatively unimportant with regard to innovation. In this generality, the argument cannot be maintained for the simple reason that obviously any new or small enterprise which survives is innovative in as far as it has opened up its own segment in the market — may it be a new product, a particular service and the like. What concerns technological and economically successful innovation, the debate is controversial. It is agreed that in average, smaller firms invest less into RaD than bigger firms do, though figures from Germany reveal, that if small firms invest in RaD at all, they spend more on it — in terms of percentages from sales or per employee — than bigger firms (Echterhoff-Severitt, 1983). Yet, disagreement rests not so much with the input to RaD, but rather with the output, the actual contribution of new and small enterprises to innovation. Freeman, while analysing 1 100 innovations in Great Britain in the 1950s and in the 1960s concluded that their share (here: enterprises with less than 200 employees) in them was much smaller than their share in employment (OECD, 1982; these informations and others are taken from OECD, 1982, if not indicated other).

The US National Science Foundation, however, came to the result that of the 319 innovations classified important for the years 1953–1973, roughly half was contributed by small enterprises (here: less than 1 000 employees). This analysis included the Federal Republic of Germany, for which one radical innovative break-through was reported; it was achieved by a small firm (less than 5 mill. US-Dollar turnover). Additionally, nine major innovations were registered of which two by small and one by a medium-sized firm (between 5 and 50 mill. US-Dollar turnover). Moreover, six improvements were acknowledged, two by small and one by a medium-sized firm. Finally, the foundation mentioned one successful imitation which a big enterprise managed to achieve. These results which — different to Freeman's conclusions — seem to indicate that small enterprise is a generator of innovation, indeed, are supported by other recent research by Armington et al. for the US showing that small, independent firms, while still accounting for only 12 per cent of employment in hich-tech, highly innovative industries, are growing two to three times faster than bigger enterprises (Armington et al., 1983).

Other evidence is equally controversial than that reported here. Presumably, the contradicting results on the role of small enterprise for innovation are to a large extent due to lacking differentiation between basic research and applied research, and between process innovation and product innovation. What concerns the planned research for basically new insights which can be used for basis innovations, e.g., a new principal in the chemical industry, it seems to be above all a matter for big enterprises (OECD, 1982). This seems to be plausible taking into account that basic research often demands for much personnel and financial resources − in the sense which Schumpeter uses characterising trustified capitalism. It is an open question, however, to what amount basic innovations which are reclaimed for big enterprises, do not go back to ideas developed in small firms or by independent individuals initially which had no opportunity to work them out further because of lack of respective resources and, therefore, came to agreements with big enterprises, to which the patented innovation is attributed. Apart from those considerations, small firms seem to be very fruitful whith applied research and, connected with it, with product innovation. The explanation could lie with the fact that virtual basic innovations can be applied in manifold areas, and that their application does not depend so much on systematic and expensive research, but on entrepreneurial intuition, on communication ways within the firm and between the firm and customers, and on entrepreneurial engagement. These all are attitudes which one may concede to a higher degree to small than to big enterprises.

Various empirical research lends ground to such arguments. In particular, it seems to be obvious that bigger companies contribute above average to process innovation, that means to procedures by which old products can be produced cheaper (OECD, 1982). If big enterprises attempt product innovation, the probability is great that they arrive at rather unimportant improvements, while small enterprises relatively often intend to supply basically new products, and are successful (Krasner, Dubrow, 1981). Typically such observations concerning the innovative behaviour of big enterprises seem to apply for oligopolistic markets. In the aircraft industry, innovative efforts on products have been concentrated on developing stretched versions of originally successful models, for long, the main technologies applied reaching back to the years immediately after World War II. The US automobile industry, for years and years undertook research above all on process innovation, and, in this context, reduced the diversity of the cars by uniformity of the design for rationalising production processes. For the pharmaceutical industry, work undertaken on behalf of the OECD, has shown that most of the biotechnological developments which may become revolutionary for the industry, have been achieved by outsiders, e.g., in the universities. Instead, firms within the industry have continued to invest in RaD on areas where the returns to investment have obviously been declining, and even today, only few firms have been backing research on biotechnologies by own expenditures (Chesnais, 1982, p. 64/65). One study for the Federal Republic also reports that small enterprises usually apply inventions, which they make, much faster than bigger enterprises. After two years, three quarters of small enterprises have made of their inventions commercially used innovations, while only one third of big enterprises has done so (Oppenländer, 1976, p. 126).

Summarising, the conclusion can be drawn that new and small enterprises are not only very important for the process of discovery, but in particular also for introducing the news to the market. Such insights have been one major reason for big enterprises for promoting the spin-off of small, independent firms, or to assist the establishment of new, small firms by others, hoping for a better usage and application of the results of own basic research and of own basic innovations. Such spin-offs and establishments of new enterprises are characteristic for the story of the Silicon Valley where the evolution of the microprocessor was effected so rapidly over the last ten to fifteen years (Lorenz, 1982).

Implications for Economic Policies

Considering the many economic arguments and empirical evidence supporting the view that small and new enterprises are one most important source for growth, structural change, innovation and employment, it seems at hand to specifically further them. As a matter of fact, many countries maintain policies aimed at the promotion of small and the establishment of new enterprises. In the Federal Republic, such policies have a long tradition being part of the so-called Mittelstandspolitik — a loose bundle of various policies which lack a clear concept as well as defined addressees and aims. In the framework of the Mittelstandspolitik which may roughly be described as the sum of policies by which those groups are promoted or protected believed representing somehow the broad middle of the society, a true plethora of programs and individual measures has been created, too, aimed at granting assistance to the establishment of new enterprises and to smaller ones. The very fact that such assistance is thought to be necessary obviously lends evidence to the presumption that the conditions are not existing under which one could refrain from public help, because it seems profitable enough to people establishing enterprises and because small enterprises are viable and can grow. In this sense, the size and the variety of aids which governments grant to them, presumably are a good indicator for the degree of a country's sclerosis and lack of vitality as is the amount and the variety of subsidies and protection in general. If this diagnosis is valid, the best remedy would be to reduce sclerosis and to abolish the causes for it, creating a climate which renders public help unnecessary. Such a climate requires profits relative to other income to be high enough providing incentives for entrepreneurial initiative. It requires, too, that competition is intensive enough destroying rents which can be obtained because of barriers against outsiders, which often are small and new enterprises and even enterprises, which are not all in the market, because under prevailing conditions it is not worthwhile to establish them or even legally or institutionally impossible.

Comparing Germany (standing for European countries in general) to the US reveals that opportunities for new and small firms are much less favourable here than they are there. In Germany, e.g., except for the service sector segment "hotels and restaurants", there is no service industry in which either prices or quantities or the production process, or market access are not subject to heavy regulation. In most cases, several sorts of regulation apply at the same time[7]. Given the US experience that roughly four fifth of the jobs created since 1970 have emerged from services, it is immediately plausible that such barriers must have hindered the supply of additional jobs in Germany. While it is true that barriers of the sort mentioned are maintained in the US, too, some of them are unknown to the US or at least not to the extent prevalant in Germany.

In particular, professional licensing for handicraft which strictly controls entry to the market is hardly known in the US. Because of this lack of barriers, it is possible, e.g., in the US to start tayloring clothes which is not allowed in Germany, except after passing the professional licensing barrier which estimatedly takes at least eight years and depends on the willingness of those to grant access who are in the tayloring business. In other respect, in the US previously existing barriers have been largely removed or become lower by deregulation. Examples are the transport sector or telecommunications which in Germany still are completely regulated at a degree partly even unknown to the US before. Also, private enterprises have hardly access in Germany to the whole area of so-called community services which never have been under public control in the US to the extent they are in Germany[8].

Another realm of significant impediments to new and small enterprises lies with the labor market. While many of those impediments are due to legal provisions, which I am not going to discuss here, at least equally important impacts are related to wage bargaining in Germany, on which I should like drawing attention[9]. Wages (and all other contract conditions) as bargained between employer associations (or individual employers) and unions directly are compulsory for all members of the association. This means that all enterprises being member of an employers association are to pay the same wage to labor, irrespective of whether labor is unionised or not. Obviously, such uniform bargains discriminate against marginal employers who have to bear the same wages than intramarginal employers. One may argue that such uniform wage settlements contribute to increasing welfare and economic growth, provided that the wages are the same for the same type of labor, and in each labor category not higher than labor's marginal product. Under such conditions, wage policies take care of full employment requirements, and together with competition on product and factor markets uniformity forces the marginal employer to either raising labor productivity or to closing down his enterprise and leaving labor to those who can make a more efficient use of it. The validity of the argument depends on the assumption that the relative scarcities of the various kinds of labor are and can be taken into account while collectively bargaining wages, and that this can be done better by collective bargaining than by individual bargaining in the labor market between individual workers and individual employers. From the rise of unemployment in Germany and from the fact that unemployment is very unevenly distributed among the various kinds of labor, one has to draw the conclusion, however, that at least since the early 1970s, wage bargains have increasingly neglected full employment requirements. These presumption is supported by empirical evidence showing, e.g., that differences of bargained wages between industries, regions, qualified and unqualified labor, or younger and older workers have been substantially reduced from the beginning 1970s (Soltwedel, 1984).

These observations are the most important, as in practical matters bargaining agreements will not only affect employers who are members of employers associations, but all others, too. For, it may be claimed that all bargaining agreements may be extended by the government to all employers which then means to all employed in the respective bargaining industry. While it is true that the percentage of the bargaining agreements declared compulsory is relatively low, it has significantly increased, making up for 7.5 per cent in 1978 (for which the most recent published figures are available) compared to 3 per cent in 1968, and in the meantime, it has presumably risen further[10]. Moreover, in practical matters, the importance of such contracts and of the mere possibility to declare contracts compulsory are much larger than these percentages suggest. For one, according to the federal government, in 1982, about one fifth of the 20 mill. German white and blue collar workers were covered by compulsory contracts. Excluded from the number of these workers is one type of civil servants, the Beamte, only. Taking into account that it is unnecessary at all that contracts have to be declared compulsory in the public sector (including the armed forces) as well as in the federal railway system and the federal postal office in order that they are applied, reduces the number of workers in sectors and industries substantially, for which needs for declaration may eventually be seen. For these reasons, in the private economy the percentage of labor covered by compulsory contracts makes up for presumably roughly 25 per cent. For another, in a number of other parts of the private economy, it can be refrained from such declarations, too; this applies, for instance, for the churches, but it is most important in a number of industries where large enterprises are dominating which determine themselves the wage bargaining on the employers' side and, hence, will hardly deviate from what they have agreed upon before. For instance, neither for mining nor for the chemical industry or energy or banking and insurance was a contract registered compulsory in 1968 or 1978. Therefore, in the "relevant" segment of the private economy, the degree of coverage must be much higher than 25 per cent.

That this segment must be small, can be concluded from evidence for manufacturing (Verarbeitendes Gewerbe). As a matter of fact, in manufacturing practically all large enterprises are members of employers associations and, hence, bound to bargaining agreements (or bargain themselves on the firm level with the unions) and presumably 80 to 90 per cent of all enterprises together are organised (Schatz, Wolter, 1982, p. 164 sqq.). For this reason, much more than the 50 per cent of labor organised in unions is covered from the very beginning by bargaining contracts; because any employer who is organised must grant labor the same contract. Figures on the industrial distribution of bargains declared compulsory reveal that it are obviously only a few industries which make up for the relevant segment requiring the government to prevent outsider competition on working conditions and to enforce uniform behavior of all employers and workers. In manufacturing, 95 per cent of all contracts declared compulsory stem from only five bargaining industries (figures as of 1st January 1978): stones and quarrying (Steine und Erden; 26 per cent); metals (Metall; 11 per cent); textiles (Textil; 20 per cent); food, beverages, tobacco (Nahrung/Genuß; 7 per cent); and clothing (Bekleidung; 31 per cent). Outside manufacturing, declarations concern above all construction (Bau; 23 per cent of declarations as existing on 1st January 1978); cleaning (Reinigung; 3 per cent; this is the industry "cleaning of buildings" – Gebäudereinigerhandwerk); gross trade (Großhandel; 16 per cent); retail trade (Einzelhandel; 7 per cent); publishing (Verlags- und Handelshilfsgewerbe; 4 per cent); and hotels, restaurants (Hotel- und Gaststättengewerbe; 2 per cent)[11]. Together, the industries mentioned account for 96 per cent of contracts declared compulsory. The industries have in common that enterprises are usually very small, and often it is relatively unexpensive to establish a new enterprise.

From the evidence, one must apparently draw the conclusion that use is made of declaring bargaining agreements compulsory for all employers (and hence employed) whenever there is the danger that individual employers or individual labor are willing to agree on wage contracts below the minimum conditions as settled in bargains, or have done so. And more use has been made with the increase of unemployment which has been inducive to offering and accepting work which is paid less than provided in the bargaining contracts. In particular, in industries which suffered from the rise of external competition or from declining demand, it was apparently necessary calling for the government to provide discipline. In textiles, e.g., the number of contracts declared compulsory rose from 2 in 1968 to 50 in 1978; for clothing, the respective figures are 2 and 75, and for construction 44 and 129.

Under such conditions, freedom to contract is neither given for individual enterprises nor for individual labor. In consequense, it is hardly possible to work on those standards which one would voluntarily accept, but only on those which the big and the well established groups in the labor market – the big companies and the unions – agree upon. This concerns at the one hand the unemployed which cannot achieve employment at the wages settled by collective bargaining, and at the other, all those who do not establish new enterprises or expand their small business or are forced to close it down, because it is unprofitable at the determined costs from bargaining results. For these reasons, those politicians calling for new and small enterprise as a remedy for present problems, should undertake efforts to abolish that the government declares bargaining contracts compulsory. At least, freedom to contract should be given to all those who are unemployed, and to all those who open up a new enterprise, and for small enterprises.

Current policies do not focus on such considerations. They rather aim at subsidising small enterprises. These policies are most likely to fail. It is true that most subsidies did and still do benefit big enterprises and distort competition at their advantage; but this does not support compensatory subsidising small enterprises, for consequently competition will be distorted in this group of enterprises, too. Because all small or new enterprises cannot be subsidised, and they should not. If at all, enterprises should not be subsidised because they are new or small or big; but assistance should be given to all those which promise the most significant contributions for future growth and employment. These enterprises cannot be known ex ante by politicians or bureaucrats who grant subsidies, and if such knowledge would be available, the faith of the companies could be let to the markets and private investors which would most voluntarily provide finance to them. If less new and small enterprises exist as would be wishful under overall economic considerations, the task is improving the conditions for enterprises in general, but not selecting specific kinds of enterprises for public assistance. Rather, the barriers should be reduced which prevent the establishment of new and the growth of small enterprises. This includes the cutting down of subsidies as well as the deregulation of the economy.

NOTES

[1] Compare the contributions contained in: Brian Hindley (ed.), State Investment Companies in Western Europe. Picking Winners or Backing Losers? London, 1983. – For Germany see also: Klaus-Werner Schatz and Frank Wolter, International Trade, Employment and Structural Adjustment: The Case of the Federal Republic of Germany. International Labour Organisation. World Employment Programme Research, Working Paper WEP 2-36/WP 19. Geneva, 1982, p. 116 sqq.

[2] The present paper draws heavily on: Klaus-Werner Schatz, Die Bedeutung kleiner und mittlerer Unternehmen für den Strukturwandel. Kieler Diskussionsbeiträge Nr. 103. Kiel, November 1984.

[3] All figures including estimates taken or calculated from: Commission of the European Communities, Directorate-General for Economic and Financial Affairs, Annual Economic Report 1984 – 85, No. 22, November 1984.

[4] In principle, however, they could be gained from Labor Market Statistics (Schatz, 1984).

[5] The census figures for 1961 showed that 98.0 per cent were small according to this definition, and the respective figure for 1971 is 97.7 per cent (Schatz, 1984).

[6] This argument applies comparing the US to Germany and other European countries. The US-minimum wage legislation leaves much more freedom to contract on an individual base as the German collective bargaining system does.

[7] For details and literature on this topic see Schatz, 1984.

[8] For details and discussions of arguments supporting deregulation and privatisation and for empirical evidence on both compare: Giersch (1983a; 1983b; 1984); Sichelschmidt (1981; 1984); Böhme, Sichelschmidt (1984); Busch (1983).

[9] For legal provisions see: Soltwedel (1984).

[10] Between the end of 1975 and the beginning of 1982, the number of existing bargaining agreements declared compulsory has increased by 32 per cent (Schatz, 1984).

[11] Figures calculated from Boedler, Keiser (1979).

LIST OF LITERATURE

Armington, Catherine, Further Examination of Sources of Recent Employment Growth — Analysis of USEEM Data for 1976 to 1980. The Brookings Institution, Washington, March 1983, mimeo.
— Candee S. Harries, Marjorie Odle, Formation and Growth in High Technology Business: A Regional Assessment. The Brookings Institution, Washington, September 1983, mimeo.

Birch, David, "Who Creates Jobs?". The Public Interest, 1981, No. 65, pp. 3–14.
— "The Contribution of Small Enterprise to Growth and Employment". In: Herbert Giersch (ed.), New Opportunities for Entrepreneurship. Symposium 1983, Tübingen 1984, pp.1–17.

Boedler, Hermann, Heinz Keiser, "30 Jahre Tarifregister". BMA, Bundesarbeitsblatt, 9/1979, Stuttgart, pp. 22–29.

Böhme, Hans, Henning Sichelschmidt, „Die Wettbewerbslage der deutschen Seehäfen und die Regulierung der Verkehrsmärkte". Die Weltwirtschaft, 1984, vol. 1, pp. 110–121.

Busch, Axel, Die Deutsche Bundespost — Bremse des technischen Fortschritts? Institut für Weltwirtschaft, Kiel Working Papers, 191, December 1983.

Chesnais, François, "Schumpeterian Recovery and the Schumpeterian Perspective — Some Unsettled Issues and Alternative Perspectives". In: Herbert Giersch (ed.), Emerging Technologies: Consequences for Economic Growth, Structural Change, and Employment. Symposium 1981, Tübingen 1982, pp. 33–71.

Commission of the European Communities, Directorate-General for Economic and Financial Affairs, Annual Economic Report 1984–85, No. 22, November 1984.

Deutsches Institut für Wirtschaftsforschung (DIW), Sind die Unterschiede der Beschäftigtenentwicklung in den USA und der Bundesrepublik in der Reallohnentwicklung begründet? Wochenbericht 33/84, Berlin, 16th August 1984.

Echterhoff-Severitt, Helga, Forschung und Entwicklung (FuE) in der Wirtschaft 1981. Forum Extra, Sonderdruck aus der Mitgliederzeitschrift des Stifterverbandes für die Deutsche Wissenschaft, Vol. 5, 1983.

Giersch, Herbert (ed.), (1983a), Wie es zu schaffen ist. Agenda für die deutsche Wirtschaftspolitik. Stuttgart 1983.
— (1983b), Reassessing the Role of Government in the Mixed Economy. Symposium 1982, Tübingen 1983.
— New Opportunities for Entrepreneurship. Symposium 1983, Tübingen 1984.

Harris, Candee S., Small Business and Job Generation: A Changing Economy or Differing Methodologies? The Brookings Institution, Washington, February 1983.
— Plant, Closings and the Replacement of Manufacturing Jobs, 1978–1982. The Brookings Institution, Washington, without year, mimeo.

Hindley, Brian (ed.), State Investment Companies in Western Europe. Picking Winners or Backing Losers? London, 1983.

Krasner, O.J., Michael L. Dubrow, "The Role of Small Business in Research and Development, Technological Change, and Innovation". In: U.S. Small Business Administration, Economic Research on Small Business: The Environment for Entrepreneurship and Small Business. Summary Analysis of the Regional Research Reports. Washington 1981, pp. 161–162.

Lorenz, Gert, "The Diffusion of Emerging Technologies among Industrial Countries". In: Herbert Giersch (ed.), Emerging Technologies: Consequences for Economic Growth, Structural Change, and Employment. Symposium 1981, Tübingen 1982, pp. 171–187.

Oppenländer, Karl Heinrich, „Das Verhalten kleiner und mittlerer Unternehmen im industriellen Innovationsprozeß". In: Ifo-Institut (ed.), Die gesamtwirtschaftliche Funktion kleiner und mittlerer Unternehmen. München 1976, pp. 119–142.

Organisation for Economic Co-Operation and Development (OECD), Innovation in Small and Medium Firms, Paris 1982.

Schatz, Klaus-Werner, Frank Wolter, International Trade, Employment and Structural Change: The Case Study of the Federal Republic of Germany. International Labour Office, World Employment Research, Working Paper WEP 2-36/WP 19, Geneva 1982.

– Die Bedeutung kleiner und mittlerer Unternehmen für den Strukturwandel. Kiel Discussion Papers 103. Kiel, November 1984.

Schmidt, Klaus-Dieter, Hugo Dicke, Juergen B Donges, Hans H. Glismann, Bernhard Heitger, Ernst-Jürgen Horn, Karl-Heinz Jüttemeier, Henning Klodt, Dieter Knoll, Axel D. Neu, Ronald Weichert, Im Anpassungsprozeß zurückgeworfen. Die deutsche Wirtschaft vor neuen Herausforderungen. Kieler Studien, 185, Tübingen 1984.

Schumpeter, Joseph A., "The March into Socialism". The American Economic Review, Papers ans Proceedings, Vol. 40, 1950, pp. 447–456.

– "The Instability of Capitalism". In: Richard V. Clemence (ed.), Essays of J. A. Schumpeter. Cambridge 1951, pp. 47–72.

Sichelschmidt, Henning, Die neue Luftverkehrspolitik der Vereinigten Staaten – ein Modell für Europa. Institut für Weltwirtschaft, Kiel Discussion Papers, 81, October 1981.

– Wettbewerb statt staatlicher Regulierung – Wege zu einem besseren Luftverkehrssystem in Europa. Institut für Weltwirtschaft, Kiel Discussion Papers, 100, August 1984.

Soltwedel, Rüdiger, Staatliche Interventionen am Arbeitsmarkt. Kiel 1984.

Szyperski, Norbert, Günter Kirschbaum, Unternehmensfluktuation in Nordrhein-Westfalen. Eine empirische Untersuchung zur Entwicklung von Gründungen und Liquidationen im Zeitraum von 1973–1979. Beiträge zur Mittelstandsforschung, Vol. 75, Göttingen 1981.

U.S. Small Business Administration, Economic Research on Small Business: The Environment for Entrepreneurship and Small Business. Summary Analysis of the Regional Research Reports. Washington 1981.

3.

Improving Economic Performance:
International Experience and Strategies

Industry Policy and Structural Change in Australia

Cedric Pugh

Introduction

The state has been involved for a long time in formulating policy measures for industry in advanced capitalist countries. Typically governments have created *ad hoc* measures in the taxation of company profits, in various tax incentives, in employment and training activities, in tariffs and other forms of assistance, and in many sorts of regulations. Viewed in this way, there is nothing new in the state's involvement with private enterprise and with policy measures to influence the economic and social performance of industry. But perhaps we should not be viewing "industry policy" simply, as it were, in this way. If we place the whole question of the aims of modern industry policy in the context of post-1974 stagflation with its interacting cyclical and structural economic problems, then we begin to see that "industry policy" must mean something more than a listing of *ad hoc* policy measures which have impacts upon industrial performance. Instead, we are addressing questions which have a bearing upon the crucial need for economic change. We need growth which is less inflationary; we need new jobs in manufacturing industry and other sectors of the economy; we need to create national "comparative advantages" via policies in technology and education; and we need a more stable economic and political context where consumers, investors, trade unionists, and policy makers can make decisions which bring shorter term aims more closely into harmony with important longer term needs for change. We have thus addressed the main sorts of problems which are addressed in industry policies. Beyond this, we must discern the essential and novel characteristics of modern policy and their wider consequences in terms of societal change and the new relations between the state and private enterprise. As suggested, modern industry policy is something more than an *ad hoc* collection of measures which influence industry. In the hands of sophisticated policy makers, it is a matter of achieving *comprehensiveness* in policy. This means that a set of policies are to be coordinated to achieve economic development, societal change, and an amelioration of the excessive inflations and unemployments from a decade of stagflation. Some of the measures to be coordinated include macroeconomic policies, policies in science, technology and education, sectoral policies for industry, trade policies, and policies in taxation and labour markets. Structural change has to be interwoven with short- and long-term policies for the economy. Comprehensiveness in policy making is a tall order, and we should not expect all societies to be equally adept at steering structural change effectively. In fact, in countries such as United States, Britain, and Australia, it is increasingly understood that competitors such as Japan, Singapore, Austria and Sweden have been more successful in using state roles in steering and inducing structural change. As our themes and arguments subsequently unfold, we shall be identifying the reasons for better policy performances in those countries which were able to deal with international stagflation at comparatively early stages.

We would be limiting our perspective if we were to consider the new state roles in industry policy as just providing amelioration to the stresses of the post-1974 stagflation. What is happening is that new state roles are being drawn into the very central areas of private enterprise. Hitherto, in conventional (neoclassical) economics state roles have been seen as largely residual to private enterprise, with some cause and reason to cover for market inadequacies in such spheres as public utilities, public goods, economic externality, and for a "social" correction to the inequalities generated by markets. Specialists in these fields will, of course, recognise that public policies have not always achieved effectiveness or efficiency, and it is not easy to achieve success and stability in modifying the outcomes of market capitalism. But the difficulties and the complexities can be expected to multiply now the state has a "hands on" approach to investment plans, technological change, profitability, and other sensitive and central aspects of private enterprise. At the very least we should expect institutional and societal changes to accompany the new forms of political economy in industry. Furthermore, in some societies we might anticipate that industry policies will add to the areas in which political and industrial frictions occur in capital-labour relations. Industry policies cannot by their very nature and purposes be politically neutral.

Our introductory discussions have identified comprehensiveness in policy development and the extended roles of the state as the major themes in this piece of writing. These themes are to be developed and elaborated in the main sections which subsequently deal with the theoretical and societal basis of industry policies, the contours of successful policy development in some Asian and West European countries, structural changes in the Australian economy since the late 1960s, and the key issues and controversies surrounding the moves to develop industry policies by the 1983 Hawke Australian Labor Party Government. Accordingly our framework for evaluation and criticism includes both the theoretical and the institutional sides of industry policy.

We begin with some summarised discussions of the main explanatory matters in societal change and in theory or basic intellectual principles.

Societal Change and Theoretical Bases

We have been arguing that industry policy is to be understood by relationship to the problems to which it is addressed, and from the perspectiveness of comprehensiveness. This approach, of course, takes us beyond any definition of industry policy which deals only with overtly selective policies for specific sectors of manufacturing industry. But by taking a broader and more societal view we need to anchor our idea of industry policy in some general principles which explain social change in modern society. Thus we proceed with necessarily brief reflections on the nature of modern society, with some specific references to technology and stagflation.

Bell (1973) and Drucker (1970) say that modern "postindustrial" society has important differences compared with older "industrial" society. Postindustrial society is characterised by:
1. the extension and sophistication of the tertiary (service) sector;
2. a heavier dependence upon research, information, and technological innovation;
3. the need to plan for change, because change is rapid and the risks of error by "muddling through" are great; and
4. a general interaction and interdependence in economic, social, cultural and political development.

As for its relevance to industry policy, a postindustrial society is less dependent upon natural resources and the "raw" conditions underlying comparative advantage in its economic structure and trade, but more dependent upon creating a technological and cultural comparative advantage from its public policies and private responses in education, in innovation, in industrial change, and in creating conditions for social and economic development. We can be more specific. Industry policies will often press for education in a postindustrial society to be both cultural and industry-relevant. An important aspect of industry policy would be its aim of making effective blends and combinations of human and physical capital. Ultimately this would translate into jobs, personal incomes from the basis of skills, and the financial viability and profitability of many private enterprises.

As another reflection on modern society, O'Connor (1973) and other authors have noted the division of the economy into three broad sectors:
1. a monopoly sector dominated by large corporate capital,
2. a competitive sector with many small- and medium-sized firms, and
3. the public sector.

Large corporations in the monopoly sector are dependent upon the public sector in its provisions of funds to create human capital (i.e. an educated and healthy work force). Governments are dependent upon the large corporations for the economic foundation of state roles. Sometimes the interdependence of these two sectors leads to conflicts over such issues as the burdens of taxation and the difficulties governments have in restraining public expenditure. But, it is the sector where there are many small firms that attracts interest in formulating industry policies. Countries such as the United States have found that during the last decade, job creation and innovation have been associated with some small firms. This points a way to economic growth and change. However, the "competitive" sector also has firms which are adrift from modern technology and management practices. Industry policy would need to address several of the varied characteristics in the small firm sector.

An important feature of modern industry policy — in its concerns for economic growth — is its interest in technological innovation. Technology has complex and many-sided characteristics, and under some circumstances the balance of considerations tends towards creating a mixture of government and private sector roles to realise potentials in economic restructuring. Along with Tisdell (1981) we can view the government aspects in the following way: First, notwithstanding some protection afforded by patent law, private firms do not always find it easy to appropriate the full returns from innovation. Technology is something akin to a public good, allowing some copying or adaptation by competitors at lesser expense than the innovator's costs. But competition itself does induce some innovation. Second, technological innovation is suffused with high risks and uncertainties. The Japanese have dealt with this problem in strategic growth sectors such as computer technology by combining government and private capital on an equal shares basis.

In its most general scope, government has a role as initiator and coordinator in developing policies in science and technology. To see what is involved, we think of three points of a triangle. In one corner we have industrial enterprises and in another the education system. The third corner is occupied by government and it has impacts upon industry and education from its policies on taxation, allocations of public finance, labour market policies, and official enquiries into the education system. As initiator and coordinator, government can be seen to further science and technology when it joins the three corners of the triangle and it persuades, cajoles and sanctions reforms in industry and education so that overall policies are cohesive and effective. All of this suggests relationship between the private sector and government which are interactive and interwined, not separated and passive. This points to the quality and character of the interaction as an important part of a really effective industry policy.

We add dimension to the societal and theoretical bases of industry policy by considering *stagflation,* which followed as a consequence of food shortages and the first OPEC crisis in the year 1973/74. This crisis undermined confidence in some key aspects of Keynesian macroeconomic policy. With experience, we have found that its competitor in the 1970s, Friedmanite Monetarism, also had problems of application to modern advanced economies. By the 1980s, Laidlaw (1982) and other Monetarists began to proclaim the essential gradualism which must attend corrective measures to stagflation, with some separated policy emphasis upon unemployment and housing. Keynesians revised their policy mix to include structural elements of economic change and a more overt stance on the *political* economy content of macroeconomics. But from the perspective of industry policy, it is the *Structuralists* who elaborated new positions in macroeconomics which more clearly could coordinate with industry policy.

The modern Structuralist position is elaborated by Maddison and Wilpstra (1982). In essence, Structuralists give equal attention to both demand and supply conditions. Along with Post-Keynesians they say that total demand has to be at a sufficiently high level to stimulate investment, profitability and change. However, the process of adjustment cannot always be smooth because on the supply side there are immobilities and inflexibilities. Thus, Structuralists favour diagnosis at the disaggregated level, accepting that labour and product markets are heterogeneous. They agree with Post-Keynesians in their view that the economy has stickiness in price and wage flexibility, with tendencies for prices to be more flexible upwards than downwards. All of this reasoning leads Structuralists towards policies aimed selectively against rigidities in the economy, at improvements in productivity, at innovation, and at improving the pattern of structural change. Policy making in technology and industry would harmonise with macroeconomic Structuralism. Post-Keynesian adaptation has moved close to Structuralist thinking, but the microeconomic foundations of Monetarism rest upon older assumptions that markets are virtually instantly flexible to new information and this flexibility is largely expressed in relation to prices.

Austria experienced less stress from stagflation than many of its competitors. It had a coordinated mixture of macroeconomic and structural policies which kept the "misery index" to less than 7 per cent, apart from the years when the 1973 and 1979 OPEC crises intensified inflation. A "misery index" is a combined index of unemployment and inflation, and for countries such as Australia and Britain this was sometimes higher than 20 per cent, even in the years which were less affected by OPEC crises. The successful mixture of policies included the following. – First, Austria pursued a policy of "hard currency", with the exchange rate gradually appreciating against those countries with which it had significant trade. As a consequence, the prices of imports were dampened, which in turn lessened the demands for higher money wages to keep pace with inflation. Export sectors were forced to be productive and efficient to maintain competitiveness in an international market where the value of the Austrian currency was appreciating. Second, in order to maintain employment and social cohesion, Austria ran fiscal deficits. But the deficits were always controlled and predictable, because general economic conditions were more stable than in other OECD countries. One aspect of fiscal policy was the maintenance of the welfare state to high standards, thus keeping the "social wage" at acceptable levels. Under Monetarist regimes in other countries, the welfare state was threatened. Third, in monetary policy the aims were to keep the quantity of money at levels which supported exchange rate policies, and to hold interest rates at lower levels than other countries. This was seen as a way of avoiding drastic reductions in the flow of new investment, but with a wariness that if interest rates were too low then short-term foreign money might take flight. Finally, Austria had a tripartite and corporate incomes and prices framework. Unions, employers, and government had developed institutional machinery for centralising determinations on prices and wages. During the stagflation, the policy was to keep average wage increases to 3 per cent, upon the assumption that productivity would increase at about that level. But differential awards were permitted within the general constraint of the 3 per cent average. The incomes and prices framework also included provisions for negotiation and agreement on structural change. Overall, the policies were coordinated and comprehensive.

We can now take our central themes a few steps further in their development. Industry policies in a context of stagflation have some important suggestive tendencies in the way new state roles are created and operated. Three key matters can be discerned. First, the new political economy seems to encourage consultative arrangements between labour, capital, and government at centralised levels. This can be regarded as a "new corporate state", with some dominant interest groups incorporated into official status and policy making in macroeconomic and structural decisions. One implication of this is that the relationship between trade union leaders and their rank-and-file membership is altered. Leaders are committed to official policies, and they would either have to persuade members that their interests were still being served, or face the possibility of internal conflicts. The membership might be more ready to accept the situation when it was long-term historical legitimisation, as in Austria, or when the unfortunate alternative is lack of job security and reduced power to the unions in an economy that might otherwise plunge into severe recession. Second, the processes of consultation in themselves provide a learning experience in practical economics and in operating the corporate institutional machinery. Consultation involves reviewing the impacts of hypothetical changes in wages, taxes, and public expenditures via sophisticated econometric and simulation models: It also involves bargaining and a willingness to resolve conflicts. Thus habits and attitudes are likely to change in the direction of the participants knowing more about economics, socio-political impacts, and the role of institutions in developing societal values. Third, dealing with structural change and industry policies is much easier when it is done within a framework of what West Germans call *ordnungspolitik*. *Ordnungspolitik* is the setting of a stable framework of inducement and constraint, operative over the medium-term for the relevant conditions (e.g. stagflation), and permitting individuals, firms, and groups in society the freedom and opportunity to set their motivations and actions to the stable framework. Of course, when conditions such as stagflation change in substantial ways, it is then necessary to reform *ordnungspolitik*.

The societal changes and the theoretical aspects of such things as industry policy, technology, the postindustrial society, and stagflation portend new state roles. These roles are more complicated than conventional interactive conditions between the state and private enterprise. They are directed towards profitability and change in private enterprise. In some respects the nature of theoretical and practical political economy begins to change. For some democratic societies, the tendencies will be towards a new corporatism and *ordnungspolitik,* or, if some countries find their historical and institutional conditions unfavourable to *ordnungspolitik,* then we can expect some difficulty in conceiving and in administering industry policies. As we shall presently see, all of this has critical implications for the progress of industry policy in Australia. Meanwhile, we can obtain some clearer understanding of successful industry policy by outlining the Japanese practice.

Japan and Industry Policy

The Japanese approach to industry policy is to incorporate it within their framework for *development* planning. Essentially a developmental stance — as contrasted with British-style regulatory approaches — enables government to use positive measures to induce internationally competitive productivity, innovation, efficiency, and continuous structural change. The developmental perspective views technology, higher education, and public policy generally as integral and contributory to economic growth and change. Patrick (1985) advises us to take a cautious attitude in assessing the respective roles of private enterprise and government in the success of the Japanese economy since the 1950s. Government has contributed to industry policy in both setting a broad framework and in selecting key industries for specific treatment. As a broad framework government has created a supportive context for saving, investment, private enterprise, and high competence in education. For treatments in specific industries, government has induced the expansion of growth industries and assisted the phasing out of industries which become unprofitable. The growth industries are selected for their comparative advantage, their high income elasticities of demand, and their price competitiveness. In specific terms this has meant the stage-by-stage process has worked through:

a) shipbuilding and heavy industry in the 1950s,

b) consumer electricals and steel in the 1960s, and

c) high technology information, and biotechnology in response to the stagflation of the 1970s.

The government's agency for industry policy is the Ministry of International Trade and Industry (MITI). MITI's interventions have been based upon arguments favouring the rationalised development of technolgy, alertness to areas where profitability fails as conditions change, and strategic pushes for long run growth. In short, MITI has advocated that these matters are necessary for supplementing private enterprise and for strategically steering some selective economic growth.

We should also appreciate that the Japanese have operated a flexible and effectively coordinated package of policies, operating as a network, to secure economic growth. In summarised outline we can specify the network as follows:

First, as Bronfenbrenner (1973) notes, capital funds have originated largely from development banks which then have a stake in the efficiency of industries.

Second, in the 1960s, government took steps to ensure that enrolements were enlarged in tertiary education, and to steer some teaching and research towards the needs of industry (Pempel 1977). Technology has been linked to smaller enterprises by coordinating trade associations, educational institutions, and government persuasion.

Third, as noted by Thurow and his co-authors (1985), industrial relations were reformed in the 1960s following disruptions and strikes. Unions were re-organised on an enterprise basis so that working conditions, wages, and the viability of enterprises were made more coherent and feasible. Some employees enjoyed "lifetime" employment. This meant that employees were given many-sided experiences in a firm, continual retraining, and a goal to achieve managerial status in mid-life. Before mid-life, the emphasis was placed upon cooperative teamwork, and the transmission of ideas for improving productivity and products from management to workers, and from workers to management. All employees (i.e. not just managers) shared in annual bonus payments.

Fourth, when stagflation struck in 1973/74, policies were reformed. Initially in macroeconomic policy, government curbed monetary and fiscal liquidity to combat inflation. However, high levels of spending in the economy as a whole were quickly restored to induce structural change. MITI moved towards R and D in "fifth generation" computer technology. For sunset industries, "recession cartels" were created to phase out those firms which were less competitive in the face of international economic trends.

Japanese growth rates have been superior to many other advanced capitalist countries. It can be persuasively argued that both broadly and specifically conceived industry policies in Japan have something to do with the comparative success. Industry policy has been operative throughout the last 30 years, and Japan has grown from contributing only some 2.2 per cent of the world's economic output in 1955 to some 10 per cent by 1980. High rates of saving and investment have also contributed to this achievement, along with competitive entrepreneurship. Having established both the general principles and exemplars we are now able to take a broad and critical perspective on the situation in Australia.

Structural Change in Australia

After World War II ended, policy makers were intent upon expanding manufacturing industry in Australia. For Australian relevance we can view manufacturing industry as being supported on what we shall describe as a "policy tripod". The first leg of the tripod was the continuation of high tariffs and other forms of protective assistance to industry. The second leg of the tripod was built upon the strong dependence of foreign investment, mainly from Britain, United States, Western Europe, and since the late-1960s, from Japan. The third leg of the tripod was migration policy, with encouragement and government assistance to immigrants to settle in Australia. Migrants became significant in the labour supply to labour-intensive manufacturing.

Manufacturing in Australia was mainly developed as import substitution in a protected domestic market. Unlike most OECD countries, Australia has never been a significant exporter of manufactured goods. The "policy tripod" stood upon reasonably secure ground until the early-1970s, though many economists doubted its qualities and efficiencies. In the mid-1970s, the ground was shaken by international stagflation, by industrialisation in Southeast and East Asia, and by a changing international economic order. Foreign investors began to divert manufacturing investment to Asian countries, and Australia found itself in relative economic decline.

Although some structural changes in favour of mineral exports and Asian trade occurred spontaneously, other sectors, including manufacturing, could not readily adapt. Moreover, from 1974 various Australian governments' slow responses to structural change were only one part of Australia's policy problems. Another part of the problem was that throughout the period 1971 to 1983 Australian governments pursued ineffective and often inappropriate macroeconomic policies. Macroeconomic policies commanded most attention, with scarcely any real significance being placed upon developing industry policy. When stagflation struck hard in 1973 to 1974, the Whitlam Australian Labor Government was expanding social policies and pursuing expansionary public budgets. Inflation accelerated, and unemployment persisted. In 1975 a disillusioned electorate voted the Fraser Liberal-National Country Party into government. Fraser became a convert to Monetarism, but he was unable to make lasting solutions to the problems of inflation, unemployment, fiscal deficits, and the profitability of private enterprise.

In the foregoing outline, we have provided the general direction and framework for the review of structural change in Australia. Our focal points in the structural changes are: *broad* sector *changes,* new *patterns of* international *trade* and changes in *productivity* in manufacturing, all variously related to the period 1960 to 1982.

Broad Structural Change

The two expanding sectors of the Australian economy have been the tertiary and the mining sectors. From the early-1960s to the late-1970s, the tertiary sector expanded from 66 to 70 per cent of GDP, and the mining sector from 1.5 to 4.0 per cent. In the same period agriculture declined from 11.6 to 5.5 per cent, and manufacturing from 30 to 20 per cent. It is the decline in the manufacturing sector which presently attracts attention from policy makers. Attention is heightened because although mining and agriculture are the main contributors to Australia's export trade, they do not employ large and expanding numbers of employees. Mining is a capital intensive industry, and over a long period of time farm output also increases without expanding employment. Agricultural products are subject to droughts and other natural hazards, and mineral products such as coal, iron ore, and aluminium experience ups and downs in prices, depending upon international economic fluctuations. Mining attracts foreign investment, especially at times when OPEC oil prices escalate and raise the relative value of Australia's abundant resources of coal and bauxite-aluminium.

The rapid growth of the mining sector has stimulated some theoretical thought on its intersectional implications. Gregory (1984) reasons along the following lines. First, with the growth of mineral exports, consumption increases and pressures are felt in wages and costs in nontradeables. Second, these costs flow on to other sectors, and this makes both the agricultural export sector and the manufacturing sector less competitive. Third, imported manufactured goods displace Australian-made goods, and the manufacturing sector declines. In short, some sectors decline to make room for the new growing mining sector. The Gregory theory assumes that some sectors do not have the flexibilities to expand or to adjust easily to cost pressures. Even without the growth of mining, Australian manufacturing would be experiencing problems because it has been slow to adapt to international changes and to rapid technological innovation.

The overall picture of broad structural change in Australia is that the tertiary and mining sectors have grown at the expense of the manufacturing and agricultural sectors. Foreign ownership has been significant, especially in mining and manufacturing. Although reliable data is not available for recent years, it is thought by informed economists that foreigners own about 35 per cent of manufacturing output and some 60 per cent of the value added in mining. However, in manufacturing, transnational corporations have been more interested in Asian investment since the mid-1970s, with some diversion from more limited and slacker Australian markets. The structural changes have mirrored changing trade patterns.

Trade Patterns

Asian countries have increased their penetration of Australian markets in the 1970s. Japan and other industrialising countries in Asia have lifted their share of imported manufactured goods in Australia from some 18 per cent in the late-1960s to 30 per cent in the late-1970s. This has been at the expense of United States and Western Europe. Australian exports have in their turn been drawn increasingly to Asian countries. By the late-1970s, 42 per cent of Australian agricultural exports were destined for Asian countries, along with some 68 per cent of mining exports. Australian economic prospects have seemed to have been tied up with Asian trade, especially in exports of processed minerals and resource-based manufactured goods.

Changing trade and structural patterns have been receiving more attention in technical economic research in recent years. Anderson and Garnaut (1983) and Anderson (1983) have explained the basis for a high intensity of regional trade in the Asian and Pacific Rim. They draw upon concepts of "complementarity" and "bias" in reviewing Australia's growth in exports to developing countries from 16 per cent of the total in the early-1950s to 35 per cent in 1980, and a reciprocal growth in Australian imports from developing nations from 21 per cent to 26 per cent. "Complementarity" arises from export oriented growth in Japan, Taiwan, South Korea, Hong Kong, Singapore, and other Asian countries during the last two decades. These countries have strong comparative advantages in manufactured goods because they have high labour/natural resources and capital/labour ratios. They have been accessible to foreign capital and their domestic savings-to-GDP ratios have been high. For Australia, the "complementarity" is the Asian high demand for minerals, processed minerals, and agricultural products, partly precipitating and partly reflecting the high growth rates in the Asian developing countries. "Bias" operates in terms of comparative advantage, reinforcing the complementarities of growth and structural changes occurring in these trading nations. Both for Australia and for the Asian countries, the future also seems secure for continuing the growth, the "complementarity", and the "bias" in the relevant sectors of the economy. But this does not mean that all is well for the Australian economy. As we have indicated, the manufacturing sector is generally rather unenterprising and lagging in technological innovation. The mining and agricultural sectors do not offer high prospects of direct employment growth, and although the tertiary sector absorbs some increasing job opportunities, it can be argued that performance in manufacturing can be improved.

Productivity

One way of assessing the performance of Australian manufacturing industry is to examine its relative productivity changes through time. It is indicative of the concentrated policy attention which has begun in manufacturing industry that the Australian Bureau of Industry Economics has recently joined an international comparative research study of productivity growth under the supervision of the eminent industry economist, Professor R.E. Caves of Harvard University. From Professor Caves' research, information will be provided on the technical efficiencies of industries in respect to input uses in production functions, and in their factor productivities from 1954–55 to 1981–82. Preliminary work by Whiteman and Harries (1984) outlines factor productivities through some 34 manufacturing industries. Using some rather arbitrary assumptions in their econometric models, Whiteman and Harris found:

1. Annual growth rates from labour inputs were statistically "significant" in 41 per cent of industries.

2. Annual growth rates from capital inputs were statistically "significant" in only 15 per cent of industries.

3. The contributions of labour and capital to economic growth varied quite widely through time. Capital efficiencies deteriorated in the years 1964–65 to 1973–74, but even with the advent of stagflation in 1973–74, capital efficiencies improved during the last half of the 1970s.

4. Technological change in Australia has been accompanied by greater efficiencies from labour, compared with capital efficiencies.

5. Capital efficiencies in some industries were negative in the 1950s and 1960s. Such results were found in iron and steel, nonmetallic minerals, leather products, footwear, tobacco, and bread industries. The reasons have not been identified in the research.

Productivity has been measured as an index of the ratio of the volume of production to the weighted sum of the factors used. The overall preliminary and tentative impression is that Australia has not gained as much from technological change and capital efficiency as other countries which operate competitively in international markets for manufactured products. If this is so, then Australian policy makers could usefully make manufacturing industry the object of attention for improved perfommance.

Structural and productivity change in Australia during the last 30 years presents a mixed picture. Manufacturing industry developed under protectionist policies, with supports from migration policies and foreign investment. However, some manufacturing industries have not shown much growth from capital efficiency and technological change. But stagflation seems to have led investors to seek greater efficiency from capital, and as we shall presently see, capital has displaced labour in some industries. Structural changes have been occurring in the Australian economy, reflecting complementary trade patterns in the Asian and Pacific Rim. Mineral and agricultural products have comparative advantage, but these industries do not offer solutions to the unemployment which accompanies stagflation. The spontaneous forces of structural change, led by recent trading patterns, are likely to continue. Where public policy becomes relevant and significant is in the more sluggish and relatively small manufacturing sector. Thus, compared with many other OECD countries we see Australia having some unusual characteristics. Its manufacturing sector is small, and its exports, with strong emphases upon primary products, reflects patterns which one normally associates with less developed countries. Although Australia ranks among the advanced capitalist nations, its relative economic position has been declining for some 25 years or so. This means that industry policy has relevance to manufacturing *per se,* and to Australia's comparative performance in economic growth. Intellectual economists have been addressing these issues since the 1970s, but as we shall see their prescriptions are in conflict.

Responses to Australia's Economic Problems

When stagflation struck hard in 1973/74, Australian policy-makers and intellectuals had no adequate and effective response. This is clearly seen in macroeconomic policies during the years 1972 to 1982. Australian macroeconomic policies have often been inappropriate to the prevailing circumstances, dogmatically contentious, and mistimed. The Whitlam Labor Governments were in office from 1972 to 1975. These Governments adopted fiscal and wage policies which heightened inflation, without having much impact upon structural unemployment. Following economic mismanagement, the Fraser Liberal-National Country Party Governments held office from 1975 to 1983. These Governments attempted to use Friedmanite Monetarism to reduce fiscal deficits, to cause reductions in real wages, and to drive inflationary expectations out of the economy. By 1982 Australian Monetarism had fallen apart. With the advent of international recession, and low tax collections, it had not been easy to reduce fiscal deficits. In the years 1979 to 1981, after some years of (partial) indexation of wages to the cost of living, a wages "blow-out" occured. Investment and consumption were despressed, and the 1981/82 "misery index" reached 21 per cent, being more than twice that of the average for OECD countries. Long term structural problems were set aside, and Australia had nothing like the more appropriate links between structural change, industry policy, and corporate features which were successful in countries such as Japan, Austria, and Singapore.

Advocates of free market solutions to Australia's relatively low growth rates focus their arguments upon the high levels of protection in Australia. The various arguments can be presented through the eyes of Kasper (1980), and Anderson (1984). Kasper takes the most expansive view among the authors, relating his themes to general economic policy and to growth. He suggests that protectionism in Australia has led to inward-looking attitudes, blocking export potential and entrepreneurship. Kasper finds that although savings ratios and investment levels in Australia have been in line with OECD averages, growth has been lagging with countries such as West Germany, the Netherlands, France, Japan, and other Asian countries overhauling Australia since the mid-1960s. According to Kasper, the problems have centred around failures to adapt to changing international demand and to a backlog of technological adjustment. Foreign industrial plants in Australia tend to be operated as restrictive "branches" of larger transnational corporations, with just a motive for filling in domestic market demands under the umbrella of protection. Old industrial structures have held back the advance of both human capital and innovative physical capital. Kasper draws upon international medium-term economic forecasting to reveal that if Australia were to follow liberalisation policies in trade its GDP would increase at about twice the rate that would prevail under continuing protection.

Anderson (1984) has set his focus more specifically on the issues of trade and protection, drawing together historical detailing and technical work in neoclassical economics. He shows that the pattern of growth and decline of manufacturing industry in Australia differs from other advanced capitalist countries. Australian manufacturing grew as a percentage of total employment through to the 1950s and then declined. It absorbed 30 per cent of employment in 1950, and less than 20 per cent in 1980. Other countries have experienced long-term declines in manufacturing job ratios for periods of 50 years and more. But these countries have nevertheless retained a higher proportion of manufacturing in their GDPs. Also, as noted earlier, Australia is less dependent upon manufactured goods for its export earnings, having a comparative advantage in primary products. Thus, whereas the EEC countries typically have some 82 per cent of their export earnings from manufacturing, Australian ratios reach only 27 per cent. The explanations for Australia's low percentages in manufacturing lie partly in the principle of comparative advantage, and partly in the policy of high protection.

Anderson found that during the 1970s effective rates of protection in manufacturing goods have decreased, though with exceptions in the textile, clothing, footwear, and motor vehicles industries. Generally, whereas effective rates of protection stood at 36 per cent in 1968–69, by 1981–82 they fell to some 26 per cent. The arguments from neoclassical economists were becoming increasingly persuasive. Both Liberal-Country Party and Australian Labor Party Governments took action to liberalise trade. In 1971 the Liberal-Country Party requested the Tariff Board to review tariffs with a view to reducing protection. In 1974 the Whitlam Labor Party Government reduced tariffs by 25 per cent as an anti-inflationary policy. The successor to the Tariff Board, the Industries Assistance Commission (created in 1974) has been a persistent advocate of liberalisation (1981). The Commission sees tariffs as an implicit tax subsidy to producers and as an implicit tax on consumption. For Anderson, reductions in protection would facilitate the intensification of regional trade and growth in the Asian and Pacific Rim, as described in our earlier reference to his explanations of "complementarity" and "bias". In short, lower protection would accelerate the deepening trade between Australia and Asian countries, consequently bringing higher growth with structural adjustment. Anderson assesses the consequences upon manufacturing industry in the following terms. – First, the manufacturing sector would scarcely decline further, if at all. Second, the more competitive sectors within manufacturing would expand. Third, the percentage of GDP which is internationally traded would (beneficially) rise. Finally, the liberalisation would come as a new awareness of the national interest, breaking down the vested interests of some sections of labour and capital which favour protectionism.

The intellectual advocates for the liberalisation of trade have the virtues of neoclassical economics. Their technical and quantitative work is firm, with good coverage in diagnosis and prognosis. But neoclassical economics needs supplementing to give it stronger societal grounding and a wider view of public policy in structural economic change. We can clinch the points by drawing upon our earlier examples of Japanese policy. The Japanese blended societal purposes with economic change by creating "recession cartels" to phase down older industrial structures. The more efficient producers would thereby survive in better economic times, but both capital and labour were given time to adjust to international economic change. Japan has placed attention on sunrise as well as sunset industries. In a mixed market and administrative guidance system, the Japanese have found that economic change can occur more readily in a policy framework which goes beyond *laissez faire*. Public policy roles can be extended to educational reform, improving training programmes, boosting technological innovation, and adopting Structuralism in macroeconomic policies. With all these policies appropriately coordinated, we find new spaces for state roles in industry policy. The advocates for market solutions could usefully extend their conceptual and intellectual range to state institutional and active structural roles.

Intellectual economists have addressed some of the main issues in Australia's structural problems. Although we cannot discern any advocate of comprehensive policy development in macroeconomics and industry policy, the intellectuals have heightened the general awareness in the community that reforms are necessary. At the political level, the election of the Hawke Australian Labor Party Government in 1983 brought economic reform firmly on to the agenda. We now turn to a review and assessment of the new moves towards industry policy.

Towards the Development of Industry Policy

Australia is at the stage where Government ministers are advocates of ideas and causes for the urgent development of industry policy. The Hawke Government inherited some *ad hoc* policies on technology, investment allowances for industry, training schemes, and other elements of policies for industry. In 1983–84, various public speeches have indicated an awareness of the necessity to collect the elements together for creating cohesive and comprehensive industry policy. To some extent, again, the major thrust of economic policy has been to correct very real short-term macroeconomic problems. However, as we shall presently see, the Hawke Government's approach to macroeconomic policies has made it possible to work for longer term economic policies to coordinate with the new macroeconomic framework. Hawke himself has been well aware of Australia's structural problems, both from his former position as leader of the Australian Council of Trade Unions and from his membership of official committees in the 1970s reviewing manufacturing and structural change. Nevertheless, Australia also faces some disadvantages in its new moves towards creating industry policy. It enters the field more than a decade behind the world's leaders. Much depends upon how the various uncertainties connected to the post-1983 incomes policies are played out in the next few years. Administrative separatism in government divides out national reponsibilities in technology, education, and trade and industry. It is not clear that performances and qualities can be raised in technological innovation and in the higher education system. Technological innovation in Australian industry has lagged behind other OECD countries, and the higher education system has neither shown the capacity for significant internal reforms nor has it enjoyed strong financial support from the Hawke and Fraser Governments in the years 1975–85.

Having set the context in the previous paragraph, we organise the remainder of this section as follows. First, we outline the findings and recommendations of various *official committees* during the 1970s. Second, we review the *new approaches to macroeconomic and incomes policies* by the Hawke Government. Third, our discussion turns to examine the Government's early work in developing *industry and technology policies.* Finally, the Government's action plans in the steel and motor vehicle industries are placed into the context of structural change in Australia.

Official Committees

Reporting in 1975, the Committee to Advise on Policies for Manufacturing Industry (Jackson) gave a dismal picture of the state of manufacturing. The Jackson Committee referred to an acute crisis with many sections of industry having excess capacity, low profitability, and low productivity. Further inadequacies were seen in education, training, and R and D. The Committee favoured reductions in protection, the reform of capital markets to create development finance, and more progressive management practices. More significantly the Committee favoured government roles in industry policy, with an urgent need for restructuring industry and for shifting the emphasis to skill-intensive new industries. The response from Fraser Liberal-National Country Party Government was rather general and lacking any commitment to urgency or to programme development. In its White Paper on Manufacturing Industry (1977) it repeated some observations from the Jackson Committee, but eschewed government roles in developing a strategic industry approach. The Fraser Government mainly relied upon private market responses, but it found some reason for creating a Bureau of Industry Economics and industry advisory councils. Further advocacy for reforms in technology and protection came from the 1979 Report of the Study Group on Structural Adjustment (Crawford). This Committee endorsed and followed the general lines argued by the Jackson Committee.

The general effect of the official reports on manufacturing and structural change was to show governments in Australia that serious economic problems existed. The two Committees fell short of setting out a fully elaborated way to create industry policy, and they did not discern the necessities to coordinate macroeconomic policies with structural policies. Australia's major political parties did not conceptualise or favour the new state roles implied by industry policy. Valuable time was lost in a world where other countries had been more adaptive and effective in response to international stagflation. Australia would be shaken out of its complacency only when in 1982 its "misery index" reached 21 per cent, and investment was very depressed.

The New Macroeconomic and Incomes Policies

Hawke fought the 1983 election campaign on the idea of "consensus" politics and incomes policies. Economic issues, with GDP falling 4.5 per cent in 1982, the "misery index" reaching 21 per cent, and industry sluggish, dominated the election. Having won the election, Hawke held a national economic summit meeting with representatives from labour, capital, and government. The new incomes policy took shape in the form of a Prices and Incomes Accord. Wages were to be indexed to the cost of living and restrained until 1985, when adjustments could take place for productivity change. Government roles were set to increase consultation with unions and employers, and to give attention to the "social wage" components of the standard of living in such fiscal spheres as taxation, health, education, and housing. In practice this meant that the Hawke Government revived a flagging housing industry and created expansionary budgets in 1983 and (rather less so) in 1984. Taxation was reduced in 1984 as a *quid pro quo* for wage restraint among the unions. On the wages front, centralisation re-emerged in the Conciliation and Arbitration Commission after a wages "blow-out" in 1979–82 when unions made leapfrogging claims in a decentralised pattern of collective bargaining.

At the institutional level, Australia has followed some of the examples we found in our earlier discussions of Austria's incomes policies. A tripartite Advisory Committee on Prices and Incomes (ACPI) monitors the Prices and Incomes Accord. Longer term economic purposes come under the scope of the Economic Planning Advisory Council (EPAC), with a focus upon reforming the tax system and industry as a first step. The restructuring of industry has the attention of a sub-committee of Cabinet, and this is supposed to be consolidated by the Australian Manufacturing Council (AMC) and by sector specific Industry Councils. In Australia, trade unionists find it easier to accept wage restraint under incomes policies if prices are also under official review. The Whitlam, Australian Labor Party, Government had created a Prices Justification Tribunal in 1973. This Tribunal had a somewhat chequered experience, with difficulty in operating within consistent objectives and criteria. For example, anti-inflationary purposes had suggested a hard line on price increases, but a depressed environment for investment had suggested that prices should be sufficient for profitability. The Hawke Government created a new Prices Surveillance Authority in December 1983, with hopes for consistency and effectiveness in a limited range of purposes.

Overall, the Hawke Government took a far more coordinative and cohesive view of economic policies in their structural and macroeconomic dimensions than its predecessors. During 1983/84, fiscal policies, "social wage" features, incomes policies, and mechanisms for dealing with structural change had been brought together in an integrated way. For Hawke, 1983/84 was a good year. His "incomes accord" held together, GDP grew by some 10 per cent, and Australia's "misery index" fell from 21 to 14 per cent. In fact, Hawke was sufficiently confident to call for an early election in December 1984, which he won. But by March 1985 the economic outlook for Australia became gloomy. The Australian dollar plunged in value; industrial relations became more contentious; the Labor Party showed more signs of factional in-fighting; and Hawke foreshadowed severe budgetary restraints for 1986. The incomes policies began to appear as just a phase in a recession, with forces poised to tear it apart when the recovery had proceeded far enough.

Policies for Industry and Technology

The Minister of Industry and Commerce, Senator Button, was busy making public speeches in 1984, advocating industry policy for Australia. It is clear that he has the sort of conceptualisation we discussed earlier in our review of practice in Japan and of the theoretical grounding for new state roles. Accordingly, Senator Button wishes to devise industry policies to facilitate structural adaptation and to make manufacturing industry internationally competitive. Building upon the Government's policies in incomes and macroeconomics, Senator Button's first active steps towards creating a new industry policy include the following. First, the Australian Industry Development Corporation has been asked to pitch its equity and loan programmes towards restructuring and revitalising industry. (The Corporation is a much smaller scale operation than leading Japanese development banks.) Second, steps have been taken to create a venture capital market under the Management and Investment Companies Act, 1983. This Act induces venture capital markets to develop by allowing a 100 per cent tax deduction for the value of capital subscribed by private industry. Venture capital will enable some small high technology companies to have access to start-up capital. But, as the Japanese know, there will still be a need for development capital for successful starters. Third, Japanese consultants have been engaged to advise on ways that Australian firms can develop exports to Japan. Finally, a miscellany of existing policies and practices are being reviewed, ranging from training programmes, through sector-specific programmes, to advisory services and assistance to small businesses. The early stages are marked by endeavour and understanding, but, as yet, with nothing as firmly committed to sunset and sunrise industries as has been done in countries like Japan and Singapore. The Department of Science and Technology was created in 1980. During the 1970s, in connection with the emphasis given by the OECD, Australia took hesitant and small steps to develop a science and technology policy. In 1977 the Fraser Liberal-National Country Party Government formed the Australian Science and Technology Council (ASTEC), with the aim of developing national policies. The Fraser Government also introduced grants for developing R and D and technological innovation. However, the OECD examiners who reported in 1974 found that Australia lagged behind most OECD countries in its R and D and technological innovation. With the election of the Hawke Government in 1983, Australian science and technology gained an energetic advocate as Minister. Barry Jones had written a popular textbook, *Sleepers Wake!* (1983), lamenting the backwardness of Australian manufacturing industry and the poor achievements in R and D. Like Senator Button, Barry Jones, has used his first two years as Minister to heighten community awareness and to signal the directions which need to be taken.

Barry Jones and senior officers from the Department of Science and Technology have been active in public speeches and in formulating policy statements in 1983 – 84. Again, the general directions for Australia which Barry Jones would like to see are much along the lines of a scaled down version of Japanese experience. This would mean that Australian performance in technological innovation would be lifted, especially in the private sector. Industry would be more closely linked with research, and educational institutions would be closer to industrial research. In terms of some facts and figures over the next decade or so, Australian performance would change. It might maintain its position of producing some 2 per cent of the world's annual general and basic research. But its contributions of only 0.7 per cent of patents and 0.1 per cent of high technology production would rise substantially.

In Australia it is easier to find aspirations than achievements. We can discern a number of problems which will inhibit the progress with industry policy. – First, the 1984 Government budget was restrictive in R and D and higher education. Second, higher education has experienced expenditure curbs for more than a decade, and it contains organisational and other difficulties. The academic community has aged, with not much regeneration from younger recruits and novel ideas. Qualities in major research are becoming more fragmented and dispersed. Third, attitudes in the business community, as evidenced by the Business Council Australia's statement on industrial revitalisation in September 1984, are rather narrow in scope. The Council mainly wants to reduce trade union power, and to take only cautious steps towards the liberalisation of trade and the taking up of entrepreneurial activities.

Fourth, the Australian system of wage determination in the Commonwealth Conciliation and Arbitration Commission is inconsistent and subject to pressures. At times when opportunity arises, the trade unions seek "leap-frogging" wage claims outside the Commission's power in a rather disorganised pattern of collective bargaining. In fact some sections of the union movement oppose Senator Button's ideas for liberalising trade, and unions are organised to pursue sectional rather than corporate national interests. Fifth, when Hawke was re-elected in 1984, he did not take opportunity to rationalise the Government's organisational aspects of industry policy. Senator Button retained responsibilities in trade and industry, and technology was added to his sphere. But science was separated from technology and came under the responsibility of Barry Jones. Finally, the Government has only recently received advice from its inquiry into labour market programmes on such matters as training schemes for the young. Australia lags behind other OECD countries in the retention of youth in education and training. Progress is likely to be slow, long term, and with more expensive impacts upon government spending than the levels which have been acceptable to the Hawke Governments.

Sector Policies

The present sector-specific policies in Australia again reflect responses to short-term considerations, and they address problems in established industries rather than seeking new high technology industries. Initiatives have been taken by the Hawke Government to improve the profitability of restructuring of the motor car and steel industries. Under the passenger motor vehicle plan, announced in May 1984, the Government will phase down the effective rate of protection from 100 per cent in 1985 to 57.5 per cent in 1992. Cars will still have double the rate of protection of manufacturing industry as a whole. It is hoped that restructuring will lead to reduction in models from 13 to 6 and that prices will be kept down in line with price movements in efficient overseas producers. Australian motor car manufacturing has been set in a context of strong international competition from Japan in domestic markets, job losses, and the infusion of overseas technology to reduce costs on production and assembly lines. The motor vehicle plan is aimed at providing a medium-term framework for continuing the change and adjustment. Basically, the Australian motor vehicle industry, which is mainly foreign owned, will continue to supply the domestic market with marginally increased competition from overseas imports.

The announcement of the Government steel plan in August 1983 indicated the serious condition of manufacturing in Australia. Australia is rich in those natural resources which are used in steel manufacturing. However, in 1982, following a decade of low productivity and the widening international recession in the early-1980s, the steel industry found itself in decline. In 1982 production was cut by 30 per cent, employment by 25 per cent, and quotas were imposed on cheaper steel from overseas producers. The Japanese had improved their labour productivity from 362 tonnes per annum in 1974 to 411 tonnes in 1980, whereas Australia's productivity fell from 181 to 174 tonnes. The Government plan covered wages, investment by the BHP Company (Australia's main producer), bounty payments, and productivity. These matters were placed in an agreement between the Government, BHP, and trade unions, with provisions for monitoring by an independent Steel Industry Authority. Wages were indexed to the cost of living under the Government's incomes policies. Bounties were paid for some products to a ceiling of $ 71.6 million; this form of assistance was chosen to keep prices down for steel users in other industries. Investment plans were aimed at expenditures of some $ 800 million over four years, with $ 500 million firmly committed in 1983. Trade unions and BHP agreed to set targets for 250 tonnes labour productivity and then to increase this above the trend rates for overseas producers.

The plans for steel and motor cars reveal that policy makers in Australia are now inclined to use disaggregative sector-specific policies. The state becomes involved in the profitability of private enterprise and uses its power in relations between capital and labour. The particular plans used combine elements of protection and restructuring. It remains to be seen whether these new state interventions will encourage more entrepreneurial moves in sunrise industries, where the real changes are necessary. Meanwhile the Hawke Government hopes for an expansion of trade and industry links with the People's Republic of China.

Perspective

Since 1983 Australia has taken a more coordinative view of structural change, macroeconomic policies, and incomes policies. The macroeconomic and incomes policies should be seen as reactions against a failed Australian Monetarism and as a response to a crisis "misery index" of 21 per cent in 1982. Policy making in technology and industry is at the preliminary stage of advocacy and with leading Government spokespersons heightening community awareness for urgent change. The real task of converting policy rhetoric into effective experience with good programmes lies ahead, if it can be achieved at all. The nature and seriousness of Australia's problems in manufacturing industry have been well put by the High Technology Financing Committee (Espie) of the Australian Academy of Technological Sciences (1983, p. 1):

> Australian manufacturing industry is in a state of decline. Employment in manufacturing decreased by 100 000 between June 1969 and June 1981, and the number of establishments employing more than 1 000 people fell by 25 per cent. Clearly, Australia is failing to generate new establishments which grow and replace those being lost in the large establishment sector of manufacturing.
>
> Studies overseas have shown that nearly all the net new jobs in the private sector have been generated by young, high growth companies and those in the high technology sector have the fastest growth. Statistics indicate that these enterprises are very economical in the level of assets per employee.
>
> Australia is failing to grasp the opportunities offered by high technology industries for wealth creation and employment growth. In fact, Australia's performance in high technology sector is being outstripped by many of its developing neighbours in the Asian region.

The Espie Committee identified the obstacles to progress as:

1. an absence of venture capital markets in Australia,
2. a general lack of managerial skills in existing enterprises,
3. the insularity of manufacturing in its general confines to the domestic market, and
4. gaps in public policy, especially in a cohesive industry policy.

Steps have now been taken to outline cohesive industry policy, and to induce venture capital markets. More needs to be done in a range of policies which coordinate with industry and technology policy. Again, taking up our themes from an "idealised" perspective and from the Japanese experience, we can see that those policies which need reform are: technology, education, industrial relations, development capital, training, wages, and sunrise industries. Our concluding section gives evaluation of prospects and possibilities in these spheres.

Summary and Evaluation

Industrie policy portends more opportunity and dilemma than appears at mere superficial levels. At superficial levels our attention is drawn to such things as policies in taxation, retraining, education, industrial relations, technology, and so on. One step further on from this superficial level, we find in Japanese experience and in theoretical principles that the qualities of industry policy depend upon cohesion and coordination. Finally, when we probe more fundamental aspects of societal functioning and of general principle, we discover the real issues and their implications. — Industry policy is aimed at improving productivity and profitability in the private sector. This means that the state is explicitly adopting new roles which interact and intertwine with private enterprise. At the very least we must revise our ideas on the theory and practice of the state in advanced capitalist societies. A somewhat related matter is the emergent new corporatism in countries which have sought consultative solutions to structural economic change and to dealing with the stresses from stagflation. The central representatives of capital and labour are "incorporated" into key decisional processes, involving government power and strategically important politics. Next, we recognise that a successful industry policy involves a process of reform and change. We shall find new economic techniques, new institutional machinery, new winners, new losers, and a whole new field of potential conflicts of interest. The costs and sacrifices of change will be justified by advocates on grounds of economic necessity and national public interest. However, the losers and the conservatives will want to protect their positions. But the reformers and the potential winners will not find the task of change easy to accomplish. They will need to formulate an effective theory of policy change, and hold a thight framework of *ordnungspolitik* to see their ideas materialise. Our summary and evaluation will address these diverse issues, beginning with the last one mentioned, the theory of public policy change.

The sorts of conditions which are necessary for key policy changes to be implemented successfully are elaborated in the literature (Downs, 1976). First, the task environment must be adaptive to change. Change is more difficult to accomplish in a socioeconomic environment which has deep cleavages of ideology and interest. Second, those who lead the change will need a high degree of political visibility, with their advocacy flowing in nonpartisan and nonideological ways. Third, innovative policy depends upon commitments of motivation, resources, incentives to change institutions, and upon access to good information. Finally, the public bureaucracies must be capable of understanding and predicting the change process.

Having stated the conditions for success in this way, we can find much for us to be generally cautious and circumspect. Although two key Ministers – Senator Button in Industry, and Barry Jones in Technology – have maintained a high political profile in 1983–84, they are vulnerable. Barry Jones lamented the low pay out to technology and higher education in the 1984 Hawke Government Budget. In addition, Senator Button has to contend with strong factional groups in the Australian Labor Party and in the trade union movement. At the Party's national conference in July 1984, the Amalgamated Metals, Foundry, and Shipwright's Union countered the Hawke-Button policy for structural change with its desire for protection for older industrial structures. Thus Senator Button is an advocate for liberalisation of trade and for economic restructuring, but his Party's policy platform has strong protectionst elements.

Senator Button and Barry Jones have not yet erected an *ordnungspolitik* structure which will enable change to proceed smoothly. In terms of resources, Jones would need more from fiscal expenditure to support science and technology. From the organisational perspective, Button would need a re-ordering of priorities in his Department, with more emphasis to industrial restructuring. Both Jones and Button would need a more dynamic and purposeful higher education sector, with education policy coordinated with industry and technology policies. The Australian Labor Party's recent approach to higher education has been to encourage enrolements of students from less privileged socioeconomic backgrounds; other problems in the higher education system have been neglected. From my own current research in organisational and educational aspects of universities, colleges, and scientific organisations in Australia (Martin, Pugh *et.al,* 1985) it is clear that policy makers should not reply upon higher education to reform itself from within.

We can sum up the prospects for useful industry policy in Australia by returning to Down's findings (1976) for adaptive change. Change will be difficult in Australia because Australia presently has deep cleavages of ideology and sectional interests. Those political leaders who advocate industrial change, namely Senator Button and Barry Jones, either face political vulnerability or some frustrations which would test the resolve of even the most deeply committed people. The Hawke Government has been somewhat hesitant and slow in making the reforms which will be necessary in education, training, and in the organisation of key departments of state. The flow of resources to high technology, to research, and to higher education is insufficient by overseas standards. Although the Australian economic crisis in 1982 provided the motivation for "consensus" politics and some attention for economic change, the future is uncertain, with the most probable outcome being that Australia will return to divisive politics and economics. Other countries are better placed to intertwine state and private sector roles in structural change. Australia's structural change will be most likely linked to market trends in resource-based minerals and manufactured goods, largely exported to developing countries in the Asian and Pacific Rim.

In prospect, Australia will remain as a "dependent" economy, with slower growth rates than many of its competitors. Industry policy in Australia seems to be destined as another theatre for capital-labour disputation. As public policy, the new steps towards formulating industry policy will probably end up in the general characteristic of Australian public policies. That is to say, by the standards of good overseas examples, policy will be less cohesive and it will be attenuated, short of success and effectiveness. Australia does not have the institutional or societal conditions for "corporatism", as represented in Japan, Austria and other countries. Also, it does not have the size or economic dynamism to rely upon *laissez faire* routes to successful change, as has been occurring in recent years in the United States. Finally, Australia began its search for a successful industry policy a decade or more after the world's leading exemplars. In a real sense, Australia has experienced lost opportunity, and if we were pessimistic we might suggest that it may be too late. Australian patriotism and nationalism places stronger priorities upon Olympic Games' gold medal counts and the results of cricket matches than with such things as high performances in technology, research, and the arts. Experience in Japan and Austria shows that all things are possible in national pride, including economic change, technology, social policies, the arts, and international sport.

REFERENCES

Anderson, K. (1983), *Intensity of Trade Between Pacific Basin Countries*, Australia-Japan Research Centre, Pacific Economic Papers No. 102, Research School of Pacific Studies, Australian National University, Canberra.

Anderson, K. and Garnaut, R. (1983), *Australia's Trade Growth With Developing Countries*, Australia-Japan Research Centre, Pacific Eenonomic Papers No. 102, Research School of Pacific Studies, Australian National University, Canberra.

Bell, D. (1973), *The Coming of Post-Industrial Society*, Basic Books, New York.

Bronfenbrenner, M. (1973), "Japan's Galbraithian Economy", in D. Marmelsteintz (ed.), *Economics: Mainstream Readings and Radical Critiques*, Random House, New York.

Committee to Advise on Policies for Manufacturing Industry (Jackson, 1975), *Policies for Development of Manufacturing Industry,* Australian Government Publishing Service.

Downs, G. (1976), *Bureaucracy, Innovation, and Public Policy,* Lexington Books, Lexington, Mass.

Drucker, P. F. (1970), *Technology, Management and Society,* Heinemann, London.

Gregory, R. J., "Some Implications of the Growth of the Mineral Sector", in P. J. Lloyd (ed.), *Mineral Economics in Australia,* George Allan and Unwin, Sydney, 1984.

High Technology Financing Committee (Espie, 1983), *Developing High Technology Enterprises for Australia,* Australian Academy of Technological Sciences, Parkville.

Industries Assistance Commission (1981), *Approaches to General Reductions in Protection,* Australian Government Publishing Service, Canberra.

Jones, B., *Sleepers Wake!* (1983), Oxford University Press, Melbourne.

Kasper, W. et. al. (1980), *Australia at the Crossroads,* Harcourt, Brace, Jovanovich, Sydney.

Laidlaw, D. (1982), *Monetarist Perspectives,* Philip Allan, Oxford.

Maddison, A. and Wilpstra, B. S. (1982), *Unemployment: The European Perspective,* Croom Helm, London, 1982.

Martin, B. and Pugh, C. et al. (1985), *Academic Suppression,* Angus and Robertson, Sydney.

O'Connor, J. (1973), *Fiscal Crisis of the State,* St. Martin's Press, New York.

Patrick, H. (1985), "Japanese Industrial Policy", in Bornstein, M. (ed.), *Comparative Economic Systems,* Fifth Edition, Irwin, Homewood, Illinois.

Pempel, T. J. (1977), *Policymaking in Contemporary Japan,* Cornell University Press, Ithaca.

Study Group on Structural Adjustment, Crawford (1979), *Report,* Australian Government Publishing Service, Canberra.

Tisdell, C. A. (1981), *Science and Technology Policy: Priorities of Governments,* Chapman and Hall, London.

Thurow, L. C. (ed.) (1985), *Effective Management: A Japanese View,* MIT Press, Cambridge.

White Paper on Manufacturing Industry (1977), Australian Government Publishing Service, Canberra.

Whiteman, J. L. and Harris, C. M. (1984), *Rates of Augmentation in Australian Manufacturing Industries,* Paper for 54th ANZAAS Congress, 1984, 17 May 1984.

The Contribution of New Enterprise to Economic Growth and Employment.
The Experience of the Scottish Enterprise Foundation

Tom Cannon

One hundred years ago, as the world faced the challenges of the "Great Recession" of the 1880s few countries appeared more able to cope with the difficulties posed by this downturn than Scotland. The industrial base appeared secure and balanced. The heavy industries of Glasgow were counterbalanced by the powerful financial sector of Edinburgh. Although the textile industry faced growing competition burgeoning electronics and chemicals industries seemed able to provide a vehicle for future economic prosperity. In contrast to the rest of the UK (and much of Europe)

> The Scottish limited companies appear to have been smaller, to have enjoyed a more lengthy existence, to have been less bedevilled by fraud, ignorance and gross mismanagement and to have been controlled by their founders a little longer, than their English counterparts; and they probably produced a marginally higher net return to their shareholders.[1]

Despite these apparent strengths the century since then has seen such a decline that

> Consistently poor growth performance has resulted in Scotland slipping gradually into the economic backwater of Europe. It now lags behind the major EC countries to such an extent that it is considered one of the poorest regions of Europe and, as such, is eligible for many forms of EC regional assistance.[2]

Traditional industries such as engineering, shipbuilding and textiles have declined while new sectors are increasingly dependent on foreign based firms. The decline has affected virtually every sector of Scottish economic life. The extent and pace of this is more remarkable given two specific assets which are seen to be critical to modern economic succes:
1. A strong autonomous financial sector,
2. Abundant energy resources.

The financial sector is relatively large, ranking fourth in the UK with a significantly faster rate of growth. The mining industry has contracted over the last twenty years. However, it is the growth of the North Sea oil industry which has excited greatest interest (Please see table next page).

Despite the importance of this sector it is clear that the multiplier effect, i.e., the influence on other parts of the economy, has been far less than originally hoped. The failure of either this "windfall" or the traditional strength in the finance sector to arrest the pattern of decline requires that policy makers look to other aspects of Scottland's economic life. This is the challenge faced by the Scottish Enterprise Foundation.

North Sea Related Employment in Scotland			
Year	Wholly Related	Partially Related	Total
1970	2 500	500	3 000
1971	3 500	500	4 000
1972	4 000	1 000	5 000
1973	5 250	1 250	6 500
1974	13 500	3 250	16 750
1975	20 000	4 500	24 500
1976	27 000	6 750	33 750
1977	28 500	7 000	35 500
1978	34 000	9 250	43 250
1979	41 750	12 250	54 000
1980	46 250	15 000	61 250
1981	49 500	16 500	66 000
1982	58 250	19 750	78 000
1983	61 000	20 500	81 500

Source: Mackay, T., "The Oil and Oil Related Sector", in Hood, N., and Young S., "Industry, Policy and The Scottish Enonomy", 1984.

The Innovative Tradition

Research into the rate and nature of new business formation in Scotland during the latter half of the nineteenth century demonstrates that relatively few, new firms were being set up to exploit new emerging technologies. Although this was a period of rapid change few Scottish companies were emerging to exploit new knowledge based industries.

New Company Formations Associated with New Technologies 1856–1895	
Sector	Cumulative Total
Mining and Quarrying	297
Manufacturing	882
Public Utilities	750
Trade	139
Service	320
Finance, Insurance and Real Estate	415
Agriculture, Forestry and Fishing	133

Source: Milne, T., and Lewis, J., "The Scottish Contribution to Entrepreneurial Studies", in Lewis, J., Stanworth, J., and Gibb, A., "Success and Failure in Small Business", Gower, 1984.

This problem has persisted despite the relatively high participation rates in Higher Education and the growing venture capital sector. The problem has been made worse in recent years by the relatively high "exit" rates.

Entry and Exit for Period 1977–1979					
	Independent		Dependent		Balance
	Entry	Exit	Entry	Exit	(negative)
Manufacturing	1 294	1 439	397	417	(165)
Non Manufacturing	1 121	951	515	389	296
Unclassified	66	20	4	3	(47)
Total	2 481	2 410	916	916	84 (180*)
* Excludes moves					
Source: Adapted from Hamilton, R., "Entry and exit of Businesses in Scotland", UK Small Firms Research and Policy Conference, Glasgow, 1982.					

Although it is acknowledged that the data has many weaknesses especially in measuring the movement of very small enterprises most evidence available today suggests that this data reflects the overall balance. There is only a marginal difference between entry and exit. It is against this background that a range of initiatives have been introduced to stimulate small business development. (Please see *Appendix A*)

The approach of working for business development through a network of agencies is central to the approach to business development in Scotland. This can be seen in three strategic areas:
1. *Entrepreneurialism,*
2. *Elite Industries,*
3. *International Competitiveness.*

Stimulating a spirit of enterprise especially in elite industries to generate internationally competitive firms is the primary goal of this network.

Entrepreneurialism

In his recent study of new company formation, Hamilton concluded that:

> In the five year period between 1971 and 1976, the small business sector was the UK's only net creator of new manufacturing jobs *by virtue of a large influx of new businesses each employing very few people.*[3]

This notion of the new formation as the primary source of newly created jobs fits in with Bannock's finding:

> Very recent research on the contribution of firms of different sizes to the growth of employment in different countries has shown that small firms have accounted for a major proportion of long-term gains, while the largest firms have been shedding labour.[4]

Appendix A

Sponsoring Organisations

Focus	IDS	SDA/HIDB	SEF	Local Authority	Private Sector	Others	Combinations
1. National	Administration of UK and EC Financing, start-up and allied services	Advisory service of Small Business Division: provision of premises: agency for ECSC funds	Graduate Enterprise: Small Firms Resources Centre				
2. Regional		As above in Regional Offices	Small Business Development Centre: EXPORTS	NESDA Small Business Enterprise Scheme: SRC			
3. Local		Special Area initiatives	Small Business Institute, Enterprise Trust Programme	Local small-firm development schemes; managed work-shops, etc. Advisory services	Enterprise Trusts	BSC Industry in steel closure areas: New Towns	Enterprise Trusts (e.g. SDA, private sector, local authorities)
4. Company-specific	Financial and Advisory packages	Individual financial premises and advisory packages	Counselling; BIG Programme	Local small-firm development scheme: managed work shops etc. Advisory services	Venture capital companies; development depts. of banks: "start up" funds, etc.	Scottish Producer Co-Operative Development project: Community enterprise projects etc.	Management buyouts (SDA, private sector)

Closer examination of the work of Birch suggests a similar significance for the very small firm often associated with the new formation.

Net Employment Change: US Manufacturing (1969–76) (figures in 000s)						
	Size, No. of Establishments					
	0 – 20	21 – 50	51 – 100	101 – 500	500 +	Total
Independents (Single est.)	+ 355	– 38	– 116	– 217	– 55	– 70
HQ & Branches of Multinats.	+ 139	+ 83	+ 41	– 43	– 247	– 28
Partnerships & Subsids.	+ 49	+ 48	+ 34	+ 6	– 190	– 52
Total	+ 543	+ 93	– 41	– 254	– 492	– 150

Source: Birch, D., "The Job Generation Process", MIT, 1979.

Despite the apparent surprise with which these conclusions were received in certain quarters, the significance of the entrepreneurial new formation has long been acknowledged by some economists:

> The process of innovation in industry by the agency of entrepreneurs supplies the key to all the phenomena of capital and credit.[5]

However, relatively little attention has been paid to the nature of the entrepreneur or the factors which stimulate or constrain their emergence. Leibenstein's definition, role statement describing the entrepreneur:

> [. . .] he connects different markets, he is capable of making up for market deficiencies (gap-filling), he is an "input completor" and he creates or expands time-binding, input-transforming entities (i.e., firms)[6]

goes some way to fitting this phenomenon into a wider theory of market adjustment. However, this and more recent work by Kirzner ("Competition and Entrepeneurship", University of Chicago Press, 1973) generally provides a marginal, short-lived role for the entrepreneur. These approaches neglect two key groups:
1. The Elite Business Entrepreneur,
2. The Revolutionary Entrepreneur.

The significance of the former is only gradually becoming recognised in studies of enterprise.

Elite Industries

The growth of the electronics industry in Scotland over the last twenty years has highlighted the importance and the risks of elite enterprises. The history of the post-war electronics industry is largely one of entrepreneurs demonstrating an ability to apply technologies and from these applications create substantial firms with large work forces. These elite businesses have had a wider importance through the generation, largely through spin-offs, of new businesses. The value added by these corporations has been very high.

However, two problems have emerged with this process. Firstly, these knowledge-based, high technology firms have not created new jobs in the numbers required to compensate for contraction in traditional sectors. The nature of the processes involved places a premium on capital, not labour intensive production processes. The resources invested in these industries seldom are likely, directly, to create the numbers of jobs needed to resolve current unemployment problems. Any policies to encourage entrepreneurship as a means of overcoming unemployment must acknowledge this.

At the same time, a second problem has become very apparent recently. This industry and the firms in it are highly mobile internationally. This is of particular significance in Scotland. The "internationalisation" of Scottish industry is now recognised as a significant factor in the current economic situation of Scotland. In recent months the potential problems of this have become increasingly apparent.

Stimulating the formation of locally owned service orientated business has been put forward as a possible response to these difficulties. However, the growth of new very small firms may worsen the international competitiveness of Scottish industry. There have been some suggestions that Scotland is already experiencing a serious non-oil balance of payments deficit. An accurate picture of the situation may prove impossible to establish, in part because of the export goods of Scottish origin through English ports. However, there is sufficient evidence to suggest that stimulating the formation of large numbers of internationally uncompetitive firms will do little to resolve the long-term problems of the Scottish economy.

International Competitiveness and the Small Firm

Britain has long depended on international competitiveness for its economic prosperity. Scotland has played a vital part in this. It is now estimated that 30 per cent of Britain's manufacturing output is exported. Although the small firms sector makes a significant contribution to this, there is a great deal of evidence that this falls short of the sector's share of the GNP. Small firms generally export a lower proportion of their output than large companies. Any increase in the importance of the small firm sector must be matched by a parallel movement towards greater small firm exports if the UK is to retain or improve its trading position.

Small firms have strengths and weaknesses in winning overseas trade. Their flexibility, short lines of communication, speed of decision-making and creativity are major assets. At the same time, resource shortages can be a major disadvantage in a resource intensive area such as exporting.

In overcoming the problems posed by this dilemma, it may be necessary to adopt solutions. In Japan the General Trading Houses provide a framework of support unmatched in Britain at present. Adapting this approach may provide a useful contribution to sustaining and improving small firm exports. Procedures exist for this.

In the last century export trading houses such as Jardine's played an important part in building Britain's overseas trade. In many ways these provided the model for the Trading Houses (Zaibatsu) in the late 19th century and early 20th century. Export Houses continue to play a part in overseas trade but to a far smaller extent than in Japan.

The Japanese General Trading Houses provide a vast array of services for the prospective exporter. These range from direct selling, marketing research through to technical and financial assistance. The integration of the financial systems with the trading sector provides a powerful basis for export trade development. The domestic trading activities of the Trading Houses are an asset in certain circumstances for smaller firms. This reduces the number of trading relations which the small firm manager needs to accommodate.

The success of Japanese exports has prompted parallel initiatives elsewhere. The New York – New Jersey Port Authority has established a Trading House based on the Japanese model. More recently, General Electric Industries in the USA have set up a similar initiative. These private sector projects may provide a model capable of being exploited in Scotland.

Scotland is well placed to explore the scope for such a scheme. The strong financial community has valuable international links. The domestic retail sector already trades extensively overseas; importing and exporting is a substantial part of their business. A number of manufacturers have compatible strength. A private sector consortium, perhaps supported by the public sector, may provide the context for a substantial development. In New York, the Trading House is based in the World Trade Centre. Locating a Scottish Trading House in the new Glasgow Exhibition Centre would provide mutual benefits. These would be greatly enhanced if the Exhibition Centre was a World Trade Centre.

A wider Context

The discussion of Trading Houses illustrates a neglected area of discussion in small firms. Much of this has focused on the role and influence of the Public sector. It is suggested here that the nature of the Private sector, particularly trading relationships, are at least as important; the retail sector.

Britain has a successful, efficient and highly concentrated retail sector. The scale of operations required to trade effectively with large retail operations places considerable pressures on small businesses. A more fragmented retail sector might provide the diversity of opportunity required by a dynamic and changing small firm sector. This is a particular problem for new starters. In a highly concentrated retail market it is both difficult to penetrate key accounts and hard to source when successfull. The scale of operations needed in such sectors as: clothing, foot-wear and food is beyond most small firms. There is an urgent need for more research into the impact of trading structures on: new enterprise formation, performance of existing firms and survival.

Support Services

The Scottish Development Agency and the Highlands and Islands Development Board perform a diverse array of roles in supporting the development of enterprise. Besides providing an "umbrella" for other organisations they provide a wide array of financial and direct support services in a variety of situations. Two recent initiatives provide some insight into the potential contribution of these agencies. The Scottish Development Agency's programme of concentrated initiatives in relatively limited areas is designed to inject sufficient resources to break the cycle of decline being experienced in these localities. Already there are signs of the benefits of this approach. In the Highlands, the HIDB's sponsorship of community co-operative developments is an attempt to combine the resources of the Board with local funds and commitment. This is indicating the value of these mutually supportive relationships.

Recent years have seen an important new factor introduced into the array of support services. Scottish Business in the Community is prompting the start of a number of Enterprise Trusts. These seek to support the entrepreneurial spirit through a strategic combination of private and public sector resources. The pace of this development illustrates the continuing power of the move to prompt enterprise in Scotland.

The Scottish Enterprise Foundation has concentrated its efforts on shaping the environment for small business development through the creation of a supportive culture primarily within the education sector. The Graduate Enterprise initiative illustrates this.

Industry and the Universities

The increasing economic importance of knowledge based industries in both manufacturing and services has increased the interest of policy makers in the potential sources of these technologies or areas of interest. This has led to considerable interest in the dissemination, development and application of university research. This has taken a number of forms. Among these the "Science Park" phenomenon has probably stimulated the greatest attention.

Although, in practice, the Science Parks vary considerably in form and character, they have some features in common. The most important of these lie in the attempt to provide high amenity facilities near universities giving elite industry firms the opportunity to develop while continuing to capitalise on their university links.

These emerged originally in the United States. The oldest is the "Stanford Industrial Park", Pato Valley, California, and includes such key firms as Hewlett-Packard and Varian Associates. Equally well known are the similar developments in the North Eastern USA often associated with Massachussets Institute of Technologies. Through these schemes, "elite industry" firms have been created. A vital element in their success has been the role of the "academic entrepreneur" and the "graduate entrepreneur". These are individuals who have applied the scientific, engineering and management knowledge developed in the universities to new company formation. In the United Kingdom over the last few years:

> There has been a rush of announcements about the inauguration of such Parks. Universities such as Warwick, Keele, Surrey, Swansea and Southampton are following in the footsteps of Heriot-Watt in Edinburgh and Trinity College, Cambridge.[7]

Graduate Enterprise

Each year over 10,000 students graduate from Scotland's eight universities. The data which exists indicates that very few consider starting their own business as a significant career alternative. This contrasts with North America where it has been suggested that almost ten per cent of graduates take serious steps towards starting their own business within ten years of graduating.

The "Graduate Enterprise" project was launched to:

Stimulate an interest in enterprise,
Provide support during the initial development period,
Supply advice and assistance,
Identify the best start up prospects,
Assist start ups during their initial development period,

among graduating students, with an overall goal of providing a framework for the development of potential elite industry firms.

Initially it was felt that the most likely participants would be postgraduate or mature students. It was estimated that almost 15 per cent of all graduating students fell into this category. At the same time it was believed that any major initiative would require tangible benefits albeit for a few successful participants. Despite this, establishing an awareness among students of the scope for entrepreneurial development was an high priority.

The programme was divided into two distinct phases:

Phase one: The Search. This involves a planned and integrated attempt to encourage and assist graduating students to formulate their business ideas and put them into a structured business plan.

Phase two: The Programme. This involves taking a small number of the "best" prospects on to a specially designed and developed training programme of the Development and Support type.

The search poses many of the greatest organisational challenges. It involves bringing together eight wholly autonomous universities, many with traditions of independence going back many centuries. At the same time data on graduate career choices indicated that most entered either the Professions or the Public Sector. A number of steps were taken to overcome the problems these challenges posed.

The first was to establish a strong private sector involvement. A number of major corporations were approached for support. This took two forms: finance and advice. Among the firms providing assistance were Ivory and Sime Limited and Associated Trusts, Coats-Patons, ICFC, IBM United Kingdom Limited and Arthur Young Mc-Clelland Moores & Co. (AYMM). Their financial support enabled the universities to make specific provision for "Enterprise Counsellors" in each university. AYMM provided a secondee to co-ordinate the project. In the event, this latter role has proved to be critical to success.

Once a structure was established all eight universities agreed to take part. The next step in the search was a one day conference in each university. All graduating students were invited personally, by letter, to the conference, which consisted of three distinct phases:

A THE ENTREPRENEURIAL INSIGHT
B THE SUPPORT SERVICES
C THE KEY ISSUES.

Initially it was forecast that about 500 students would take part at this stage. In the event 1 009 students took up the opportunity to become involved.

The composition of these groups was monitored carefully. Although there is inevitably considerable variation between institutions, some patterns emerged. Post-graduate and mature students were disproportionately represented as was expected. There was a surprisingly high level of participation by science and engineering students, estimated at 50–60 per cent. Women were represented in proportion to their numbers in the university population. Early indications were that potential "elite industry" involvement would be high.

Following the conferences, each enterprise counsellor set aside one day per week for personal assistance to prospective entrepreneurs. This was designed to help the participants in developing their business plans. It had been estimated that no more than eight or ten potential entrepreneurs per university would take part at this stage. In fact an average of twenty students per university took advantage of this opportunity.

The next stage in the search involves the selection of up to forty projects for the programme. It was anticipated that these would be drawn from approximately sixty proposals. The actual number of proposals already submitted is 130. A significant proportion of these relate to elite industries.

Once the full list of proposals have been submitted local panels of businessmen and academics will select a number for final consideration by a National Panel, which will be looking for a maximum of forty to go to the next stage.

The Programme

This consists of six distinct stages:
- *Pre-programme preparation,*
- *A Foundation Programme,*
- *Field work,*
- *Long weekend,*
- *Field work,*
- *Long weekend.*

Pre-programme Preparation

This is a specific, company based placement designed to give each participant the chance to get a real world view of the small firm.

Foundation Programme

This is designed to give each graduate entrepreneur a secure base in terms of *knowledge, skills* and *personal development* on which he can build his future work. This will include formal training, personal tuition, project work and work on his business plan.

Field Work

This provides the potential entrepreneurs with the opportunity to work on setting up their business. They will be able to turn to programme tutors for advise and assistance.

Weekends

This will give participants a chance to review their progress while getting specific advice and assistance. A special emphasis of this period would be placed on formalising their final business plan.

The Implications

The achievements of this initiative illustrates the potential impact of targeted and networked initiatives. The target group in this instance were graduating students whose attitudes and skills made them responsive to the notion of enterprise. The network consisted of participants from within the system, educationalists and supporters from outwith education, public agencies and private firms. It is too early to provide a conclusive statement of achievements. However it has:

1. Generated considerable interest and participation among the key target group.

2. Provided a supportive environment for potential entrepeneurs.

3. Stimulated a significant number of start ups.
4. Created a support model which is generalisable.

The nature of the start ups has not been a clearly "elite industry" as orgininally hoped.

Nature of Business

		No.	Per cent
Manufacturing	Elite	12	13
	Traditional	11	12
Services	Elite	28	24
	Traditional	32	33
Other	Elite	5	6
	Traditional	11	12
Totales		94	100

However these are the short term results of an initiative which is necessarily a long development.

In other areas of development a similar model based on specific targeting has obtained more spectacular short term results. The EXPORTS Programme of the Foundation is designed to reach existing firms currently adopting a passive approach to export market development. It draws together university, private and public sector agencies. It consists of three stages:
1. Search and Selection of suitable firms,
2. Action based training,
3. Overseas Workshop.

During recent years, over 200 firms have participated with an average increase in direct exports of 300 per cent. Similar initiatives in other areas have generated equally spectacular results.

These programmes highlight the importance of recognising that the small firm community is not the homogenous group that much of the literature describes. The diversity and scale of this sector needs to be recognised in development programmes. At the same time the dynamic nature of the individual enterprises requires that support is on-going and changing. The combination of these factors with the size of the category of enterprise calls for either a massive increase in the provision of support or more effective use of existing resources. The experience of the Scottish Enterprise Foundation suggests that in the current economic environment the former is very unlikely even if desirable. It is suggested meaningful long term progress calls for more effective networking of existing resources. There are institutional and attitudinal barriers to this. Despite this, this route offers perhaps the best prospect of effectively mobilising indigenous resources to ensure that Scotland emerges from the current recession on an upward trend in economic development.

NOTES

[1] Payne, P. L., "The Early Scottish Limited Companies 1856–1895; An Historical and Analytic Survey", Scottish Academic Press.

[2] Bell, P., "Trends in Scottish Industry", in Hood, N., and Young, S., "Industry, Policy and the Scottish Economy", Edinburgh University Press, 1984.

[3] Hamilton, R., "New Business Formation: Theory, Evidence and Policy", Stirling Economics Teaching Paper no. 10, August 1982.

[4] Bannock, G., "The Economics of Small Firms", Oxford, Basil Blackwood, 1981.

[5] Schumpeter, J., "The Instability of Capitalism", in N. Rosenberg (ed.), The Economics of Technical Change, London, Penguin Books, 1928.

[6] Leibenstein, H., "Entrepreneurship and Development", American Economic Review. Papers and Proceedings, Volume 58, 1968, p. 74.

[7] Financial Times, Special Report, 21st January 1983.

The Envisaged Revised Industrial Development Strategie of South Africa

Nicolaas van der Walt

Introduction

Although South Africa may be regarded to be a developed country it is probably more correct to define the country as one which has a dual economy with a semi-developed industrial sector. It is a *dual* economy because of the relative importance of existing traditional economies which are mainly situated in the rural regions of the country. It is semi-developed as far as the industrial sector is concerned, mainly because the developed sector is not capable of meeting its own investment demands in order to reach a level of selfsustained growth. Surplus income from the primary sectors as well as investments from abroad are still very important determinants for the overall development of the country. Due to the importance of gold in South Africa the production structure is relatively undiversified. This implies that the developments in the single-product market have an overwhelming effect on what is happening in the rest of the economy.

At present duality in South Africa is experienced through extraordinary pressures from the traditional sectors which are to be absorbed into the developed sector of the economy. These pressures are intensified by a relatively high population growth which is, in certain cases, as high as 2.7 per cent per annum, whilst the primary sectors as such have reached their maximum levels of production and growth. Seen against this background the intensified development of industry is a major priority and an industrial development strategy is therefore a matter of necessity. However, the question is how to develop a strategy in a country which believes the free market economy to be the best of economic systems.

In order to answer this question as far as South Africa is concerned, this contribution will start off by devoting attention to the free market economy as it operates in this country. Naturally it is impossible to discuss this matter in great detail, and attention will be given only to those factors which are directly related to industrial development. Secondly, the structural problems of the country on both the supply and demand sides will be identified. Furthermore the envisaged industrial development strategy for South Africa will be discussed with particular reference to policies which are intended to reduce the effects of the existing structural distortions. Finally, the proposed industrial development strategy will be evaluated.

Role of Market Mechanism and Economic Order

Economic development creates socio-economic instabilities in order to transform societies to higher levels of socio-economic wealth. This process is not without social costs and hardships. However in South Africa the basic point of departure as far as industrialization is concerned is that the free market mechanism must be used as far as possible to solve the problems of development. In this profits and prices are the main indicators of the direction of development, and the success of this approach depends on a system of effective competition.

When creating a system of effective competition it should be borne in mind that the developed sector of the economy is still relatively small and that monopolies and oligopolies are more readily created than is normally the case. This imbalance demands a rather strong policy of effective competition, with the following three aims, namely:

— the combating of structural distortions in the market place itself, i.e. limiting rules and regulations which are detrimental to the effective operation of the market place. Naturally this is easier said then done, especially at the lower levels of government. As is the case everywhere in the world, rules and regulations ultimately form the power base of governments and officialdom, and they do not give these up willingly;

— taking action against those factors which tend to increase structural distortions in the market place via unnecessary and detrimental concentrations due to takeovers and amalgations; and

— limiting government participation in the production sector of the economy.

The free market system is the sole navigator of the country's economic destination. However, sometimes the route is unfortunate and unstable, and in the last instance the South African government finally intervenes in the market place in order to ensure some form of structural stability in the industrial development of the country. The question is how? Should the development strategy be one of balanced versus unbalanced growth? If imbalances are to be created where should these be? Could a situation of balanced growth finally be achieved?

Without going too deeply into the theory of balanced versus unbalanced growth the following points may be made: the original exponents of the balanced growth doctrine ask for large-scale investments to overcome indivisibilities on both the demand and supply side of the development process.[1] On the supply side these indivisibilities refer to the lumpishness of capital (especially social overhead capital) and the fact that simultaneous investment in a large number of activities can take advantage of various external economies of scale. On the demand side reference is made to the limitations imposed by the size of the market on the profitability, and hence feasibility, of economic activities.

South Africa is not capable of following the approach of balanced growth. Though large-scale investments are recognised as an important determinant for industrial development, there is simply a shortage of other resources such as skilled manpower, entrepreneurs, and decision-makers, and more important, "decision-makers who are not just able to make decisions, but who are also able to put their decisions in a feasible form into practice". South Africa is also not capable of following a "development process via excess capacity" simply because in the past this approach led to the non-optimal allocation of scarce resources. A unique example of this may be the teaching profession in South Africa where the price mechanism is not fully allowed to establish the remuneration for different teaching professions in the country. As a result there is a shortage of scientists and engineers whilst historians, for example, are in abundance.

As in the case of price mechanism, industrial development in South Africa seems to follow the Hirschman argument of "succesive adaption" with the system itself, through the market mechanism, pointing out developing shortages and bottlenecks.[2] However, the timeous identification of structural shortages and bottlenecks creates a serious problem as far as the stable development of industry and the economy as a whole is concerned. As is the case with fiscal policies and the stabilization of the business cycle, there are also lags concerning identification, decisionmaking, and the introduction of precautionary measures. In order to identify these structural shortages and bottlenecks in time South Africa has devised an economic development programme which keeps government and industry informed on the economic development of the country. A series of structural econometric models is used, and to a certain extent these make it possible to identify shortages and bottlenecks in the medium and long term. An indicative approach is followed, meaning that no corrective measures are enforced directly but that the market mechanism is influenced indirectly to produce the required results.

Envisaged Revised Development Strategy

If a free market approach to development is pursued and if it is accepted that the development path will not be stable or that development of industry may move in the wrong directions from time to time it is only necessary to simulate the development process for occurring bottlenecks and shortages in an effort to develop a strategy for industrial development. This can only be achieved through a intimate interaction between sections of the private sector and government, sometimes over extended periods of time. This also implies that a total strategy is not developed instantly on the drawing board of some central office but that the strategy comes together through various sub-strategies generated from the offices of those who are responsible for the development of industry. In the end someone has to co-ordinate these sub-strategies into a total strategy as well as evaluate it in order to avoid duplication of conflict situations which may arise.

Against this background it may justifiably be argued that the development strategy in South Africa goes back to the 1920s and has developed over the years to something formidable, although "blueprints" in the autocratic sense of the word do not exist. Clearly the most important aspects of this strategy at present are the existing bottlenecks and shortages for which sub-strategies have been developed. It will not be possible to discuss each of these sub-strategies in detail. Only the most important will be discussed briefly for the purposes of illustration.

Seen against the background of the pressures applied to industry due to the absorbtion of traditional people into the modern sector, it becomes clear that the industrial development strategy of South Africa differs from that of modern industrial powers such as the USA or West Germany. The development strategy of South Africa can therefore, for the sake of convenience, be divided into two separate parts. The *first* consists of those strategies which are directly related to the absorbtion process of traditional economies and corresponding production technologies which have to be enforced, and the *second* consists of those which are more concerned with the development of the modern industrial sector. As far as the traditional sector is concerned there are mainly two sub-strategies, namely:

1. small business and informal sector development strategy which is aimed at those formal and informal businesses which do not normally qualify for the services of banks and other financial institutions;

2. a manpower strategy which is aimed at
   - eliminating the shortage of skilled manpower through continued immigration of skilled labour from countries where are surplusses. Immigration of this nature was recently revised so as not to be curbed during periods of recession in South Africa;
   - increasingly educating the illiterates in the country to a level at which they are trainable for specific jobs. Particular importance is attached to technical, occupational, and non-formal education. As training is an endogenous variable in the production process, education of this nature is undertaken by the private sector in close co-operation with the government which subsidises this form of education and training;
   - introducing various measures to promote and maintain peaceful labour relations and to ensure the mental and physical well-being of the work force;
   - retraining those who are unemployed by means of an Unemployment Insurance Fund during recession;
   - negotiating agreements among participants in the labour market concerning shortened working hours or introducing job sharing rather than retrenchment;
   - rechanneling government funds to create or maintain more jobs during periods of recession.

The industrial development strategy for the modern sector can again be divided into several sub-strategies of which the following are singled out as the most important:

strategy concerning technology, in which the aims are:
- to adapt modern technology to the capabilities of the South African labour force, i.e. the use of more labour-intensive techniques in such a way that commodity exchange rates favour the South African production activities;
- the substitution of domestic technologies for imported technologies and;
- effective incentives created by government for the private sector to develop new technologies or to replace imported technologies, and to sponsor technological research to the highest degree possible;

strategy concerning demand factors as far as internal industrial development is concerned; namely that:
- the process of import substitution should cover a wide range of raw materials, capital goods, and strategic products; and
- the level of exports should be increased mainly because of the decreasing contribution of import substitution to economic growth.

The strategy regarding the demand factors calls for a more prominent combination of import substitution and export development. This combination is effected for various reasons of which internal structural development of industry and the external earnings of capital for the overall development of the South African economy are the most important. In certain instances these two aims are in direct conflict which will be pointed out at a later stage.

strategy concerning the spatial development of industry which is aimed at the regional deconcentration of industrial activities in order to
- prevent the depopulation of rural regions and unnecessary urbanization of mainly unskilled people, thereby causing urban unemployment; and
- ensure that the traditional peoples, who reside mainly in the rural regions of the country, also develop industrially.

This is done by indirect control over the existing metropoles in South Africa through the elimination of subsidies which were paid for transport, water, and electricity in the past. Programmes to introduce a differentiated tax system, in which the cost of developing infrastructures in these metropoles will be borne by the metropoles themselves are also underway. This is done to achieve a more market-related cost structure as far as the location of industry between the existing metropoles and rural regions are concerned.

strategy concerning international regional development in Southern Africa which is aimed at:

- the acceptance of free international trade, though many of the countries with which South Africa trades and which also subscribe to this principle deliberately act in a directly, opposed manner either by forming trading blocks from which South Africa is excluded or by boycotts, which is of course a political matter;
- developing Southern Africa in its entirety and not South Africa as sub-element of a region. This policy led to the Nkomati Accord with Maputu which is of tremendous importance, not just for industry in Mozambique but also for South Africa;
- co-ordinating South Africa's own development policies with those of her neighbours by means of timely consultations in order to achieve the optimal development of the region.

The interdependence of the Southern African economies is accepted as a fait accompli due to market-related forces and much is being done to improve this structural relationship within the reasonable limits of the economic and political aspirations of the countries concerned.

Evaluating of Industrial Development Strategy

The industrial development policy of South Africa is best evaluated against the background of the historical development of the free market concept in South Africa. Possibly the greatest achievement of the recent South African past is the survival of the free market in an society which was, in 1948 for example, in the position (and which at that time needed) to change the system into a socialist or centrally planned economy. At present there is a growing feeling that even more should be done to move to an even freer economy. This is mainly due to the realisation that the development mistakes of the past originated from the fact that the importance of the market and its forces was not recognised; all the signs for optimal development were not identified in time, nor were the appropriate corrective measures and actions taken.

The revival of the free market principle in South Africa also led to the belief that past industrial development strategies were inadequate and that the strategy should be changed to suit the present South African needs. As a result of this the Kleu Report was released indicating some of the main factors of a revised industrial development strategy.[3]

The indications given by the Kleu Report were largely based on the development of industry to achieve the macro-economic aims of the creation of long term full employment, the structural development of a stable balance of payments, long term income creation, as well as an increase in productivity in the most general terms, whilst relative price stability in the structural sense of the word was left to the monetary authorities. Together with these indications the report was also concerned with where industrial development in a regional sense should take place. This was mainly due to the pressures brought about by the expected increase in urbanization.

Only the backward linkage effects of industry were taken into account to calculate the relative income, import, capital and labour intensities of the different industrial sectors. The same procedure was followed in establishing the potential of the different industrial sectors for earning foreign capital. The forward linkage effects were not identified and as a result the internal structure of industry was not explicitly acknowledged. The indications, therefore, were not clear as to how the internal structure of industry should be developed.

Because the aim of relative price stability was left to the control of monetary authorities the effects of price changes were not explicitly analyzed and therefore there were no indications of the internal and external competitiveness of industry. This information is a prerequisite for the development of an internal and an external development strategy involving industry. However, indications were that exports would play a prominent part in the future development of industry. The internal structure did not receive the same attention.

This approach to a development strategy in South Africa must be seen against the backdrop of the particular phase of industrial development. The industrial structure is still not fully developed and until recently there was still a vast amount of empty cells to be filled in terms of the input-output table of the country. In the past these cells were mostly filled by means of import substitution which did not depend on the internal structure of industry as such but on the relative feasibility of substitution projects with regard to the market. As a result the internal structure developed by chance, more specifically at those points where domestically produced final consumption goods were substituted for imports.

As was pointed out earlier, South Africa has reached the stage where these substitution opportunities are exploited so that many of the still existing empty interindustry cells are related to the production of certain intermediate and capital goods. This is of course a more difficult stage of import substitution and it is more directly related to the internal structure of industry. However, how these cells will be filled still depends on the relative feasibility of substitution projects in the domestic market. On the export side, exports originated mainly from existing industrial structures, and the exploitation of interindustry cells in this regard again depends on the relative competitiveness of production output in the international market, leaving the exploitation process at random. In the final analysis the development of the internal structure of industry must be seen as an endogenous factor which depends on the market opportunities for import substitution and exports.

At this point the South African experience tends to question the Hirschman approach to the internal development of industry which calls for the stimulation of those sectors which have the most extensive backward and forward linkages.[4] This is particularly true of import substitution. However, when taking the different phases of import substitution into consideration it appears that it is only natural that in a free market system those industries with the most extensive backward linkages will be stimulated in the first phase of import substitution, i.e. the substitution of final consumer goods. The second phase of import substitution, which is mainly concerned with intermediate and capital goods, also concentrates on industries with relatively extensive forward linkages. The South African experience therefore differs from but does not totally reject the Hirschman theory of industrial development. The policy of creating definite structural imbalances by stimulating the demand of a few industrial sectors is a powerful source of inflationary pressure, with cost and price increases eminating from the bottleneck sectors and spreading throughout the economy. There is increasing evidence that the so-called Latin American debate on inflation may also be valid for South Africa. The structural inflation rate of approximately 10 to 12 per cent per annum since the beginning of the seventies is relatively low in comparison with that of the countries in Latin America. This is mainly due to the partly successful monetary policies which were followed during the last fifteen years. However, the average growth rate of the South African economy has also decreased significantly during the past decade and it is an open question to what extent the decreasing rate of growth is attributable to the monetary authorities' efforts to keep the inflation rate as low as possible. Against this background there are two questions which are still waiting to be answered in South Africa, namely:

— What is the highest level of structural inflation which can be accepted before this type of inflation becomes detrimental to economic growth?
— How should the approach of unbalanced growth to industry be rectified to keep structural inflation as low as possible?

The answer to the first is a matter of empirical research. The second calls for the balanced growth version of the linkage model which was used to identify certain industrial sectors for increased development, i.e. every linkage of the identified sector must be developed in a balanced way so that supply meets demand.

In order to achieve the balanced growth version of the linkage model, experience in South Africa has shown that there are two prerequisites for this type of industrial development strategy to be put into operation. The *first* calls for an integrated organization consisting of all sectors of government and the private sector which are responsible for identifying shortages and bottlenecks among the linkages, if an approach of "development via shortages" in certain industrial sectors is followed. *Secondly* this structure has to be built from the "bottom upwards" i.e. the structure has to be founded in the market place itself where these shortages and bottlenecks occur.

In addition to the above-mentioned prerequisites, an industrial development strategy which is based in the market also calls for the most dynamic revisions of the rules of the game. Rules and regulations which are necessary for the development of industry today may be obsolete tomorrow. The problem, however, is that when the rules of the game are institutionalised through central government these become rigid and politicized and in the end hamper rather than help the development process. This is mainly because of the power base these rules and regulations afford to government officials. As far as South Africa is concerned, the country still has a long way to go, and many of her industrial development problems can be attributed to the rigidity towards the rules of the game as far as the market system is concerned. A solution to this may be a greater decentralization of institutional powers.

Conclusion

A this point it is clear that an industrial development strategy in a free market system cannot be developed instantly. This is mainly due to need for the identification of bottlenecks and shortages if the Hirschman approach to industrial development is followed. The development process is also a process of such a dynamic nature that the existing development strategies are always due for revision. The success, however, depends on the success of the identification processes, as well as the steps taken to rectify developments which are not beneficial to the overall economic growth of a country. This also applies to South Africa, and the present revision of her industrial development strategy is being carried out mainly because of bottlenecks which developed recently due to the absorbtion of traditional economies into the modern sector of South Africa and the semi-developed state of the modern industrial sector.

NOTES

[1] Thirlwall, Growth and Development, p. 177.
[2] Hirschman, Strategy of Economic Development.
[3] Kleu, Summery of Report of Study Group on Industrial Development.
[4] Yotopoulos, et. al., Economics of Development: Empirical investigations, pp. 229 – 306.

BIBLIOGRAPHY

Hirschman, A. D., *The Strategy of Economic Development,* New Haven, Yale University Press, 1958.

Kleu, B., *Summary of Report of the Study Group on Development Strategy,* Government Printers, Pretoria, South Africa, February 1983.

Lewis, W. A., *Economic Development with Unlimited Supplies of Labour,* Manchester School of Economic and Social Studies, May 1954.

Thirlwall, A. P., *Growth and Development with Special Reference to Developing Economics,* The Macmillan Press Ltd., Unwin Brothers Ltd., Great Britain, 1978.

Yotopoulos, P. A., and Nugent, J. B., *Economics of Development; Empirical Investigations,* Harper and Row Publishers, New York, USA, 1976.

The Meaning and Validity of a U.S. Industrial Policy

Siegfried G. Karsten

A consciously-oriented broad industrial policy for the United States has both "meaning" and "validity" in that it would address itself to actual socio-economic concerns or issues and could be implemented. A narrowly structured industrial policy, especially one that would involve central planning or direction of the economy, is not in the cards. In a mature industrial society, the focal question centers not only on efficiency and productivity but also on human values, especially the rights for freedom, for a productive and creative life, and for a life in dignity. The basic question no longer is whether the United States should have an industrial policy; it already has one. The question is what kind of an industrial policy the United States should actively pursue in order to strengthen the market system and to maximize social welfare as effectively as possible.

I.

Alfred Marshall opened his *Principles* with *"political economy or economics* is a study of mankind in the ordinary business of life"[1]. That is, any economic analysis has to start with "what is" at the time and place in question and not necessarily according to some formulated paradigms or theories. It is the economic structure of a society which determines how economic and social challenges are resolved.[2] However, no socio-economic structure is permanent; it needs to adapt itself to changing circumstances and requirements. Popper and Dahrendorf are essentially of the same opinion.[3]

This brings us to the question of how economic theories or policies should be evaluated. The best criteria which are available for this task are the ones which Leo Rogin formulated. He postulated that economic theories or policies need to be relevant to the socio-economic order in which they are applied, i.e., as a reflection of events current at the time in question. He recommended, therefore, that theories and policies be analyzed in terms of their "meaning" and "validity", according to their relevance to socio-economic issues or challenges as strategic factors, and their potential for implementation.[4]

It is commonly held that an enterprising market system achieves productivity gains and economic growth through inventions and innovations, i.e., through new technology, new methods, and new products. However, economic growth per se neither is sufficient nor does it alone bestow strength and vitality on an economy. A dynamic society, no matter at what stage of its development, grows through continuous experimentation. It is experimentation not only with regard to new products and new ways of producing things, but, most importantly, experimentation with regard to new socio-economic and institutional processes.

One result of such experimentation was the paradigm of a social market economy. The latter, in essence, is defined as a "functional" market economy, which is responsive to those challenges for which the existing market mechanism does not provide satisfactory answers.[5] Walter Eucken, influenced by his associates at the Freiburg School, especially Franz Böhm, Müller-Armack, Erich Preiser, and Wilhelm Röpke, developed the conceptual framework of a social market economy. It aided Ludwig Erhard to materialize his ideas and plans for West Germany's economic recovery and post World War II socio-economic system.[6]

Eucken's central thesis is that the evolution of a functional market economy, as the guarantor of freedom, human dignity, and justice, cannot be left to chance but must be *consciously guided*. Contemporary institutional arrangements, e.g., monopoly powers exercised by business, industry, and labor, and the way fiscal and monetary policies are influenced by special interest groups, interfere with the market to effectively resolve questions of unemployment, inflation, and economic growth. Therefore, there is no assurance that prices continue to function as efficient allocation and rationing devices, leading to increasingly greater intervention by the state in socio-economic processes. Other issues such as the environment, poverty, and an inequitable distribution of income, are beyond the reach of the market. However, the desire for economic security, for a life in dignity, for protection from economic calamity which is beyond the individual's control, is universal.

Eucken's paradigm prescribed a "functional" market economy, the guiding framework of which he defined in terms of eight "structural" and five "regulating" principles, based on concepts of freedom, liberty, and social justice.[7] He advocated the position that contemporary society demands a "right order" in economic relationships, in the interrelationships between capital, labor, and government. This was to be achieved through:

1. The primacy of a neutral monetary policy – to stabilize the value of money as a necessary condition for a functionally competitive economy.
2. Open competitive markets, both domestically and internationally.
3. Stable and predictable economic policies which are essential for long-term decisions.

    (The preceding three are part of his "structural" principles, the following ones are formulated under his "regulating" principles.)

4. The establishment of a monetary numeraire to depoliticize and to stabilize monetary policy.
5. Reduction and control of monopoly power.
6. A functional price mechanism which reflects both internal and external costs.
7. An incomes policy.

8. An integrated countercyclical policy approach which reflects the interrelatedness of all socio-economic problems, e.g., unemployment, inflation, growth, investment, poverty, the environment, etc. And, by inference,

9. An industrial policy could be added to the above list.

This new "order", which is to combine the advantages of competition with concerns for justice and equity, is to facilitate solutions to socio-economic challenges which are economically and ethically justifiable and which enhance man's opportunities for a "productive" life.

II.

Although the socio-economic system of the United States cannot strictly be classified as a "social market economy", it is inching closer to that paradigm. For one, the Preamble of the Constitution states: "We the People of the United States, in order to form a more perfect Union, establish Justice, insure domestic Tranquility, provide for the common defence, promote the general Welfare and secure the Blessings of Liberty to ourselves and our Posterity, do ordain and establish this Constitution for the United States."

What is meant by domestic tranquility, social and economic justice, and by general welfare? It appears that these concepts, which essentially define the fundamental premise of the paradigm of a social market economy, form the "imaginary" battleground between the so-called conservatives and liberals or between monetarists and Keynesians.

The premises of social and economic justice, however defined, that each citizen should be able to lead a "productive" life, that inflation, unemployment, an unsatisfactory rate of growth, poverty, and a polluted environment, to mention some, are undesirable, are commonly accepted in the U.S. Where the disagreement arises is how to solve these problems. Many of these objectives are explicitly expressed in the Employment Act of 1946, the Humphrey-Hawkins Act of 1978, and in the platforms of the political parties. The consensus is that a healthy and dynamic free enterprise economy needs to be supported by an efficient and human public sector, the two being complementary to each other.

Traditional approaches have relied largely on the manipulation of monetarist and Keynesian-type policies to increase the level of output, partly by increasing the productivity of labor, and thus raising the level of employment and incomes, while at the same time attempting to maintain price stability — an almost Herculean task.

What does the record show for the post World War II period? There appears to be no fundamental difference with regard to the results of fiscal and monetary policy changes, regardless of which administration had occupied the White House. Both the Democratic and the Republican parties (with the possible exception of the years of the Eisenhower administration) have presided over worsening rates of unemployment, rising rates of inflation during the 1960s and 1970s, increasing rates of growth in the money supply, and rising shares of federal spending as a percentage of GNP. For example, the average inflation rate rose from 2.1 per cent during 1949/52 to 9.7 per cent for 1977/80. The unemployment rate increased from an average of 4.4 per cent in 1949/50 to 8.5 per cent during 1981/84. Federal spending as a per cent of the GNP rose from 2.7 per cent to almost 25 per cent with the federal budget surplus falling from an average rate of 0.8 per cent of GNP to about −5.0 per cent of GNP by 1984 and getting worse. At the same time, the rate of growth in the money supply has been increasing from an average annual rate of 2.7 per cent in 1949/52 to almost 7 per cent by 1981/84.[8]

Major changes in the American society are under way. For example, the so-called middle class is shrinking in size. Whereas in 1970 53.4 per cent of families enjoyed incomes between $15,000 and $35,000, only 43.9 per cent did so by 1982.[9] Well-paying blue-collar jobs are being replaced by lower-paid service jobs. A recent report, prepared by the "Physician Task Force on Hunger in America", called attention to the fact that "hunger is more widespread and serious than at any time in the last 10 to 15 years."[10] It labeled it a "national health epidemic" which affects 20 million Americans, young and old alike, calling for increased spending on food programs for children and the elderly.

The U.S. Census Bureau published information which revealed that the poverty rate reached 19 per cent in 1984, compared to 11.1 and 15.2 per cent in 1973 and 1983, respectively. 66 million Americans or nearly 30 per cent of the non-farm population benefits from direct government assistance in one form or another. Or, about 20 per cent of the population receives some aid based on low income levels.[11]

Problems are intensifying in other areas of the economy as well. The number of bank failures is sharply up. For example, for the years 1979, 1980, and 1981, 10 banks failed each year, with significantly fewer failures prior to 1979. Bank failures dramatically increased from 10 in 1981 to 42 in 1982, 48 in 1983, and 70 in 1984. The number of business and farm failures also have reached their highest levels since the Great Depression.

These unwanted developments in the economy contributed greatly to the publication of the first draft of the American Catholic Bishops' Letter on the U.S. economy,[12] which caused considerable public controversy. In this pastoral letter the Catholic Bishops, in essence, reemphasized some of the tenets of a social market economy, i.e., of a "functional" market economy. They stressed that the relevant yardstick for economic life and policies is to be found in the dignity of the people. That is, a socio-economic system must be structured in such a way that enables man to find employment which would permit him to express initiative and creativity in his work. But which also provides him with a sufficient income to meet his daily needs and which facilitates the development of his potentials.

Among other measures the letter calls for an incomes policy to lessen the inequality in the distribution of income and wealth. In the narrower sense, the Bishops' Letter suggests the broadening of the income base for the general population. The self-interest of every segment of the population and the economy would be served by this approach. In other words, the better off people are in general, the more prosperous every individual and business is going to be. What the Bishops are saying is that the pursuit of greater economic justice and equity also creates new wealth. The suggested reform proposals do not advocate the abolition of capitalism or of a free enterprise economy, but their transformation into "capitalism with a conscience" and a "functional" market economy.

The fundamental questions that need to be asked are, therefore, how well does our socio-economic system provide access to humanizing work and how well does the system care for those who cannot work?

III.

As the previous section pointed out, serious socio-economic challenges need to be resolved in the United States. Current trends in public opinion and in the political processes discourage solutions which mandate increases in social spending and taxes. Presently, Keynesian-type policies to solve socio-economic problems are neither socially nor politically acceptable. The long-term solution, therefore, is to be found in policies which will strengthen the productive potential of the American economy. This avenue, in the form of a rational industrial policy, although controversial in nature, could muster majority support by the general public and the body politic. As Dahrendorf points out, economies are still oriented primarily towards "stability" and "growth".[13] If these do not materialize, all kinds of problems arise. Not only are individuals' well-being affected, but the social balance is called into question.

No socio-economic policy is viable in the long run which does not address itself to social "bads", i.e., to problems of instability, poverty, unemployment, and inflation.[14]

> The state has to consciously shape the structures, the institutional framework, the order, in which the economy functions. It has to set the conditions under which a functional and humanly dignified economic order evolves. But it is not to direct the economic process itself. ... government planning of the structure – yes. Government planning and directing of economic processes – no.[15]

The above quotation from Eucken essentially sums up the type of industrial policy that is feasible and implementable in the United States. As Marshall would have it, the function of government is to govern as little as possible; but not to do as little as possible.[16] In other words, the dictum is to have as much direction as necessary with as much "laissez faire" as possible. Individuals and business firms are to be motivated to change things which are in their power to change. However, social action is called for when causal factors are beyond the reach of individuals and businesses.[17]

What is meant by an industrial policy? For one, an industrial policy cannot be divorced from fiscal or monetary policies. According to Chalmers Johnson, it forms the third leg in the economic policy triad consisting of fiscal, monetary, and industrial policy. Furthermore, he sees it primarily as an "attitude" and secondly as a technique. Industrial policy, in the opinion of Johnson,

> involves the specific recognition that all government measures — taxes, licenses, prohibitions, regulations — have a significant impact on the well-being or ill-health of whole sectors, industries, and enterprises in a market economy.[18]

Industrial policy may be explicit or implicit; it may be positive or negative in nature.

> Put negatively, industrial policy refers to the distortions, disincentives, and inequities that result from uncoordinated public actions that benefit or restrain one segment of the economy at the expense of another.[19]
>
> In a positive, explicit sense, industrial policy means the initiation and coordination of governmental activities to leverage upward the productivity and competitiveness of the whole economy and of particular industries in it. Above all, positive industrial policy means the infusion of goal-oriented, strategic thinking into public economic policy. It ist the attempt by government to move beyond the broad aggregate and environmental concerns of monetary and fiscal policy of the market system.[20]

In other words, the objective of an industrial policy is to increase overall economic activity and not simply to rearrange the existing economic pie. It should be oriented towards serving the national rather than special interests.

In the United States industrial policy has been mostly of the implicit variety, i.e., its existence is official denied, e.g., in the "President's Economic Report". However, various legislation, regulation, fiscal, and monetary policies have influenced enonomic development in a similar manner as an explicit industrial policy would have.[21]

Examples of industrial policy offer themselves in the anti-trust legislation, the Reconstruction Finance Corporation of the 1930s and 1940s, the Tennessee Valley Authority, the Employment Act of 1946, the 1976 National Science and Technology Act, the Humphrey-Hawkins Act of 1978, and the establishment of the Department of Energy, to mention a few. At the micro level, the following come to mind: land grants to the railroads, subsidies to farmers, business, and industry, tariffs and quotas, loan guarantees (e.g., Chrysler and Lockheed), etc. With regard to the public sector implicit exercises in industrial policy manifest themselves, for example, in the tax code, government regulations, government expenditures for the social infrastructure, defense, research and development, and the space program.

Whether industrial policy is exercised in an explicit manner, its aim is to activate the capacity of the market economy. Furthermore, it is almost impossible to separate industrial policy from an incomes policy, at least in the wider sense of the term. A formally announced industrial policy would be beneficial in that it would make "hidden" choices open and explicit.

There is no question that an implicit industrial policy has been pursued in a haphazard fashion. As a result, resource allocation has become distorted with insufficient attention being paid to the long-term growth potential of the economy. For example, tax shelters, investment tax credits, depreciation allowances, etc., have interfered with real long-term investments in plant and equipment in favor of short-term financial investments. The huge defense budget channels resources into defense-oriented industries, with the potential of a net reduction in employment opportunities. Massive federal deficits, inducing high interest rates, have also interfered with real investment decisions, domestically as well as internationally, manifested by the rising foreign trade deficit. The imposition of tariffs and quotas on imports grants inefficient industries protection from competition for which consumers pay in higher prices, forcing them to reduce other expenditures. As a result, jobs are being lost in other industries. Actions which were intended to maintain jobs in uncompetitive industries yield opposite results in other more efficient industries. The net effect is a redistribution of jobs, if not a net loss; every one loses in society except those directly related to protected industries.

IV.

A meaningful industrial policy cannot be left to chance but must be consciously guided. As Robert Solo points out:

> Faced with a precipitous decline in its technological preeminence, with even basic industries in seeming danger of collapse, the United States needs a policy and the capacity to upgrade its industrial perfomance.[22]

What form should this industrial policy take? Present social and political trends call for vital economic growth through injecting new vitality into the market system. This essentially has two implications, namely the achievement and maintenance of satisfactory rates of economic growth and the reduction of government spending as a percentage of the GNP.

It is also recognized that neither the government nor the private sector can alone create a competitive environment in which business can flourish, technology can expand, and people can work and prosper. Government and business need to be united in one goal, namely to bring about a healthy economy that brings about growth and prosperity for all. Kevin Phillips, in issuing a conservative call for an industrial policy, demands government action to bring about a more competitive economy.[23] He calls on government to take a pro-business position, to coordinate economic and trade policies, to bring about a new kind of business-labor-government collaboration, or to do whatever is necessary.

In 1983, 153 democratic members of the U.S. House of Representatives issued a statement: "A High Production Strategy to Rebuild America".[24] Among other proposals, this statement outlined:

(THE) NATIONAL GOVERNMENT MUST NURTURE INVESTMENT, INNOVATION AND GROWTH AMONG PRIVATE BUSINESS WHILE ENSURING SUFFICIENT PUBLIC INVESTMENT TO BOTH MEET THE NEEDS OF BUSINESS AND PROVIDE THE JOBS AND SERVICES THAT BUSINESS MAY NOT PROVIDE.

> Economic growth and maximum production require a healthy and dynamic private sector aided by an efficient and humane public sector. Under federal leadership, business, labor, and government must be brought together to work cooperatively to create a climate of growth.

Specifically with regard to a national industrial policy, the statement proposes:
1) A national investment facility.
2) Expanded support for research and development.
3) A renewed commitment by government and business to provide education and training programs.
4) An aggressive campaign to increase exports.
5) Strategies to encourage worker participation in management, profit-sharing, and ownership in U.S. corporations, to improve the quality of work life and enhance industrial productivity and innovation.

The statement further stressed public investment efforts as part of the proposed industrial policy:
1) Maintenance of highways.
2) Expansion and renovation of mass transit systems.
3) A modern and competitive railroad system.
4) A program to ensure adequate water supplies.
5) Programs to improve energy efficiency.
6) Maintenance of watersheds, protection and conservation of land and resources.
7) Programs to stimulate the construction and renovation of housing.

With regard to an incomes policy:

With an anti-inflation program, the government must seek a consensus with labor and business to achieve an "incomes policy", in which a balance is achieved among wages, productivitiy, the prices of necessities, lower interest rates, and resumed growth in investment and job creation.

Sar Levitan and Clifford Johnson, in their study on the social safety net, advocated a similar approach.[25] This call for action by a significant number of the representatives in the U.S. Congress is very much in line with the paradigm of a social market economy.

With regard to stable and predictable economic policies, one of the structural principles in the paradigm of the social market economy, substantive tax reform and significant reductions in the federal deficit are called for. The demand for an incomes policy recognizes the fact that mass production also requires mass consumption, which can only be facilitated with a broadening of the income base.

V.

The foregoing analysis pointed to the facts that an industrial policy for the United States has both "meaning" and "validity". It has "meaning" in that it addresses itself to relevant concerns of broad sectors of society. It possesses "validity" due to widespread support by a broad cross section of society and by the willingness of politicians to enact relevant legislation. In the contemporary world, a free market economy has to be understood in terms of a "functional" market economy, i.e., as a social market economy.

The challenge of an industrial policy is how to depoliticize the economic process. One major obstacle to the paradigm of a "functional" market economy is to be found in continuing discontinuities in economic policies. This holds not only true between but also within given administrations. Each administration attempts at first to do things differently than its predecessor as though national economic interests and objectives changed every four years with a change of the guard in the White House.

The real factors which influence the level of employment in society are to be found in foreign trade relations, technological development, the magnitude and type of investment spending, currency exchange ratios, fiscal policy, monetary policy, economic fluctuations, socio-economic structural changes, the distribution of income and wealth, and, of course, in the values and expectations of people.

Inventions and innovations in a high technology society tend to be associated with substantial costs and high risks, which private industry often cannot or is unwilling to assume. If for no other reason, a public policy with regard to research and development needs to set up a framework within which the private sector, in partnership with the public sector, can realize its potentials.

Despite the controversy surrounding the idea of an industrial policy, what is in the making is how to formulate a broad consensus among business, industry, labor, the financial community, government, and consumers, with regard to the long-term goals of the American society and how best to promote these. It is within this framework that an industrial policy is feasible for the United States.

NOTES

[1] Alfred Marshall, *Principles of Economics*, 9th ed. (London: MacMillan and Company, 1961), p. 1.

[2] Walter Eucken, Das Ordnungspolitische Problem, *Ordo-Jahrbuch für die Ordnung von Wirtschaft und Gesellschaft*, Vol. 1 (1948), pp. 60–62.

[3] Fons Elders, ed. *Reflexive Water* (London: Souvenir Press, (1974), pp. 116, 130–31. – Ralf Dahrendorf, *Die Chancen der Krise* (Stuttgart: Deutsche Verlagsgemeinschaft, 1983), p. 222.

[4] Leo Rogin, *The Meaning and Validity of Economic Theory*, (New York: Harper & Brothers, 1956), pp. 1–13.

[5] Wilhelm Röpke, Das Deutsche Wirtschaftsexperiment, Beispiel und Lehre in *Vollbeschäftigung, Inflation, und Planwirtschaft*, Albert Hunold, ed. (Erlenbach-Zürich: Eugen Rentsch Verlag, 1951), p. 266.

[6] Bodo B. Gemper, „Die Jenaer Wegbereiter der Freiburger Schule", *Orientierungen zur Wirtschafts- und Gesellschaftspolitik,* 18 (4/1983).

[7] Walter Eucken, *Grundsätze der Wirtschaftspolitik,* Edith Eucken-Erdsiek und K. Paul Hensel, eds. (Hamburg: Rohwolt Verlag, 1959), pp. 160–77. – Eucken, „Das Ordnungspolitische Problem", pp. 76–77. – Walter Eucken, „Die Wettbewerbsordnung und ihre Verwirklichung", *Ordo-Jahrbuch für die Ordnung von Wirtschaft und Gesellschaft,* Vol. 2 (1949), pp. 32 ff. – Siegfried G. Karsten, "Eucken's 'Social Market Economy' and Its Test in Post-War West Germany, *American Journal of Economics and Sociology,* April 1985.

[8] Michael Parkin, *Macroeconomics* (Englewood Cliffs, NJ: Prentice-Hall, 1984), pp. 544–46.

[9] *U.S. News & World Report,* March 12, 1984, p. 16.

[10] "Hunger Called U.S. Epidemic", *Atlanta Constitution,* February 27, 1985.

[11] "66 Million in U.S. on Government Aid", *The Atlanta Constitution,* September 27, 1984. – "What Recession did to People's Incomes", *U.S. News & World Report,* August 15, 1983, p. 8.

[12] The U.S. Catholic Bishops Ad Hoc Committee, "Catholic Social Teaching and the U.S. Economy", *Origins* (November 15, 1984).

[13] Dahrendorf, *op.cit.,* pp. 68–69.

[14] Eucken, „Wettbewerbsordnung", p. 88.

[15] *Ibid.,* p. 93, my translation.

[16] A. C. Pigou, ed. *Memorials of Marshall* (New York: Augustus M. Kelley, 1966), pp. 336, 363.

[17] William M. Dugger, "Social Economics: One Perspective", *Review of Social Economy,* Vol. 35 (December 1977), pp. 308–9. – Eucken, Grundsätze, pp. 179–87.

[18] Chalmers Johnson, *The Industrial Policy Debate* (San Francisco: ICS Press, 1984), p. 7.

[19] *Ibid.*

[20] *Ibid.,* p. 8.

[21] U.S. President, *Economic Report of the President* (Washington, DC: U.S. Government Printing Office, 1984), p. 87–111.

[22] Robert Solo, "Industrial Policy", *Journal of Economic Issues,* Vol. 18 (September 1984), p. 713.

[23] Kevin P. Phillips, *Staying on Top* (New York: Random House, 1984).

[24] U.S. Congress, National Economic Recovery Project, *A High Production Strategy to Rebuild America,* March 8, 1983.

[25] Sar A. Levitan and Clifford M. Johnson, *Beyond the Safety Net: Reviving the Promise of Opportunity in America* (Cambridge, MA: Ballinger Publishing Co., 1984), pp. 159–61.

4.

Social and Industrial Relations Aspects

Views of Both Sides of Industry on an EEC Industrial Policy

Egon Schoneweg

Historical Account

There is no provision in the EEC Treaty for a comprehensive industrial policy along the lines of the Community's agricultural, transport or commercial policies. However, Article 235 could provide a legal basis for such a policy, as it has done already for others (e.g. regional policy).

Frequent calls have come from various quarters for a Community industrial policy, but the framing of this policy has come up against problems of definition and economic philosophy, i.e. deciding how economic systems are to be organized. The Community budget is also indicative of these problems; with less than one per cent of the total of 25,000 million units of account being earmarked for industrial policy measures in 1985.

During the first twelve years of its existence the Community was extremely inactive in this area. The first blueprint, the "Colonna" Memorandum on Community industrial policy, was not presented till 1970.

The Commission's Colonna Memorandum highlighted five basic objectives:
1. Achievement of the single market,
2. Unification of the legal, fiscal and financial system,
3. Closer links between companies,
4. Control of change and adaptation,
5. Extension of Community solidarity in economic relations with third countries.

In July 1970, on the basis of the Colonna Memorandum and papers drawn up by the French, German and Italian Governments, the Council entrusted a panel of senior civil servants who were to report to the Committee of Permanent Representatives with the investigation of nine major issues. These nine questions, which reflected the concerns of the governments were:

1. Introduction of a common market in various advanced-technology and capital-goods sectors.
2. The promotion of industrial progress and technological development in the Community.
3. Measures to facilitate transnational industrial mergers within the Community:
   a) establishing a Community advisory bureau for companies wishing to establish closer links,
   b) extension of the role of the European Investment Bank (EIB),
   c) drawing up a procedure for the Community-wide coordination of questions relating to industrial restructuring.

4. Development of Community solidarity with an eye to improving technological cooperation with non-Member States.
5. Cooperation between Member States on the question of foreign investments.
6. The possibility of establishing, in addition to the "European company", a more flexible, legal vehicle, which will facilitate closer links between companies.
7. The regional aspects of industrial policy.
8. The coordination and streamlining of Community funds earmarked for economic development.
9. The role of public enterprises in the industrial policy of the Community.

In retrospect, there was something idyllic about the philosophy underlying these proposals. This is borne out by the following excerpt from the Commission text:

> To reconcile industry and society means first freeing the industrial worker from the curse still weighing down on him; this no longer means material squalor, even though this is still with us, but the intellectual poverty bred by monotonous jobs, the ever growing pace of work, conveyor-belt production methods, the inconveniences of transport, the harmful effects of city life and above all the lack of recognition.
> It means bringing work to the people and not vice-versa. Europe must not become a continent full of people without roots or a melting pot in which national and regional traits are lost.
> It means an economy focussed more on the fulfillment of basic human aspirations: comfort and security at home, attractive towns to live in, a protected countryside accessible to everybody and mass culture not corrupted by snobbery or elitism.
> It means a Europe economically open to the world but still in charge of its own destiny, its influence based not only on a cultural heritage without equal, but also on the efficiency of its economy and its institutions.
> And lastly, it means a Europe relying on its own capabilities and concentrating its new energies on a more equitable distribution of wealth, the reconciliation of nations and the organization of peace.

Nothing much came of the Colonna Memorandum and the subsequent work based on it, or of the declarations of intent made at the October 1972 Paris Summit.

From 1973/74 onwards, however, the crisis triggered off by the oil shocks forced the Community to regard industrial policy as an exercise in crisis management. This policy, to which further reference will be made later on and which was focussed on the steel, textile and shipbuilding sectors, was essentially a reactive rather than an active policy. Subsequently, in more recent years the industrial change set in motion by new technology has further impaired the Community industry's competitiveness and produced upheavals on the labor market to which no satisfactory solution has yet been found. One point worth noting in this context is the consensus among employers and unions that even if optimum growth rates were to be achieved, the unemployment problem is unlikely to disappear automatically. Hence the renewed, urgent need for a Community industrial policy. Before such a policy is discussed in detail, its objectives and possible instruments need to be defined.

Definition and Inventory

The main objectives of an industrial policy are:
— to bring industry into line with market conditions
— to improve industrial competitiveness
— to make rational use of resources
— to keep the social impact of technological change under control.

These objectives can be pursued by:
1. Creating the right general climate.
2. Direct and indirect intervention.

The right general environment can be created by

a) Abolishing non-tariff trade barriers. In the main this means the technical barriers which impede the free movement of goods and the creation of a single market. The Commission has submitted 180 draft Directives, targeted to motor vehicles, electrical appliances, measuring instruments, chemical products (in particular, dangerous substances), textiles, foodstuffs, etc. Many of these draft Directives have not (or have not yet) been adopted by the Council. Mention should also be made in this context of the problem of standards whose application is a *de facto* trade barrier. This has caused friction between Member States which, basically, can only be settled by introducing Community-wide standards. There are also signs of a new approach to the drafting of Directives; in the past these have tended to be too heavyhanded and bureaucratic.

b) Abolition of legal and tax barriers. This covers three areas:
   1. patent law, trade mark law and competition and anti-trust law (with special reference to Article 85);
   2. in a wider sense, company law measures, such as the setting up of a European company and the harmonization of national legislation on joint-stock companies;
   3. tax harmonization, which so far has not progressed beyond the general introduction of the VAT principle, and even then with widely varying rates. This means in practical terms that the tax treatment of transnational cooperation ventures is unfair.

c) Opening up of the award of public contracts. Public procurement policies are highly protectionist in all Member States. Evidence of this can be found, for example, in telecommunications and in the railway sector. In order to break down these national barriers, it has been the rule for some time now that invitations to tender must be published in the Official Journal of the European Communities if they exceed a certain value. However, this is only an initial step.

d) Support for high technology. The Community hesitated about acting in this field for a long time, and the first practical steps were not taken until recently, when the ESPRIT programme (European Strategic Programme for Research and Development in Information and Technology) was launched.

Community and industry have committed themselves to spend 1,500 million ECUs over five years. The programme was drawn up following consultations with industry, universities and national authorities. The general aim is to create a technological base for Community industry.

Five priority areas have been selected in the light of current trends:
- advanced microelectronics
- advanced information processing
- software technology
- office automation
- computer-controlled manufacture.

In each area the Commission will select the most interesting projects which are submitted by research establishments or companies, regardless of their size. It will be assisted in its work by administrative and consultative bodies on which the Member States, science and industry are widely represented. The contracting parties must be based in the Community and, generally speaking, offers must come from several Member States. One major aim of ESPRIT is to set up an information system to which all interested parties have access, so as to ensure that research findings are disseminated as widely as possible.

c) Finally, mention should be made of supportive trade measures, e.g. agreements under GATT, international textile agreements such as the multi-fibre arrangement and voluntary restraint agreements in the motor vehicle trade.

Direct and indirect intervention covers four areas:

a) The most far-reaching measures are those taken to regulate the market in certain areas. Naturally, the possibilities afforded by Article 58 of the ECSC Treaty for fixing steel quotas and prices spring to mind first and foremost.

b) Subsidies. The treaties (i.e. Art 54 of the ECSC Treaty and Art 92 of the EEC Treaty) adopt different approaches to subsidies. The ECSC Treaty is basically dirigistic and is therefore more favourably disposed towards subsidies, while the EEC Treaty bans public subsidies to companies or sectors. Practical problems are also caused, for example, in the steel sector by specific provisos, such as the one stating that subsidies can only be used for the reduction of capacity – something which is naturally difficult to monitor.

c) Regional policy. The structural measures taken by the Community in the field of regional policy since 1975 are one form of indirect intervention. These measures are mainly designed to reduce the structural disparities to be found in the Community between central and peripheral areas and also, more recently, between prosperous and structurally-weak areas. The original aim was to aid individual projects. However, this led to such a vast number of applications that the basic principles of Community regional policy had to be revised and greater prominence given to large-scale programmes. Particular mention should be made here of "Integrated Operations", which involve all the available Community financial instruments being concentrated on a concerted package of measures covering structural improvements, vocational training, improvement of infrastructure etc.

d) Social Policy. Although there is no Community social policy as such, since 1958 there has been a European Social Fund which operates mainly in the fields of training and retraining. Here too it is clear from the level of funding, approximately 5 per cent of the Community budget, that these activities are largely symbolic. It should not be forgotten, however, that up to the present time some 1.5 million workers in the Community have benefitted directly or indirectly from European Social Fund measures.

So far the Member States have been unable to agree on the future course of the Community's subsidiary programmes in the fields of regional and social policy. A further complication is the fact that the prospect of the Community's enlargement southwards poses new problems in the regional policy sector which will necessitate special programmes. All the controversies about economic philosophy governing Member States' industrial policies also apply at community level, of course. However, because of the *de facto* principle of the unanimous vote at the Council of Ministers decision-taking there is more difficult than it is nationally. In addition, industrial traditions vary a great deal. Take, for example, countries such as France with its colbertism or Italy, where more than 53 per cent of industrial production is state-controlled. Consequently, the public sector is more important in these Member States than elsewhere.

The Impact of New Technologies

It has taken the advent of new technology to get the industrial policy debate off the ground again. The Community is faced with a challenge which will determine whether it will have a future role to play worldwide. Because of their closer links with the grassroots the two sides of industry are probably more aware of this situation than the political powers that be. This was borne out at the Economic and Social Committee's new technology conference held on 6–7 November 1984, which was attended by all of Europe's leading trade associations. There was a large measure of agreement between the two sides of industry. With regard to the new technologies it also became apparent that the participants' analyses of the situation were broadly in line, and there were clear indications of possible approaches to tackling the problem.

Although concern was expressed in one of the opening speeches that the trade unions' presumed desire to safeguard jobs might prejudice them against new technology, these fears had been allayed by the end of the conference.

First of all it was clearly established that the new technologies have become a testing ground for Europe's ability to maintain its international position. This was the first main point. The second was the realization that the sums involved in developing and introducing advanced technologies far exceed the financing capacity of European companies and even individual Member Staates; the European dimension is essential to enable the branches of industry to compete with the United States, Japan and other countries.

The leading American computer manufacturer spends $ 10 million on research and development each day. In other words the amount spent by a single company in two months is equivalent to the Community's entire annual budget allocation for research, information, innovation and industrial policy. The Community is greatly handicapped by the lack of a fully developed internal market and divisions in public purchasing policy. It has been calculated that the manufacturing cost of the development of a new generation of digital telephone exchanges would be between $ 700 million and $ 1,300 million. Turnover of roughly $ 14,000 million would be required to amortize development costs of $ 1,000 million. Although these are only approximate figures it is clear that no individual Member State could provide the necessary demand. And yet public sector initiatives and purchasing policy are enormously important in the field of advanced technology. Joint research can put Europe at the forefront of developments, as in the case of high energy physics and nuclear fusion, and joint manufacturing projects such as the Airbus, ARIANE and Spacelab have shown that Europe can compete successfully.

The ESPRIT programme which I mentioned earlier was indeed a sensible and farsighted initiative; the only question is whether the decision to set up the programme was taken too late. Less than 1 per cent of the 1984 Community budget was spent on industrial policy, information and innovation and the funds for research are about to be cut in the 1985 budget. These are definitely not steps in the right direction.

All this points to the need for a European industrial policy which would not be limited to supporting industrial sectors in crisis as a result of difficulties in adapting to structural change but, rather, designed to encourage growth sectors. This does not imply dirigistic intervention in industry by government — not even in the fields of research and development. It is nonetheless true that the development of new technologies entails particularly heavy costs and considerable risks. Programmes like Joint European Torus (JET) in the field of nuclear fusion and ESPRIT in information technology should be followed by other programmes for telecommunications and biotechnology, in order to prevent energies being dispersed by duplication of work. It is also necessary to create a climate favourable to the development of the innovatory skills of small and medium-sized enterprises.

The Social and Industrial Relations Aspects

The social aspects of the problem are, however, just as important as the economic and industrial aspects I have already mentioned. The question arises as to how our society can control the development of these technologies, how they can be made acceptable and how the two sides of industry should react to them. In this context I should like to point out that the Economic and Social Committee expressed a number of fundamental conclusions on new technology and social change in a recent — and unanimously adopted — Opinion.

The Committee established that the introduction of new technologies in products and production processes was changing both the level and structure of employment. Although opinions differ on the implications for employment, there is, however, general agreement that the introduction of new technologies in industry is destroying more jobs than it is creating. Wider use of the new technologies will accelerate structural changes in employment in the years to come.

In this context it is to be expected that traditional forms of employment in many areas of the tertiary sector will be wiped out; the sector will cease to fulfil to the same extent as hitherto its traditional function of compensating for job losses in the industrial sector.

For virtually all groups of workers new technology will mean significant changes in the nature of work and the qualifications required. Less qualified workers in particular will face the risk of not having the right skills and be in greater threat of being put out of work. The hardest hit will be groups like women and migrant workers — who are already at a disadvantage in the fields of training and employment.

On the other hand, however, new technologies offer greater opportunities than conventional office and manufacturing technologies for new, and most importantly, more flexible ways of organizing work, coupled with higher qualification requirements and improved working conditions. Such positive achievements depend, however, on the way in which new technologies are introduced in manufacturing and administration. Finally it should be stressed that the individual use of new technologies can affect the right of workers and their representatives to be consulted and kept informed by management and to participate in the running of their industries.

The centralization or decentralization of corporate planning and decision-making, the introduction of inter-company computer networks and the growing monitoring potential of the new technologies could upset the traditional balance of power between the two sides of industry. There is, therefore, a clear tendency for the degree of consultation between the two sides of industry on questions of information and worker participation to be adjusted to reflect the extent of technological change and the size of the company. This means a discernible increase in worker participation at company and inter-company level. It should be borne in mind that the introduction of new technologies requires that workers and their representatives be fully informed and consulted at an early stage. It is also in the interests of management to take the necessary steps to ensure that workers are involved in the introduction of new technologies and that humanly acceptable working conditions are safeguarded. This can only be achieved through the participation of workers in the planning and design of technological systems and if measures to counter the new technologies' impact on working conditions and employment are negotiated and introduced in good time.

The role of the two sides of industry is thus spelt out. It is a well-known fact that both sides have their umbrella organization at Community level and are also starting to organize themselves on a sectoral basis. The Union of Industries of the European Community (UNICE) is the leading organization for the employer's side and, more especially, for industry. Its trade-union counterpart is the European Trade Union Confederation, which however is not confined to the Community. In recent years several attempts have been made to get both sides to go further than top-level formal meetings and to hold negotiations, i.e. engage in collective bargaining, even if this term has been avoided because of the sensitivity of the subject. UNICE has opposed this demand time and again, arguing that it has not been authorized by its members to enter into negotations. Recently, however, there have been signs of a break in the deadlock for the first time. The new Commision presided over by Jacques DELORS has made closer cooperation with both sides of industry one of the priorities of its policies.

In this connection it held a meeting on 31 January 1985 with the Community umbrella organization at which it asked them to examine whether there could be closer contacts between both sides in two fields,
a) employment policy and work organization,
b) the impact of the new technologies.

Here the Commision did not commit itself, envisaging only the provision of technical support. It seems as though this initiative marks a breakthrough in the catalogue of taboos which has held sway for so many years; for the first time a form of collective bargaining at Community level might get off the ground. Even though wage agreements at Community level are inconceivable, there is plenty of scope for outline agreements in the two fields mentioned above. If the Community-level umbrella organizations were to be involved in such agreements, however, a further step would be bound to follow, namely the fleshing out of such outline agreements at sectoral level. Even if we seem at present to be a long way away from such agreements, collective agreements at Community-level are a logical sequel to the establishment of the EC internal market and genuine European integration. Such economic integration is clearly not a viable proposition unless it has a counterpart in the labour-relations field.

Some Reflections on Industrial Policies Based on British Experience

Hilde Behrend

Introduction

The discussions at the Walberberg symposium have indicated that the topic of industrial policies cannot be discussed without taking into account social policy goals. As pointed out in several of the papers this fact has been recognised by the use of the concept of the "social market economy" and, in practical terms in West Germany, by Erhard's economic policies.

One implication of this definition of our topic is that the market is not wholly free in western industrial democracies because government industrial policies can and often do intervene in the free market. In addition, in a mixed economy, we must not forget that the public sector is more liable to be controlled by government action than the private sector. In Great Britain, for instance, governments have at times controlled the pricing policies of public corporations as part of their anti-inflation policies. They have also subsidised nationalised industries. These considerations strengthen the case for using the term social market economy and for examining the social as well as the economic objectives of industrial policies.

In Britain social policy objectives for the post war period were discussed during the war and given shape in the 1942 Beveridge Report on Social Security and Allied Services and in Beveridge's 1944 book on Full Employment in a Free Society and in the 1944 Coalition Government White Paper on Employment Policy which laid down as one of the objectives for post war economic policies the attainment and maintenance of full employment – an objective accepted by the leader of the Conservative Party, the Prime Minister Winston Churchill and the leader of the Labour Party, the Deputy Prime Minister Clement Attlee who became Prime Minister after the 1945 election.

Attlee's Government as well as subsequent British Governments have pursued four major social objectives: rising standards of living, stable prices (a goal later referred to as the control of inflation), full employment and better social services. Other industrialised countries, as the Walberberg symposium has shown, pursued similar goals.

The question which I want to raise here in this stock-taking exercise is whether the conflicting claims on our economic resources which arise from the four objectives can be reconciled or whether the goals are too ambitious so that expectations will have to be lowered.

General economic policies

It is important to point out first of all that the four objectives which I mentioned have been formulated as targets for solving existing economic and social problems and that these problems have been the trigger for government action at specific points of time. Thus it was the problem of unemployment which hit the western industrialised countries at the end of the 1920s which gave rise to the goal of establishing full employment after the second world war and to the British Government's commitment to it. In Britain this target was achieved by the end of the 1940s when the transition from the war economy to a peace time one had led to full employment; indeed, in some of the regions, to overfull employment; in the Midlands, for instance, to an unemployment rate of 0.3 per cent for men in July 1951 and to an average unemployment rate for men in Great Britain of 0.9 per cent. It is interesting to note that Beveridge's view was more pessimistic; he estimated that an achievable target for full employment would be a reduction of the unemployment rate to three per cent. However, there were marked regional differences and in some regions of Great Britain unemployment remained a source of concern requiring industrial policy attention.

By 1947 the shortage of labour associated with full employment had led to wage increases in undermanned and prosperous industries and the Government began to express concern about the danger of inflation. In February 1948 therefore it sought the nation's support for a policy of wage restraint which received qualified support from the British Trade Union Congress (the TUC) until September 1950. This policy was accompanied by a devaluation of the pound in September 1949 to cope with balance of payment problems.

These developments shifted the focus of British economic policies from the preoccupation with unemployment to that of the fight against inflation. The problem of rising prices and wages began to come to the forefront and has remained there to the present day (April 1985). Thus Margaret Thatcher who became British Prime Minister in 1979 has stated repeatedly that the reduction and containment of inflation is the major objective of her economic policy. I should add that in the past, British Government concern with inflation was particularly marked at times when the British economy ran into balance of payment crises.

Successive British governments have used two major types of approach in the fight against inflation: monetary and fiscal controls and incomes policies. On the monetary front, when they thought it neccessary, they introduced measures to restrict credit facilities and to make it more difficult and expensive to borrow money, for instance, by raising the bank or minimum lending rate. On the fiscal side they increased taxation, for instance, by raising purchase tax or VAT or income tax or corporation tax and by government expenditure cuts.

The consequences of these deflationary measures were that they halted economic growth by harming industry. Investment plans were upset and retarded by the imposition of monetary controls; the willingness to take risks, to innovate and expand was discouraged and the making of plans for the future was overshadowed by uncertainty and rising costs. The monetary and fiscal anti-inflation policies and their stop-go effect, therefore, constrained and disrupted industrial development; and, in impeding economic growth, they threatened the goals of rising standards of living and of maintaining full employment.

For these reasons, it has been argued that the second type of measures which British governments used, namely incomes policies, whether pay freezes or pay restraint policies, would be less disruptive, especially if they were based on concensus, that is, if the policies were supported by the employers and trade unions. On this point it was easier for a Labour Party Government to win support from the Trade Union Congress than for a Conservative one. Nevertheless both parties used such policies. Furthermore, within the ups and downs of the economy there was a kind of continuity and evolution in the policies which were used. In the attempts to find a workable incomes policy, for instance, the notion that an incomes policy should link pay increases to productivity increases, which had been mooted in 1951 by a Conservative government, became a major frame of reference while it was in office in the 1960s. Furthermore, the scope of the policies was extended. The policy concept was enlarged to include all incomes and eventually was referred to as a prices, productivity and incomes policy.

On the industrial relations side attempts were made to bring the employers and trade unions closer together in tripartite discussions. One example, for instance, in 1962 was the establishment of the National Economic Development Council (later renamed National Economic Development Office or NEDO) by the Conservative Government. It was set up to pursue the objectives of "keeping the rate of increases of incomes within the long-term rate of growth of national production, improving the basis for consultation and forecasting and for creating a climate favourable for economic growth". This organisation has survived to the present time as a forum for tripartite discussions.

Two strategies were used with regard to incomes policies: temporary halts to all pay increases, referred to as pay pauses or pay freezes and pay restraint policies; both were based on persuasion and voluntary co-operation or, on two occasions, on statutory powers.

The rules for pay restraint policies were based on the objective, already mentioned of linking pay increases to productivity increases. The aim was to lay down guidelines or norms which would keep the size of pay increases at a level just below that of the economic growth rate. The use of norms was bases to begin with on admonition and persuasion and the setting up of "watch dog" organisations. For example, the Conservative Government backed its 1962 "guiding light" policy by establishing under Royal Warrant a National Incomes Commission to watch over the observance of the guidelines for incomes by enquiring into and expressing views on wage claims of special importance. However the trade unions refused co-operation with this commission. The succeeding Labour Government therefore replaced it in 1965 by setting up the National Board for Prices and Incomes. Its terms of reference were to examine particular cases of prices and incomes behaviour, report on its findings and make recommendations in the national interest. This body was abolished by the Conservative Government which came into power in 1970.

In passing I should perhaps mention that during some of the incomes policy stages certain groups of employees were exempted from the pay restraint rules, for instance, lower paid workers, workers who had genuinely increased their productivity and cases of acute labour shortage or of gross pay anomalies.

One other issue is of importance in the context of incomes policies. The economic growth rate measures the increase in the gross national product in percentage terms and for this reason, it would appear, pay restaint norms were usually expressed in percentage terms. Thus they were often set 0.5 or 1 per cent below the economic growth rate. However, the use of percentage norms poses problems of equity: the lower the income is, the lower is the cash award and yet the needs of the lower paid workers are greater than those of higher income groups. This point should' not be wholly ignored in a social market economy where it can be argued that it should not be the poor who make the greatest sacrifices in adverse conditions.

My inflation studies[1] have highlighted this problem. In a national sample survey which I directed in April 1966 the great majority of the British respondents who had received a pay increase of less then £ 1 per week said that it had made little or no difference. By contrast, the men who had received £ 2 a week or more considered that this amount had made a difference. At that time, the majority of manual workers were earning less than £ 21 per week. The findings thus indicated that with a 3.5 per cent norm in operation a large proportion of the population was receiving pay increases of well below £ 1 and therefore fell into the category of those who perceived that no visible benefit had resulted from their pay increases. The low awards therefore carried in them the seed for further pay demands. The frustration that resulted may well have been an important factor leading to the 1969 pay explosion.

It should also be noted that the majority of our respondents in the 1966 survey and in our later Irish surveys described their last pay increases as an amount per week and only a very small minority expressed it in percentage terms. I would argue, therefore, that it is important that economists and politicians should take account of the fact that people do not think in percentage terms in everyday life when they grumble about pay increases which are too small or prices which have risen. The choice of a pay award formula therefore has to assess carefully what is appropriate in a particular situation. It seems that a flexible approach is required as was adopted by the Labour Government in its social contract incomes policy in which a fixed pay increase amount norm was introduced for the 1975 phase and for the 1976 phase a percentage norm with a floor and ceiling, i.e. with minimum and maximum amount entitlements.

What has been the approach of the Thatcher Government in the fight against inflation? When the new Prime Minister came into power in 1979, she declared that the reduction of inflation would be the major goal of the government's economic policy. To achieve this they would use a purely monetary policy and no incomes policy. The strategy adopted has been that of control of the money supply by expenditure cuts and by control of the public sector borrowing requirement (PSBR). However, the Government has also used indirect controls of incomes based on spending limits imposed on the public sector and in 1984 and 1985 three to four per cent limits for public sector pay increases have been mentioned in government pronouncements as well as general admonitions that pay demands should be restrained. During the period of office of the Government the rate of inflation has decreased from a peak of 22 per cent in April 1980 to five per cent in May 1984 so that one can say that the policy has so far been fairly successful on the inflation front although the rate has crept up to 7 per cent in May 1985. However, critics hold that the price paid for it in unemployment is unacceptable. Unrest and concern about pay offers which are considered to be too low are reappearing, particularly in the public sector. Settlements are higher in the private sector and this adds to feelings of unfair treatment. It would seem that the question of whether Britain needs a general incomes policy is in the air. In April 1985, for instance, the Bank of England expressed the view in a report that there is a need for wage restraint.

Regional Policies

Regional policies have been a major feature of British economic policies since the 1920s. Before the second world war attention was focused on so-called "special areas" of high unemployment. After the war the 1945 Distribution of Industry Act was passed. This enlarged the assisted areas and designated them as Development Areas. Regional policies have remained in existence, in various forms, to the 1980s although they have been curtailed by the Thatcher Government.

In their book on Regional Policy (1978) Armstrong and Taylor[2] present details of 46 policy measures and note that 23 of these were major ones (Appendix C, pp. 309–317). In summarising them Armstrong and Taylor report (p.182) that "various 'carrot and stick' policies have been used in Britain to bring about a geographical reallocation of capital and labour, with most emphasis being placed on policies to induce the movement of capital towards the depressed areas". To a large extent the policies followed the lines of the Barlow Report recommendations made in 1940 in a white paper that a policy of decentralisation or dispersal, both of industries and industrial populations from Greater London and other conurbations should take place.

Professor Gordon Cherry, in a conversation I had with him recently, called the British approach a "policy of positive discrimination". The main feature of the policies has been the provision of favourable terms for setting up new firms or branch factories in specified development or assisted areas. These were usually areas of high unemployment and contracting industries where the work was brought to the workers. But some projects were more ambitious they combined the relocation of enterprises with the relocation of workers, for instance, by the creation of New Towns or by measures to prevent depopulation. The inducements used for promoting change may be described as variations on a theme.

There were financial incentives for firms to move to particular locations such as investment and building grants, rents and rates subsidies and tax concessions and, at times, in special cases direct financial assistance. There was migration assistance for displaced workers and for moving key workers and provisions of housing in New Towns; and training and re-training facilities; also the provision of factory premises and leases. Another important measure was the setting up of Regional Ecconomic Planning Councils to co-ordinate and develop regional economic policies. Some of these are still very active, for instance, the Scottish Development Agency.

In the prosperous cities and urban areas, by contrast, expansion was made dependent on planning permission, building licences and Industrial Development Certificates which were often not granted in those areas to put pressure on companies to move to the development areas.

However, in the first half of the 1980s, under the Thatcher Government with its expenditure cuts, aid to the assisted areas has been run down and regional planning has been demoted. The economic philosophy behind this has been that regulation and subsidisation induces inefficiency and that, therefore, the more successful and prosperous South Eastern industrial region of Britain should be allowed to develop and expand without restraints in a free market and that this will bring about economic growth and will spread from the south to other areas through competition and greater efficiency.

In terms of specific general rather than regional schemes to foster economic growth and reduce unemployment the Government has encouraged the setting up of small firms and of Enterprise Zones in different parts of the country through financial concessions and aid. It has also sponsored and financed various types of work experience and/or work training schemes for unemployed school leavers and re-training schemes for older age-groups.

Can we evaluate the effectiveness of regional policies? Armstrong and Taylor (2, Ch. 11) discuss this question from the economist's point of view and point out that it is a complex and difficult task involving social cost-benefit analyses, planning balance sheet methods and goals achievement matrix approaches and that it is, therefore, a task for future research to estimate "the full economic and social welfare effects on all regions and citizens". However, I doubt whether such a time and resource consuming exercise is worth while.

It seems to me that a historical case study approach which examines the fate of individual enterprises which have moved to, or been set up in, development areas would be more rewarding. It could provide insights with regard to successful and unsuccessful support of industrial and management strategies and could pinpoint more general lessons about mistakes made in different stages in the development of a firm and whether they were identified and dealt with before it was too late.

Important parts of such evaluations would be comparisons of the records of British and foreign firms who took advantage of development aid. Originally, as I have mentioned, British industrial policies aimed to redistribute industry and industrial populations by relocating British enterprises. But in later periods foreign firms were encouraged to come and set up factories. One must also ascertain how many completely new enterprises were set up. Another aspect, of course, is that of the question of the types of industry that took advantage of the aid and how they coped with adverse economic conditions. I believe there is considerable scope for case study research in this field.

Nationalisation and Privatisation

The fact that the state has become a major owner of enterprises in many western industrialised countries suggests that there can never be a wholly free market economy. What we have is a mixed economy of public and private enterprises and therefore economic growth and development depends on the performance of both sectors and on the interaction between them.

It would appear that the size of public sector involvement in manufacturing industry depends largely on the ideology of past governments and therefore on past history. Thus, the size depends on political decisions which may or may not have been made on economic grounds. One could argue, therefore, that ownership and changes of ownership for which strong economic arguments can be put forward have a better chance of becoming effective than those which are backed mainly by ideological considerations.

However, in my view, a change of ownership by itself does not improve the production and market performance of an organisation; improvements depend on the ability and drive of the new management, the previous performance of the organisation, the capital which is available for investment and the economic climate. If the state provides necessary f nance or if the new management can raise money in the open market the organisa ion may be in a position to do better than before. If an industry consists of many small and often inefficient and high cost units a reorganisation of the industry by rationalisation through nationalisation can be successful. On the latter grounds I believe that there was a strong economic argument for the nationalisation of the British coal industry in 1945 and that much was achieved during the first periods of nationalisation. This is illustrated by the peaceful re-organisation of the job-classification and pay-structure carried out during this period by a Joint Committee of the National Coal Bord and the Union of Mineworkers. A one year study had revealed the existence of 6 500 "different" jobs at the time of the take-over! This list was first reduced to a standard list of 400 jobs and after further study the two sides agreed that a classification into 13 grades would be satisfactory[3]. How the British coal industry has fared in the later stages of nationalisation and particularly during the crisis period of falling coal demand in the 70s and 80s is another question. The period brought to the forefront the problem of the size of the industry; that it is too large and that the market has shrunk. Since the change in the economic situation has also affected private coal mines abroad one can argue that the fate of coalmines highlights problems associated with the size of organisations which can arise in both public and private sector enterprises.

It seems that there is an optimal size and that some public and private enterprises are too large, too bureaucratic and too inflexible when adjustments are needed to be efficient and that expansion beyond the optimum can lead to higher cost, inefficiency and trouble in adverse conditions.

In addition one can argue that the success and efficiency of public enterprises does not only depend on the economic climate, size, management skills, employee attitudes and a good industrial relations climate but also on government attitudes: whether they are supportive and democratic or not. An important question in this context is whether enough freedom of action is given to the management. In Britain, it has often been fettered by government restrictions and interventions.

Kenneth Boulding[4], in referring to the public sector as a "Grants Economy" has pointed out that its performance depends on the goodwill of the grantgivers rather than on the market. If governments are prepared to give financial and other aid, this helps to create positive responses and performance while hostile attitudes are liable to result in negative responses.

Another consideration which is particularly relevant and worrying in the British context is whether successive policies of nationalisation and denationalisation, further nationalisation or renationalisation and privatisation make sense. With the current programme of privatisation we may be able to get a better picture in ten years' time. The case for it has been that competition in a free market economy forces management in the private sector to be efficient; and yet one government aim has been to slim down and improve the management of public enterprises with a view to selling them when they have become efficient and profitable. In the case of British Leyland, for instance, the Government sold the most profitable unit in the organisation, Jaguar, and so the profits of the group are now lower than before the sale making its position more difficult.

Policies for improving labour productivity

I want to turn now to the problem of low labour productivity. This topic refers to problems which arise at the level of the firm and poses questions with regard to their industrial and employment policies. However, these may be influenced by admonition and information from governments and also by legislation.

After the second world war considerable concern was expressed by government spokesmen and managements in western industrialised countries about low worker productivity. This led to various recommendations for motivating workers to work harder. The International Labour Office in Geneva, for instance, recommended in 1951, in a report entitled Payment by Results, the use of such payment schemes.

That higher productivity is important for economic development and rising standards of living cannot be disputed. However, not all the remedies suggested are necessarily effective. As research has shown, for instance, the use of payment by results can raise production standards but it can also misfire and lead to restriction of output. What is important for the effectiveness of such schemes is the bargaining process about the appropriate rewards for different standards of effort. Thus, as my incentives enquiries have shown[5], the introduction of a payment by results scheme represents the conclusion of an effort bargain in which workers agree to raise their standards of effort in exchange for the guarantee of higher earnings. To be successful the effort bargain must be based on mutual agreement with regard to the terms of the bargain.

This is just one example of a frequently used scheme among many other measures and approaches which have been advocated and tried to improve worker motivation and productivity. What is important, therefore, is to assess what is appropriate action in a particular situation. In such an evaluation employee attitudes and the climate of industrial relations need to be taken into account. In addition, a well thought out personnel and wage policy to establish good performance and attendance standards may have to be formulated at company level. Furthermore, the assessment should not be a once only exercise. It is important to assess regularly what is appropriate in the particular situation of a firm at a particular moment of time and not to imitate what others are doing. What is effective elsewhere may not be effective in the situation which is being reviewed.

This is so because a firm's overall industrial policy including its employment policy must depend on the stage in its development which it has reached. The needs are different in the setting up and expansion stages from those in the stabilisation stage or in periods of recession and cutbacks when a company has to adjust to adverse conditions. This means that it is important for the viability and profitability of an enterprise to adopt policies which are appropriate for their particular situation and stage of development. If unsuitable policies are in operation or chosen trouble may ensue.

In the assessment of what is appropriate evidence from historical case studies of the company policies of industrial enterprises could be useful as I already suggested earlier in the context of regional policies. If we can diagnose past mistakes and their effects through case studies managements could examine their relevance and could perhaps learn to avoid them.

Evidence, for instance, which I obtained in an investigation of the employment policies used by a number of factories in the central belt of Scotland revealed that some of them had made major starting up mistakes. One firm, for instance, had built up its workforce in the early stages at a rate of 300 a month to meet production targets. This resulted in overmanning and a slow pace of work which was not properly controlled by the measured daywork payment system which the firm started off with. A number of other firms started off with inappropriate payment systems and had to change them.

Pay structure reforms which I have argued are necessary from time to time were carried out successfully by a number of firms. These reforms dealt with rationalisations of the pay structure and with problems of piece rate drift.

Some of the lessons management learned were also spelt out; for instance, that the setting of the right pace of work should be watched from the start and that attendance standards should also be watched and that wage rates should not be raised before production is up to the appropriate standard. Overall it would appear, however, that the quality of management is a critical factor and that it is, therefore, very important that experienced managers should start up or be appointed to start up large enterprises. Among the qualities required is the ability to tackle the task of establishing good working relationships and a good industrial relations climate in the firm. Another critical factor is that of the outlook of the employees (and in a unionised plant of the trade unions) because their perceptions, attitudes and expectations can further or hamper the effectiveness of an enterprise.

Finally we should not forget that industrial development depends on the success of individual enterprises as well as on the economic climate which is, in turn, affected by Government economic and industrial policies.

Concluding Comments

In the introduction I raised the question whether the conflicting claims on our economic resources which arise from the four economic and social policy objectives of rising standards of living, stable prices, full employment and better social services can be reconciled or whether the combination of these goals is too ambitious so that expectations will have to be lowered.

As my report of the history of the measures taken in Britain has shown we reached the objective of full employment at the end of the 1940s. However, full employment and economic growth led to labour shortages, to pressures for higher pay and to rising prices. Thus, inflation became a major problem and its containment has been a major government objective from 1948 to the present time (1985). With inflation came the emergence of regular patterns of pay increases, often referred to as the annual wage-round. This practice gave rise to employee expectations that every present pay increase will be followed by another and larger pay increase and that this will happen as a matter of right, not of work contribution – a right which assumed the property of a regular entitlement not easily amenable to change. As a result changes in the cost of living became the major frame of reference for employee expectations. Incomes policies were only accepted as temporary measures and big increases were expected when they came to an end.

How did all this affect the objective of rising standards of living? If we take 1945 as a frame of reference we can say that we have witnessed considerable improvements in standards of living; for instance, better housing and a great increase in house ownership, improved social services, higher incomes and longer holidays. The moderate economic growth rate and the availability of credit made this possible.

However, the problems arising from the 1973 oil crisis led to a period of zero growth in Britain and the problems of depression and rising unemployment together with inflation i.e. stagflation. High unemployment has become a major problem but the Conservative Thatcher Government still lays greater emphasis on the fight against inflation. As regards the objective of rising standards of living it would appear that the standards of living of the majority of those who have jobs have risen since 1973 although many members of the employed population complain that they have fallen in the last few years and it is therefore important to note that it is their perceptions of the situation which affects their attitudes to work and to pay increases. The lower paid and the unemployed have been the main losers. In addition, they, as well as others, have been hit by cuts in social services and public spending.

As my account shows successive governments have only made partial and temporary progess in the pursuit of one or other of the four objectives. The evidence suggests therefore that the simultaneous achievement of the four objectives represents an unattainable goal in the present situation.

One reason why the problems of inflation and unemployment have been so difficult to deal with, so intractable that we have not found lasting answers in the course of four decades, is that they belong to a class of human problems which Hardin[6] described as "no technical solutions problems". This means that psychological and political attitudes, expectations and moral values as well as economic strategies may have to be changed to cope with, or adapt to, the demands which arise in new economic situations. In the present situation, for instance, policy-makers should not only take account of economic resource constraints but also of people's perceptions of the situation and of the moral dilemmas created by the differences in the standards of living of the better off and the lower paid.

Margaret Thatcher, the Prime Minister, demands frequently that people should be more realistic. However, one reason why they are not is that there are communications gaps. As my research enquiries have shown (see note 1) ordinary citizens often do not understand economic terms and interpret situations differently from politicians and economists. To be effective, therefore, economic policies may have to overcome psychological obstacles; for instance, those of deeply rooted pay increase and standard of living expectations which cannot be met by existing resources. Several recent and current pay disputes have illustrated this. However, people may have to learn to accept that standards of living cannot rise every year and may fall at times; and that their employers may not have the necessary financial resources to give regular, as well as higher, pay increases every year.

It is perhaps possible that industrial regional policies which pursue social as well as economic objectives could help bridge the communication gap because they incorporate human considerations. They could create local confidence and changes in outlook and could thus act as a catalyst to motivate people to cooperative and positive action. It is relevant to note in this context that the EEC has acknowledged the social need for giving regional aid in specific cases. The psychological encouragement which this can provide, I believe, could be important.

At the present time people in many regions of Britain feel that their needs have been neglected. It is therefore conceivable that some well thought out industrial policy measures to stimulate industrial recovery and development and to reduce unemployment, could play a major role in creating a more favourable psychological (and industrial relations) climate for economic recovery.

NOTES

[1] For details of my inflation, incentives and absence enquiries see Hilde Behrend, Problems of Labour and Inflation, Croom Helm Ltd., Beckenham, 1984.

[2] Harvey Armstrong and Jim Taylor, Regional Economic Policy and its Analysis, Philip Allan Publishers Ltd. Oxford, 1978. See also Regional Industrial Policy, Cmnd. 9111, HMSO London. December 1983.

[3] See W. H. Sales and J. S. Davies, Introducing a New Wage Structure into Coal-Mining, Bulletin of the Oxford University Institute of Statistics, vol. XIX, No. 3, August 1957,

[4] See Kenneth Boulding, The Economy of Love and Fear: A Preface to Grants Economics, Wadsworth, 1973; and Redistribution to the Rich and to the Poor, editors Kenneth Boulding and Martin Pfaff, Wadsworth, 1972.

[5] See Note 1.

[6] G. Hardin, The Tragedy of the Commons, Science Vol 162, New York, 1968. Hardin applied the term "No technical solution problems" to population control problems.

Labororiented Managementpolicy in Industry within a Social Market Economy

Herbert Schmidt

Preliminary remarks

The German economic miracle of the postwar era was achieved under the conditions of an economic system that is called the social market economy.

So it seems useful to pin down the ambiguous concept "social market economy" and to interpret it. Our governmental policy and also our private entrepreneurial policy, the industrial policy, are shaped by the principles of this economic and social systems. Certain forms of manpower and social policy within our business firms, and the influence on each other of employer and employee, are hardly to be understood without the help of referring to these key ideas. One such central idea is our graduated system of management-employee co-operation and co-determination — including the institutional framework within which it operates.

But it should be made clear that not every aspect of labor relations wihtin a firm is regulated by the state, as undeniable as the influence of social legislation on entrepreneurial and industrial policy is. Autonomous decisions of a business enterprise, whatever the orientation towards labor productivity, can also be motivated by efforts to provide humane working conditions.

In general our economic system has functioned well in the past. Only in the last few years have an increasing number of voices been directing attention to negative aspects of the evolution of productivity in the Federal Republic of Germany. So recently the Bonn correspondent of the Financial Times (London) wrote (Carr 1981): "West Germany is gaining a new and highly unflattering image abroad. It is that of the ageing champion boxer — a bit fatter and slower — who mumbles he is still the greatest, even as he sinks groggily onto the ropes. What has become of the 'land of the economic miracle', it is asked, where current-account surpluses, a hard Deutsche Mark and diligent workers seemed as much a part of the natural oder as beer and wurst?" The Japanese export offensive, new technologies, the oil shock, rising prices, unemployment and last not least high wage and supplemental wage costs — revealingly referred to by business as "social burdens" — raise the question of efficiency and of whether there are limits on the social market economy. The times in which everybody wants to earn more and wants to work less are past.

The Socio-economic Components of the Social Market Economy

A mainstay of the social market economy is the concept: "to link the principle of the free market with an approach to social balance".

The term "social" in the social market economy represents an obligation for all participants in this system. The implementation of social justice and social behavior in this system must always be evidenced and proved anew. Here too the foundation to begin with is the concept of the liberal market economy. But that economic concept saw the human being as a labor force and labor as a factor of production. So it is inherent in this market-economy system that socially undesired phenomena should emerge.

The transformation from market economy to social market economy is carried out by setting and recognizing social, ethical values. Social policy, legislation, entrepreneurial leadership, behavior and responsibility in line with these demands give rise to an economic system strived for by the ideal concept of the social market economy with a high degree of social freedom and development.

The Principle of the Socially Conscious State
as a Tenet Rooted in Constitutional Law

The principle of the socially aware state finds expression in the norms that obligate it to civically and socially conscious action and that are stated in the Constitution. The Constitution's declaration that the Federal Republic of Germany "is a democratic and social federal state" — the so-called "social-state clause" — is a determining and obligating norm.

Here is the expression of the idea that the state may and should shape the social order. All constitutionally guaranteed basic rights have to be seen and interpreted in the light of this social-state declaration. From that requirement is derived the right and the obligation of the state to engage in socio-political activity and social legislation. This activity and legislation is also of significance to the employer-employee interrelationship and to the social responsibility within a firm.

Which basic rights have, in the perspective of the social-state clause of our constitution particular significance for a labororiented industrial policy? They include, in particular

— the protection of human dignity, for example by humane working arrangements and the humane integration of the human being within the working process,

— the right to free development of the personality,

— the ban on discrimination, according to which no one may be denied equal treatment because of sex, age, origin, etc.,

— the freedom of association — e.g. the right on the basis of free choice of the purpose behind the association to establish common-interest groups, labor unions, co-operatives and other organizations,

— the freedom to choose a career, the place of work and the place of training, and

– the guarantee of private property – with, however, an explicit social responsibility, as a result of which limitations are permissible if the use of the property does not also serve "the common good".

With the establishment of such a systemic framework, corresponding to the idea of the social market economy and the obligation of the state as of the individual to adjust conduct to these norms, the fathers of the Federal Republic of Germany's Constitution distanced themselves from the "eclectic principle". This principle is to be taken to mean the way of carrying out an in part pragmatic, uncoordinated and only reactive policy and legislation that consists primarily of correcting mechanisms for avoiding social inequities and insecurities. The handed-down, traditional social policy received a new orientation; modern social policy – and derived from that entrepreneurial labororiented policy obtained constructive goals. As formative policy, prevention gained significance through the conceiving of forward-looking measures in private business as within the framework of industrial policy and governmental social policy. Corrective, completing socio-political measures to abolish social injustices are considered secondary where forward-looking planning and influencing can avoid or check undesirable influences on the society or on the personnel in organizations.

Influence of Legal Activities on Labororiented Industrial Policy

Let us assume that the social-market-economy concept is fully capable of implementation. In that case, based on Kant's principle of the categorical imperative, we could ascertain the following situation: Provided that everyone active in the economy and society behaves according to the tenets provided by the state, then economic and social progress must result, in equal measure, and without further governmental activity – to the satisfaction of all.

But, in industry – in the organizational practice – we know a lot of problems. The social duties as well as the existence of an efficient network of social security alone do not resolve the problem of the variety of productivity-restricting phenomena that can arise day by day at the place of work. High rates of turnover, absenteeism, illness and invalidism, strikes, sabotage, waste production, and behavior patterns in restraint of performance are caused by the conditions under which work has to be performed in the various firms. Legally guaranteed or voluntarily granted employee rights as a means of co-operating in the modification of working conditions in the direction of improving productivity and avoiding undesirable social hardship now can look back on an nearly 70 year-long tradition in Germany. The first law on works councils was passed in 1920.

The Differentiated System of Co-determination

Here reference should be made to the principles of the currently valid law as to the norms in the Federal Republic of Germany for co-operation between management and employee in a firm. This system envisages
- institutional and
- substantive

arrangements. The institutional conditions delineate the framework within which problems between the "social partners" — labor and management — are to be discussed. The employees' substantive rights consist of detailed and graduated rights ranging from information, counseling, initiative and co-operation to qualified co-determination. The laws regulating these rights and duties of employer and employee are:

1. The act respecting co-determination by employees in the supervisory boards and managing boards of undertakings in the mining industry and in the iron and steel industry. 1951.
2. The act respecting workers' co-determination (Co-determination Act). 1976.
3. The Works Constitution Act. 1952. (Including participation in the supervisory boards.)
4. The Works Constitution Act. 1972.

The two first-named laws and the part of the Works Constitution Act (1952) that is still valid today — which guarantees workers in firms with less than 2,000 employees an one-third participation of their representatives on the supervisory board — regulate the economic or qualified co-determination within the company (see figures pp. 197–200). These laws embody the employee's true co-determination on the partitatively constituted supervisory boards of all policy decisions regarding a firm, i.e. equal representation of management and personnel.

In contrast to the British and American board system, we have a system of company management at two levels:
- management via the board of directors and
- management via the supervisory board as the firm's superordinated organ of control.

In regard to the direct increasing of human resources productivity, I attach secondary or indirect significance to the system of co-determination within business or industrial enterprises. But not to be overlooked is the role of the labor or personnel director appointed by a firm as a member of the board with status equal to that of the commercial and technical directors. This director supports managerial policies that have equal regard for the economic and social efficacy of the company. The employees' representation on the supervisory board can exert influence in the same direction.

To be distinguished from co-determination within firms is the so-called simple or social co-determination, as it results from the Works Constitution Act.

This law is of highest importance for an organizations personnel management and the character of our type of industrial policy. This kind of co-management involves the influence of the employees on only the social and personnel aspects of what happens in a firm. Here we in the Federal Republic of Germany differentiate between two levels of organization: the industrial company and the works or plant. The company or firm is defined as the unit that is organizationally, economically, financially and legally superordinated to the works or plant. As a rule, the firm consists of numerous individual plants that are economically or legally dependent on the firm. By contrast, the plant or works is to be characterized as a unit of production of primarily local organizational and technical scope. The site of operations is the location at which the company management realizes its goals, purposes and strategies. Here, too, the specific measures, oriented towards individual employees or groups, involving the working force, personnel policy and socio-economic aspects are implemented. Accordingly, this is also the place at which measures to increase human resources productivity can be introduced and can become socially and economically effective. The ways and means of co-operation between employer and employee result from written and unwritten (unwritten in the sense of being sociological, ethical, moral, religious or social usages) norms that are symbolized by the existing works constitution. The Works Constitution Act sets only minimum requirements that are binding on both labor and management. These requirements can be broadened by agreements within the firm, by collectively bargained contracts or by voluntary social acts on the part of management.

The Works Constitution Law applies to private firms with, as a rule, five regular employees. But only 6 to 10 per cent of all firms qualified to have a works council have such an organization. These firms, however, employ about 75 per cent of the total working force. The works council is the institutional representative of employees vis-a-vis employers.

Humane and Participative Entrepreneurial Management

It is not intended here to spell out in detail the individual rights of the employee of a firm and the comprehensive activities, rights and duties of the works council. These rights and activities extend basically to

— the establishment of humane working conditions, and the doing away with on-the-job accidents and dangers to health,
— co-determination in social matters (working regulations, working hours, social facilities, wage scales, the patterning of social plans),

- participation in corporate manpower planning, occupational training, hirings and dismissals,
- rights of obtaining information and advising in regard to economic matters (especially investment and rationalization projects, the introduction of new technologies and working methods, organizational changes, etc.).

In addition, control functions have been granted to the works council. It is, in particular, to ensure adherence to laws and regulations that serve the interests of and the protection of the employee. This function applies, for example, to occupational training, as well as to the variety of regulations in regard to on-the-job protection and accident prevention.

Through these specific forms of co-operation the ways and means available to management and the personnel director are enhanced by impulses that permanently reinforce employee motivation. One aspect here has been the new orientation of entrepreneurial policy as a result of legal regulations. Another has been a rising interest on the part of the employer in the form of a readiness to take on responsibility. As a result of this legislation, too, a variety of activities in the field of social science began to contribute to a firm's qualifications for discharging its tasks. Governmental concomitant or "flanking" measures, too, have been promoting this process of development.

The Works Constitution Act (1972) in the Federal Republic of Germany introduced a process in industry, within firms, of a growing awareness of the purpose and possibilities of new management styles, and the practice of new forms of patterning and organizing work. To be sure, many perceptions afforded by the ergonomics and social sciences in this area were already available. But the necessity of putting these perceptions into practice had only been recognized in the past to very differing degrees. Now for the first time a law provided that "the employer and the works council shall have regard to the established findings of ergonomics relating to the tayloring of jobs to meet human requirements". This provision led to a comprehensive taking of inventory as to what the engineering sciences, psychology, occupational medicine, sociology, economics, the science of nutrition, pedagogics and the other sciences had to offer in the way of research results in regard to working life. The law has been an enduring, non-material promotion of labor-oriented research.

Within this conjunction, the strong American influence on social and motivational research within the behavioral sciences in the Federal Republic of Germany is impossible to overlook. Otherwise than in the U.S. itself, in the Federal Republic of Germany it was hardly necessary to search for firms willing to apply the new insights, or to seek for a readiness for interdisciplinary co-operation with other branches of learning. Obligated anyhow to socially oriented conduct, since the 1976 co-determination law firms had been required to appoint labor directors who, within the co-determined pattern of the firm's management, would give emphasis especially to these workoriented methods in ways that would also cause the measures to promote productivity. This interest included, besides matters of working organization, new methods of personnel management and the implementation of preventive forms of personnel and social policy on the part of the firm. Forward-looking personnel, training and work planning were an integral part of the dynamic concept of the works constitution. No longer were technically and organizationally necessary requirements within a firm to be only reacted to by the personnel. Henceforth these requirements were to be planned simultaneously and discussed with the works council. In part, the works council, besides these new rights of initiative, also obtained the possibility of exercising a co-determining function in regard to the new requirements.

Persistently the research and teaching in the sphere of business administration seeks to liberate people from the concept of the "homo oeconomicus", oriented towards factors of production and costs. The new orientation, along lines traced by the behavioral sciences, of business operations finds particular expression in the field of personnel management.

Influence of the Collective-bargaining Partners

Besides the state, the agreements between employers and unions are contributing increasingly to the planning of plant and corporate organization. Employers' associations and labor unions, the collective bargaining partners, are important implementers of social policy.

The employer-employee relationship, along with the freedom, guaranteed by the employers' association's and unions' autonomy, to conclude collective-bargaining agreements, are integral and indispensable components of the social market economy's structure. Besides the previously dominant wage agreements, increasing significance is coming to be attached to over-all collectively bargained agreements — agreements that also go into matters of working conditions, protection in regard to rationalization measures, or participation in ownership of the firm or corporation.

Efficiency of Labororiented Measures
under the Conditions of the German Economic Order

The Thesis of Decreasing Readiness to Perform on the Job as Social Security Increases

The legally prescribed social services by firms and those voluntarily granted or negotiated in collective-bargaining sessions currently amount, within the manufacturing branch of industry, to some 80 per cent of the effective compensation of an employee. These amounts are paid as supplemental — or, better, as additional — wage costs by firms. All such payments taken together plus the wages themselves make up the employee's gross wage. Labor costs have risen considerably in the last 15 years.

Besides the negative effects of higher wage costs on international competitive ability, this critical observation is increasingly being made: that a firm's outlays largely for the benefit of the employee's social security, and the concomitant claims enjoyed by personnel, reduce working morale and inhibit readiness to do a job. The value of these financial services as a motivation to work performance is challenged. But, for the moment, under the conditions of a high rate of unemployment (February 1985: 10.5 per cent; 2.6 million unemployed workers) there is a new change in the worker's behaviour. Nobody likes to go the risk to loose his job.

A representative survey of 500 firms by the Chambers of Commerce and Industry in Koblenz revealed that the firms questioned about the effect of social safeguards on their personnel
- 48 per cent reported no change,
- 16 per cent an increase and
- 35 per cent a decrease

in the employees' readiness to do the job. The decreases were reported, in particular, by large enterprises. As causes of a decrease in work performance, the firms mentioned high tax and social-security burdens on employees, with the effect of reducing readiness to put in overtime. Further symptoms were given as being unjustified sick leave and the high degree of social security. Components of the extensive social-security system include unemployment insurance, continuation of wages in case of illness, rules about dismissal to avoid socially unjustified and mass dismissals and the safeguarding of the validity of claims for old-age provisions by the employer. In a number of branches, supplemental agreements regarding protection against rationalization exist, either as part of collectively bargained agreements or within a firm by internal accord. One of the main complaints of German firms is about the high rate of absenteeism, of almost 10 per cent compared with 3.5 per cent in the U.S. and 2.7 per cent in Japan. These figures stand in juxtaposition to annual working times (and hours actually worked per employed person in manufacturing industry) for 1983 of
- 1,760 (1,635) hours in the Federal Republic of Germany
- 1,920 (1,860) hours in the United States
- 2,094 (2,061) hours in Japan.

In this regard, too, the German worker can point to major social progress.

But the international comparison offers no reason to suppose that countries with more limited provisions for unemployment care have had better results in doing away with unemployment. The German Institute for Economic Research suggests that, in contradiction to the expressed suppositions, the quantitatively large quota of social-security benefits functions as an economic stabilizer. Social security can give a lot of chances for more flexibility in personnel management. Nevertheless there are governmental activities under way and in discussion in our parliament to reach more flexibility in firms and creating more workingplaces.

A further indication of deficient readiness to perform the work is the strike. In regard to strikes, too, it emerges that the Federal Republic of Germany, probably because of its effective social-security network, makes a good showing. A considerable tendency to strike is evident particularly in those countries in which the levels of social-security benefits and incomes are relatively low.

Measuring Social Responsibility by Human Resource Accounting and Social Reporting

In measuring the efficiency of Government-Business-Labor Relations and the social responsibility of enterprises the Federal Republic of Germany is still in Kindergarten. Government measures for the "Humanization of Working Life" include also the working out of data about protective measures, standard values, minimum requirement as to machinery, installations and place of work. Completely comparative data and internal social indicators are inadequately collected and inadequately used by management.

A Human Resource Accounting Movement has developed in the Federal Republic of Germany which has been heavily influenced by American initiatives (Brummet, Flamholtz, Gustafson, Herrick, Lawler, Woodruff)[1]. This has the goal of contributing systematically

- to the justification of decision making for management,
- to the creation of objective information for the improvement of industrial relations by means of
- controllable measurement of social responsibility and the productivity of human resource management in the framework of social accounting and auditing.

Initial investigations have shown that greater attention is being payed to the workload placed on employees in larger and modern factories when the consequences are high due to higher capital intensity and production interdependencies. This is being achieved mostly by increased use of machinery and labor saving technologies. The economic relevance of medically perfomance reductions, motivation, or work satisfaction is increasingly recognized. Tradeoffs between professional pride and income maximizing are being analyzed as regards their relevance to productivity.

Whereas in France rigorous requirements for collecting social data and creating a social balance sheet have been set the Federal Republic of Germany has depended more on the self-initiatives and sense of responsibility of enterprises and the social partners. The unions have made proposals for the collection of data. The government signaled its position in a proposed law for the coordination of corporation law in the European Community in which it recommended the voluntary delivery of information concerning human resource management in enterprises. Labor Unions have signaled interest, in a legally prescribed form of social balance sheets and social reporting and auditing. This law shall become finished by the parliament up to the end of 1985 and bring new impulses for more social responsibility and social accounting in German industry — we hope.

NOTE

[1] Humanvermögensrechnung. Instrumentarium zur Ergänzung der unternehmerischen Rechnungslegung – Konzepte und Erfahrungen. Edited by Herbert Schmidt, Walter de Gruyter Publ., Berlin, New York 1982.

Co-determination in the mining industry and in the iron and steel production industry
Model

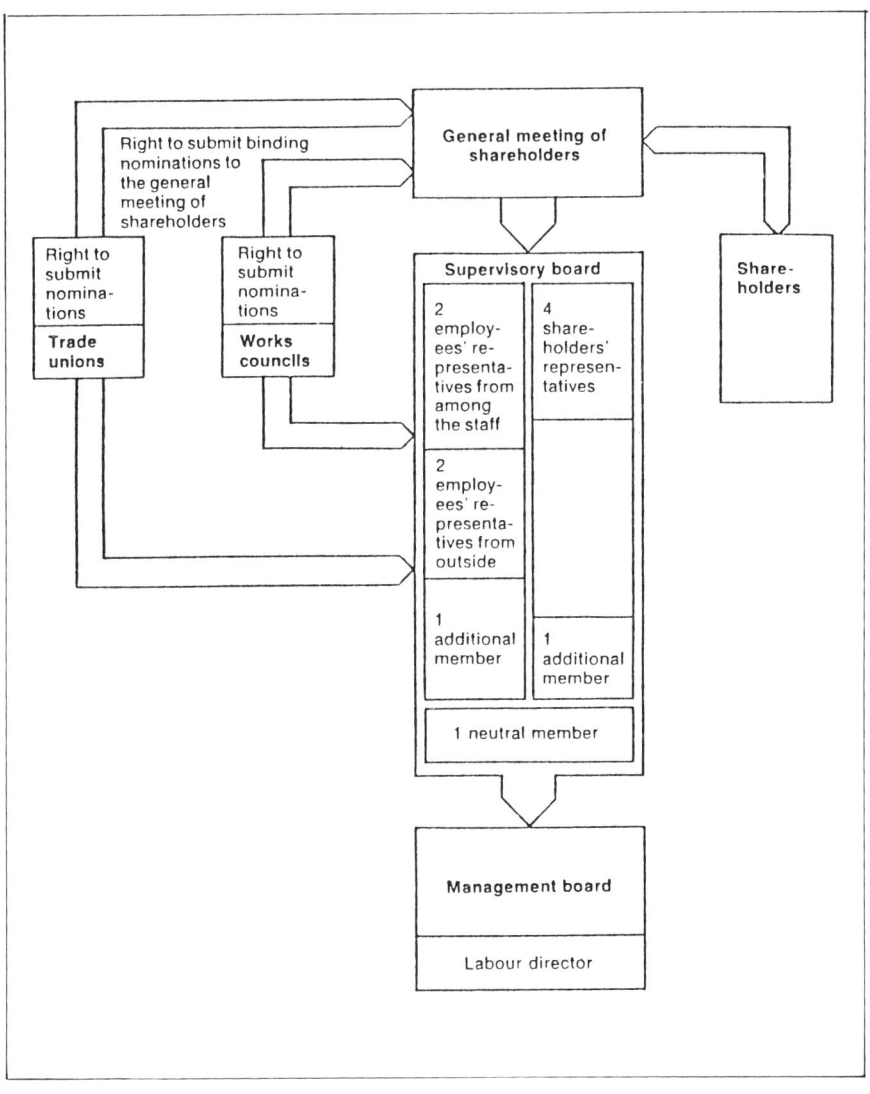

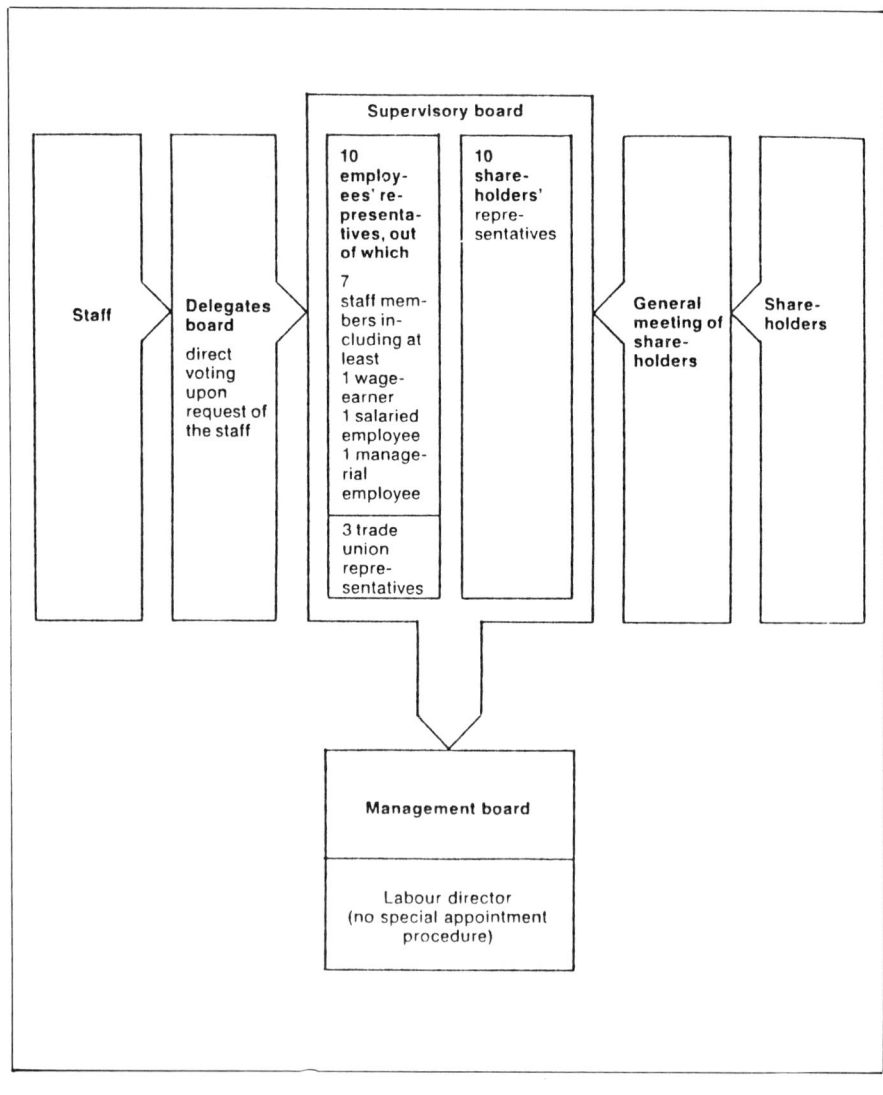

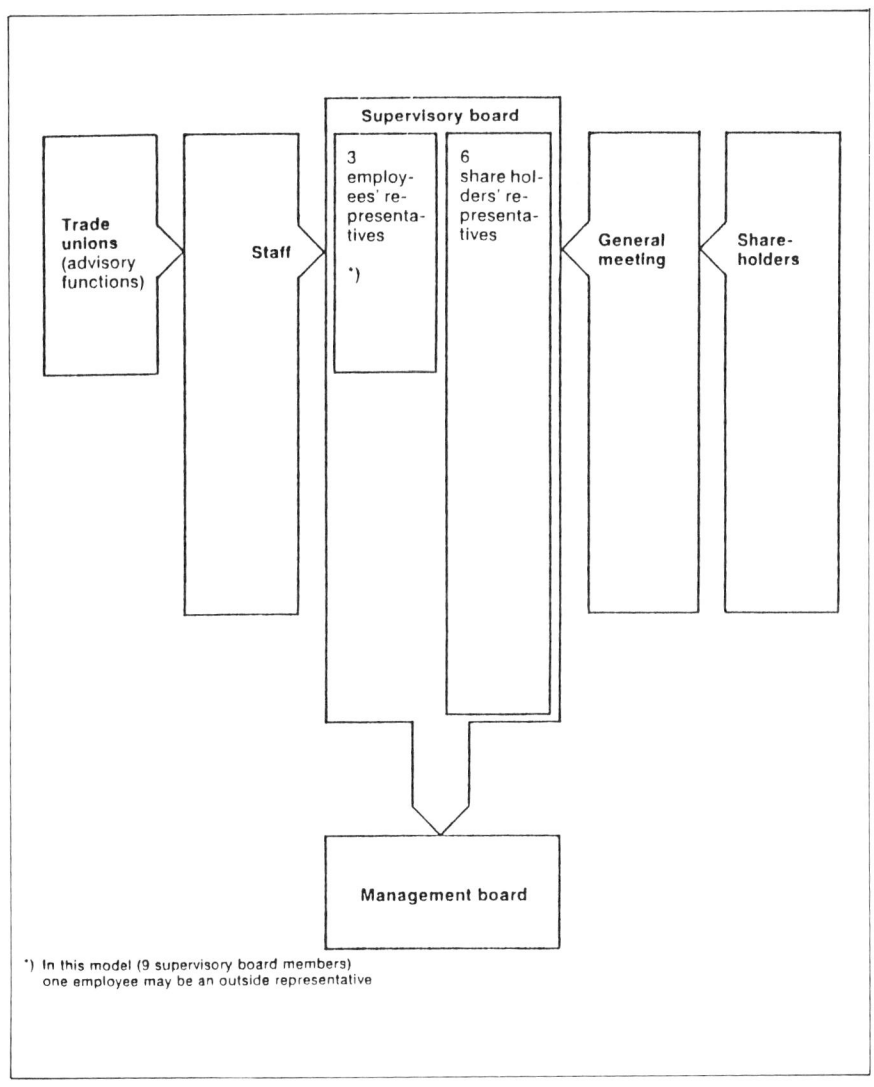

Co-determination under the Works Constitution Act of 1972
Works constitution

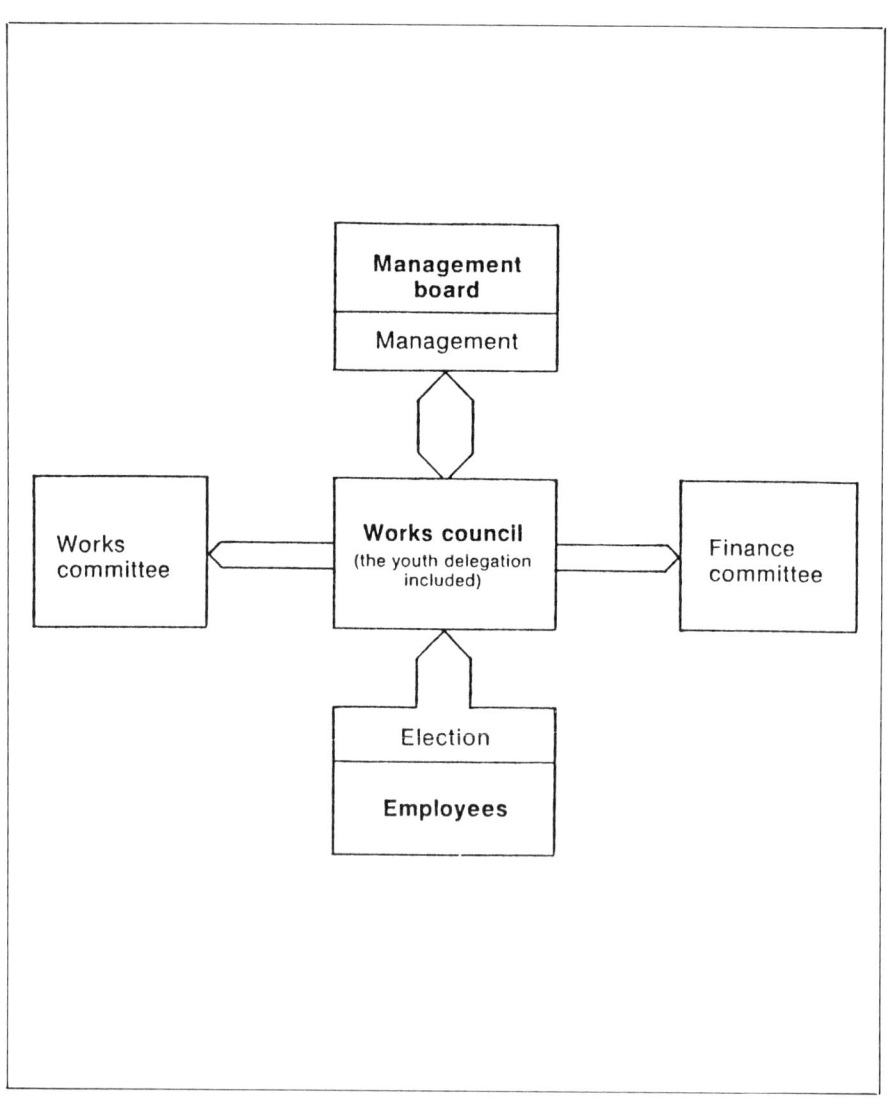

Index of Names

Adenauer 67
Alinson 30
Anderson 116, 119
Armington 96
Armstrong 179
Arrow 40
Attlee 175
Ayres 34
Bannock 133
Barlow 179
Barnes 34
Bastiat 57
Behrend VIII, 175
Bell 34, 109
Beveridge 175
Bevin 63
Birch 91, 135
Boehm 38, 156
Boehm-Bawerk 39, 40
Boulding 34, 182
Brinkman VIII, 21
Bronfenbrenner 113
Brummet 195
Button 123

Cannon VIII, 131
Carr 187
Caves 117
Cherry 179
Chesnais 97
Churchill 175
Clay 64
Colbert 4

Dahrendorf 155
Debreu 40
Delors 174
Downs 128
Drucker 34, 109

Eisenhower 157
Erhard 16, 19, 20, 37, 38, 39, 40 ff., 58 f., 68, 75, 156
Eucken 38, 43, 156
Eulenburg 39

Feldstein 3, 22, 33
Fels 15, 20
Flamholtz 195
Fleming VI
Fraser 115
Freeman 96
Friedman 110

Galbraith 34
Garnaut 116
Gemper VII, VIII, 11
Gibb 132
Giscard d'Estaing 3
Gompertz 24, 34
Grapin 3
Gregory 115
Grinder 39
Gruchy 30
Gustafson 195

Hamilton, A. 21
Hamilton, R. 133
Hardin 185
Harris 92, 117
Harrod-Domar 24
Hart 34
Hawke 120 f.
Hayek 38, 39
Herrick 195
Hicks 40
Hirschman 147
Hood 132
Huber 60
Humphrey-Javits 32

Jackson 121
Jenkis VI, VIII, 57
Jenner VI
Johnson, Ch. 33, 159
Johnson, Cl. 162
Jones 124

Kant 189
Karsten V, VIII, 155
Kasper 119
Keynes 24, 110, 157
Kirschbaum 93
Kirzner 135
Kleu 150
Knapp-Simmel 40
Kriegel 3
Kuehn 76
Kuznets 25, 34

Lachmann 39
Lasalle 4
Lawler 195
Leibenstein 135
Leibniz 58
Levitan 162
Lewis 132
List 38
Lorenz 98

Mackay 132
Magaziner 33
Marshall 155
Martin 128
Marx 4, 26, 34, 38, 91
McCloy 68
McCracken 3
Menger 39
Meyers 75
Milne 132
Mises 39
Mitterand 3
Molitor VIII, 3

Mueller-Armack 38, 58, 156
Myrdal 24

O'Connor 109
Ogburn 34
Oppenheimer 38
Oppenlaender 97
Orville 28

Palmer 29, 33, 34
Patrick 113
Pempel 113
Phillips 161
Popper 155
Preiser 156
Price 34
Pugh VIII, 107
Reagan 3, 23
Reich 29, 30, 33
Rieger 38
Rodbertus 38
Roentgen VI
Roepke 38, 156
Rogin 155
Rostow 26
Ruestow 38

Sahlins 26, 34
Samuelson 40
Sawhill 29, 33, 34
Schatz VIII, 89
Schiller 77
Schmidt VIII, 187
Schmuecker 75
Schoneweg VIII, 167
Schultze 22, 29, 33
Schumpeter 34, 91
Service 26, 34
Smith 19, 38
Solla Price 27
Solo 34, 161
Soltwedel 100

Spann 38
Stanworth 132
Steinberg 7
Szyperski 93

Taylor 179
Thatcher 176
Thiel VIII, 47
Thurow 22, 33, 113
Tisdell 110
Tool 30, 34
Trezise 33
Tylor 24

Veblen 34
Vershofen 39

Wachter 23, 33
Wallis 33
Whitehead 34
Whiteman 117
Whitlam 115
Wolter 100
Woodruff 195
Wright 28
Wuensche VIII, 37
van der Walt VIII, 145

Young 123

Subject Index

AEG 18
ARIANE 172
Adjustment assistance 18
Adjustment, inadequate 47
Advantage, comparative 107
Airbus 172
Allocation 41
Armaments policy 57
Australia 107
Australian Bureau of Industry Econ. 117
Austria 107, 112
Austrian School 39
Automobile producer 6

Back-up support 18, 19
Bank failures 158
Banking System 18
Bargaining, collective 193
Barriers, technical, legal, tax 169
Boycott 150
Breaking-up assistance 18
Business-labor-government 161
Buy-out 18

Canada 4
Capital formation 140
Capital-labor relations 108
Catholic Bishops' Letter 158
Change, societal 107
Change, structural 107, 163
Change, technological 27, 117
Civitas humana 38
Co-determination 190
Coalmining 57 ff.
Colonna Memorandum 167
Community service 99
Competition 4, 18, 19, 43, 99, 157
Competition, national and internat. 9

Competitiveness 21, 136
Concerted action 6
Conciliation and Arbitration Comm. 122
Confiscation 41
Constitution, German Federal 58, 189
Cross-cultural 21
Cultural Economics 24, 34
Culture 24, 27
Czechoslovakia 68

Decline, economic 32
Deprivation effects 41
Deregulation 21
Development planning 113
Development programmes 142
Development, economic 25
Development, technological 163
Disparity 50
Dynamics, qualitative 22

ESPRIT programme 170
EURATOM 5
Economic order, international 115
Economic policy, discretionary 17
Economics, Keynesian 29, 30
Economics, demand-side 29, 41
Economics, neoclassical 29
Economics, supply-side 29, 41
Economy, American 21, 22, 29
Economy, dual 145
Economy, monostructured 74
Employment 19, 41
Employment Act 157
Energy Crisis 67
Enterprise, graduated 139
Enterprise, small and new 89 ff.
Entrepreneurialism 133
Entrepreneurs 6

Entrepreneurs, Keynesian 5
Entrepreneurs, Schumpeterian 5
Environment 37
Europe 3, 91
European Coal and Steel Community 5
European Community (EC) 5, 91, 195
European Currency Union 68
European Currency Unit (ECU) 170
European Economic Community (EEC) 52, 167 ff.
European countries 47
Evolution, cultural 27
Evolution, economic 24, 32
Evolution, general 28
Evolution, specific 26, 28

Forecast 5
France 6, 7, 70
Free-enterprise system 41, 73
Freiburg School 156
Future 20
Future growth industries 89

GATT 10, 170
German economic miracle 187
Germany, East 63
Germany, West 11, 12, 13, 14, 15, 16, 20, 21, 22 f., 23, 42, 47, 57 ff., 89 ff., 175, 187 ff., 195
Gestalt 24 ff.
Government spending 125
Great Britain 23, 70, 89, 107, 136, 175

High-tech industries 89
Historicism 39
Homo oeconomicus 193
Homo sapiens 32, 34
Human Resource Accounting Movement 195

Humankind 27
Humphrey-Hawkins Act 157

Industrial Development Certificates 180
Industrial adjustment 30
Industrial development strategy 145
Industrial policy 28
Industrial policy, conceptual 17
Industrial policy, coordination of 53
Industrial policy, function of 17
Industrial policy, infrastructural 43
Industrial policy, innovative 17
Industrial policy, labororiented 188
Industrial policy, market-oriented 8, 11, 12
Industrial policy, structural 19
Industrial revolution 25
Industrial revolution, third 16
Industrial (coal-)policy 77
Industrialized Countries, Newly (NIC) 4, 11
Industries Assistance Commission 120
Industries, knowledge based 132
Intervention 21
Intervention, state 48
Investment help 68

Japan 3, 4, 5, 8, 10, 11, 21 f., 22, 23, 33, 34, 42, 107, 136, 172, 194
Job creation 92
Job-classification 181
Joint Task, programme 50, 51

Labor Unions 195
Labor market, German 94
Labor-management 15
Latin America 152
Linkage, foreward and backward 151

MITI 8, 22, 113
Management, entrepreneurial 191

Markets, grey and black 6
Measures, flanking 192
Meiji Restoration 21
Misery index 118
Mittelstandspolitik 98
Mozambique 150

Nationalisation 181
Netherlands 119
New Deal 32
Nightwatchman state 57
Nkomati Accord 150
Nobel Prize VI, 24, 40
North sea oil 131

OECD 114
OPEC 5, 83, 110
Oil shock 83
Opportunity costs 53
Ordnungspolitik 12, 112
Ordoliberals 38

Pacific Rim 116
Paris Summit 168
Pay-structure 181
Planning, democratic 30, 32
Planning, economic 30
Planning, indicative 30
Poland 63
Policy of adjustment 85
Policy of preservation 85
Policy tripod 114
Policy, anti-inflation 177
Policy, competitive 19
Policy, countercyclical 157
Policy, fiscal 29, 123, 163
Policy, incomes 177
Policy, innovative industrial 19
Policy, monetary 156, 163
Policy, regional 47 ff., 170, 179
Policy, sectoral 47 ff.
Policy, social 171, 175

Policy, structural 19
Policy, technological and research 19
Pragmatism 16, 19, 30
Price mechanism 147
Primacy of industry 17
Privatisation 181
Protection 8, 119
Protectionism 7
Protectionist 4, 6

Reaganomics 22, 29
Redistribution of jobs 161
Reenforcement assistance 18
Responsibility, entrepreneurial 14
Responsibility, social 195
Restructuring, economic 128
Risk taker, Schumpeterian 28
Ruhr district 57 ff.

Schumann Plan 67
Science 28, 32
Science park 138
Sclerosis, economic 91
Scotland 131, 183
Scottish Enterprise Foundation 131 ff.
Scottish Development Agency 138
Sector, competitive 109
Sector, monopoly 109
Sector, public 109
Selfhelp 19
Sequestration 63 ff.
Silicon Valley 98
Singapore 107
Social balance 187
Social market economy 11, 16, 17, 19 f.,
    37, 38, 39, 156, 187 ff.
Social safety net 13
Social state 60
Social technology 26
Social-State Clause 188
Society, economic 39
Society, postindustrial 109

Solution, market-oriented 13
South Africa 145
South East Asia 47
Spacelab 172
Spin-off 18, 98, 135
Stagflation 110 ff.
Starting-up assistance 18
State planning 4
State, semideveloped 153
Structural change 19
Structural change, declining 85
Structural change, rising 85
Structural change, waning V, VI
Structural change, waxing V, VI
Structural distortions 146
Structural policy 12
Structural policy, market-oriented 37
Subsidy 7, 49, 170
Sunrise industries 28
Sweden 107
Switzerland 7

Targeting, industrial 7, 48
Tarifpolitik (wage settlements) 15
Technological gap 89
Technology 27, 43
Technology policy 127

Tennessee Valley Authority 160
Trade Union Congress 176
Trade Unions 73
Trade barriers, non-tariff 169
Transformation 26
Transportation 24
Trojan horse theory 12

US Small Business Administration 95
USA 4, 6, 11, 21, 23, 30, 32, 47, 64, 70, 90 ff., 107, 155, 157, 172, 194
Unemployment 99, 176

Venture capital 123

Wait-and-see mentality 19
Walberberg, System Symposia V
Wealth of nations 19
Weapons technology 16
Wharton School study 23
Winding-up assistance 18
Works Constitution Act 191
Works Council 193
World War II 28
World War II (post era) 21

Yugoslavia 68